jeremy evans

plain sailing

how to sail dinghies and catamarans

southwater

This edition is published by Southwater

Southwater is an imprint of
Anness Publishing Ltd
Hermes House, 88–89 Blackfriars Road,
London SE1 8HA
tel. 020 7401 2077; fax 020 7633 9499
www.southwaterbooks.com; info@anness.com

This edition distributed in the UK by
The Manning Partnership Ltd, 6 The Old
Dairy, Melcombe Road, Bath BA2 3LR
tel. 01225 478 444; fax 01225 478 440
sales@manning-partnership.co.uk

This edition distributed in the USA
and Canada by National Book Network
4720 Boston Way, Lanham, MD 20706
tel. 301 459 3366; fax 301 459 1705
www.nbnbooks.com

This edition distributed in Australia by
Pan Macmillan Australia, Level 18
St Martins Tower, 31 Market St, Sydney
NSW 2000; tel. 1300 135 113; fax 1300 135 103
email customer.service@macmillan.com.au

This edition distributed in New Zealand by
The Five Mile Press (NZ) Ltd
PO Box 33–1071 Takapuna, Unit 11/
101–111 Diana Drive, Glenfield, Auckland 10
tel. (09) 444 4144; fax (09) 444 4518
fivemilenz@clear.net.nz

A CIP catalogue record for this book is
available from the British Library.

Publisher: JOANNA LORENZ
Managing Editor: JUDITH SIMONS
Project Editor: MARIANO KÄLFORS
Designer: GOWERS ELMES LTD
Photography: OCEAN IMAGES
Illustrations: CREATIVE BYTE
Production Controller: CLAIRE RAE

Previously published as part of a larger
compendium, *The Practical Encyclopedia of Sailing*

10 9 8 7 6 5 4 3 2 1

Even though some of the photographs in this
book show people sailing without a lifevest or
buoyancy aid, the author and publisher advise
their use for all sailing situations. In most
cases there are no laws or regulations
regarding the use of lifevests, although they
are invariably mandatory for dinghy racing
and at sailing schools. Sailing is above all
about taking responsibility for your own
decisions and actions.

plain sailing

Contents

Introduction

Sailing began as a sport for wealthy gentlemen at the end of the 19th century, at a time when steam and diesel were making sails redundant for both commercial and naval use. A historic race was staged around the Isle of Wight off the south coast of England on 22 August 1851 with sixteen yachts taking part, and The Royal Yacht Squadron's Hundred Pound Cup made by Garrard of London as the prize. Its name was changed to the America's Cup in honour of the winning schooner *America*, and this was the start of international yacht racing as we know it today.

Since those early beginnings the rich have continued to enjoy the sport at racing events such as Antigua Race Week, the Aga Khan Cup at Porto Cervo or La Nioulargue Regatta for vintage racing yachts at St Tropez, while at the other end of the spectrum the growth of dinghy sailing and affordable cruising has made the sport available to all. You don't even need to own a boat to experience sailing, since willing crews are in

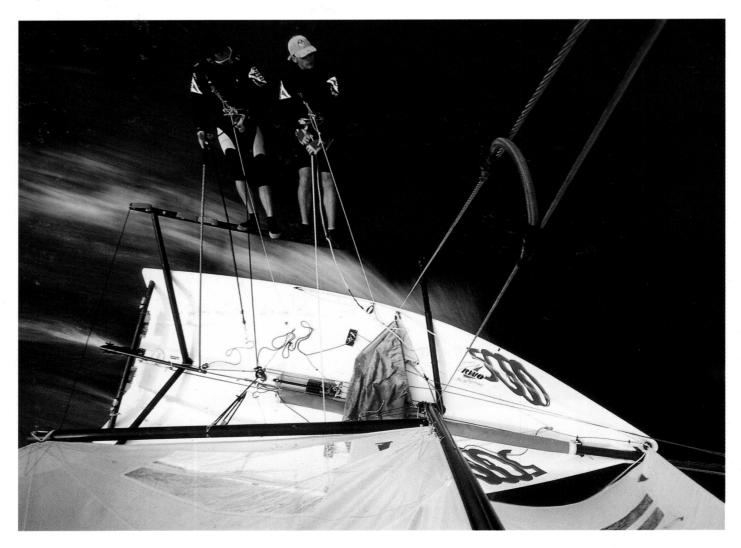

demand at every level of the sport, and time rather than money is the commitment that is required.

So why sail? It all comes down to experiencing the exhilaration of two elements – wind and water – and learning to contain and control them. The basic skills are easy enough to acquire, but beyond that a lifetime of experience awaits.

OPPOSITE **The twin wire skiff represents the ultimate expression of what was first conceived at the end of the 20th century – the high performance racing dinghy.**

RIGHT **Twin-hulled catamarans are a modern re-working of an ancient concept that provides an unrivalled combination of stability, power and performance.**

ABOVE **Sailing a modern dinghy can be an athletic and challenging pastime, with crews using their skills to balance the power of wind and waves.**

ABOVE **The challenge of mastering the elements under sail reaches its full potential in an event such as the Vendee Globe Race.**

Sailing
Basics

For many people, the first introduction to sailing comes via small open dinghies that provide an immediate and thrilling response to wind and waves. Dinghy sailing began to establish itself as a popular concept in the 1950s, when a new breed of relatively light, fast and responsive, marine plywood designs began to make sailing widely available at reasonably low cost. The sport prospered mainly as a competitive pastime, and clubs were established wherever there was sailable water and racing was organized on a regular basis.

Learning the basics is sufficient enough to provide endless hours of fun and pleasure. For those who want more, modern technology has also made high performance sailing readily available, with dinghy and small boat racing providing the bedrock of an international sport that ranges up to the heights of Olympic competition.

Taking up dinghy sailing

A sailing dinghy can be defined as a small, open boat powered by sails, which is usually crewed by one or two people. Unlike a sailing cruiser, it has no cabin to provide any kind of overnight or foul weather shelter and, unlike a keelboat, it lacks a weighted keel to help keep it upright. More than any other type of sailing craft it relies on the skills of the crew to keep it balanced against the force of the wind, sailing forwards efficiently rather than leaning on its side, and heading where the helmsperson directs it.

A century of design evolution has ensured that modern dinghies are as user-friendly and easy to sail as is possible. At one end of the scale internationally popular boats such as Optimists, designed for children's use, or Toppers, perform an entry-level role, and are just about perfect so long as you accept that the business of learning to sail must start well before you even think about launching on to the water.

ABOVE **Nothing can beat learning to sail in an open dinghy as it brings the crew into the closest possible contact with the elements.**

Harnessing the forces of nature

Sailing is all about learning how to harness the natural forces of wind and water, and a small dinghy brings you closer to them than any other kind of sailing. Dealing with the forces of nature should never be undertaken lightly, particularly when the combination of too much wind and cold water temperatures can threaten life. To deal with them efficiently and ensure that sailing is both enjoyable and safe, all sailors have to accept that learning to sail is a lifelong process in which experience is built on basic knowledge.

LEFT **Different sizes of boat suit different sizes of people. The International Topper is small, light and forgiving, ideal for younger sailors.**

RIGHT **The Laser Pico is a modern, slightly scaled up rival to the International Topper.**

Why take up sailing?

The reasons for enjoying sailing are many, but the following points cover most of them:

Healthy for you

Lots of exercise and clean, fresh air make it a top choice for children and adults alike.

Meeting people

It's a camaraderie sport, where half the fun is enjoying sailing with others and talking about your experiences.

Seeing new places

There are all kinds of options for travelling and viewing places from a different perspective.

Inexpensive

While the sky is the limit for those indulging in offshore racing in keelboats, costs can certainly be kept reasonable with a small dinghy. At dinghy sailing level the costs of the sport compare favourably with other pastimes.

Challenging

That's what is so good about it. While virtually anyone can kick a football or even jump on and ride a bike at a basic level, almost no one could just get in a dinghy and sail without some help. The skills required and the time spent learning them are all part of the attraction of the sport.

Feeling great

The wind in your hair and the sun (sometimes) on your face contributes to an indefinable feeling of wellbeing as you skip across the water.

Continual learning

There is so much to learn, and the continuous learning process, which owes so much to experience, invariably makes sailing a sport for life.

Variety

There are all kinds of boats and types of sailing available. The choices range from state-of-the-art, knife-edge performance to traditional, relaxed cruising. Just pick whatever suits you best.

Competitive satisfaction

If you are that way inclined, dinghy racing is widely available at all levels and for all ages from seven onwards.

A safe sport

It is rare for anyone to drown or get seriously injured while sailing, and properly organized schools and clubs, which are backed by national authorities, can boast a near unblemished record. It is however vital to start by getting proper tuition; while experience is built up you can continue to enjoy the sport in a controlled environment such as a sailing club.

ABOVE **Capsizing is all part of the fun of sailing, and modern equipment and clothing allows the crew to stay safe and warm.**

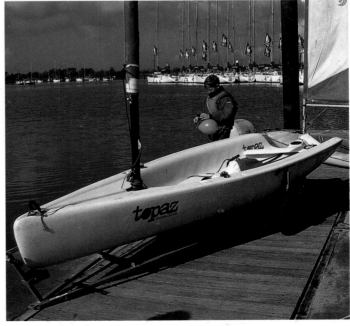

ABOVE **The Topaz continues the Topper/Pico theme, with a blow-moulded plastic hull, which is virtually unbreakable, and the option of different rigs.**

Starting to sail

Children can learn many things quicker than adults, and the 10–14 age range is an optimum age for fast learning. Some children – often from hard-core sailing families – are encouraged to start much younger, which is acceptable so long as parents realize that they run the risk of putting them off. Six is the youngest realistic age to sail a small dinghy such as an Optimist, and then only in perfect Force 2 conditions or less with close supervision at all times. Do not take chances as the child may feel out of control and become scared if the wind blows harder.

Adults can take up and enjoy dinghy sailing at any age, including those who are well into their retirement years. A modicum of physical fitness is necessary, and the level required is directly related to the type of sailing being pursued – hanging from the trapeze while controlling the power of a 49er bears little resemblance to enjoying the staid comforts of a family-style dinghy such as a Wayfarer or Laser 16.

It is also important to accept that factors such as fitness, strength, maturity and experience, which age may or may not confer, have to be compromised with sailing conditions. Ideal conditions for learning probably mean warm air and sea temperatures, light winds and flat water, none of which are demanding, while colder, windier conditions will require considerably more resilience and hardiness if you are to enjoy the experience.

Join a sailing club

When it comes to dinghy sailing, the ideal solution is often to join a sailing club where you can enjoy organized activities, exchange views with like-minded people, learn about racing, sail with safety cover available, and have a permanent launching and boat storage facility.

It is not even necessary to own a dinghy to join a club. Many successful dinghy sailors, such as boat designer Phil Morrison who has boats such as the Laser 5000 and

ABOVE **A club provides an opportunity to meet and socialize with fellow sailors, to sail in company and enjoy the camaraderie that the sport offers.**

RS 400 to his name, learnt their skills by offering to crew for local dinghy owners. This can be an excellent and very cheap way to gain experience, so long as the owner is a good sailor who will actually pass on the right way to do things. A phone call to a local club, a word with the secretary, or a look at the notice board is the best way to find people seeking crew.

Geographical location can pose problems, and the cost and hassle factor will obviously increase if you have to drive long distances to find a suitable club. Most well-populated areas with good sailing waters are well served by sailing clubs, but in some cases over-subscription and high costs of membership can put up a barrier for newcomers.

The boat

Dinghies are widely available new or second-hand. A new boat comes with all the usual guarantees, but the second-hand supply means that boats are available at all prices and really start very cheaply.

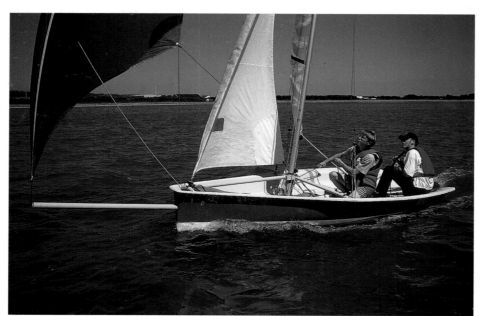

ABOVE **The Topper Sport 14 provides an ideal modern mix of learner-stability combined with gennaker-performance. This medium-size dinghy is suitable for both adults and teenagers.**

Buying a second-hand boat is considerably less dangerous than buying a second-hand car, but there are still plenty of pitfalls with rigging, sails and hull materials, all of which suffer from wear and tear, and replacement parts are generally expensive. This means that good advice is necessary for anyone considering buying second-hand.

Boat accessories

Your boat will probably require a launching trolley to push it to and from the water. It may also need a road trailer or roof rack bars depending on size, and a boat cover for protection and storage.

Personal accessories

A buoyancy aid is the most vital accessory. It must be the right size for the sailor's weight and allow maximum freedom of movement. In most conditions the crew will need a minimum of a wetsuit and spray top to keep warm.

As in most sports you can pay a lot of money for the very latest technical clothing. As a minimum requirement, you may also need to buy special dinghy shoes or boots, which are recommended for good grip, warm feet and ankle protection, a woolly hat in a synthetic

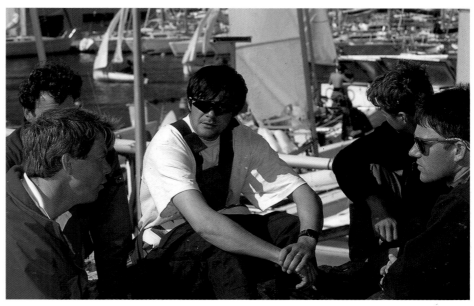

ABOVE **Find opportunities to talk to more experienced sailors to gain more knowledge and learn by your mistakes, which will take your skills to the next stage.**

thermal material to prevent heat loss in colder weather and reinforced sailing gloves for hand protection.

Maintenance

Modern mass-produced polypropylene dinghies, such as the Pico and Topper, should require little more maintenance than cleaning and the very occasional replacement of fittings. Otherwise, the

great majority of modern dinghies are built in fibreglass, which is virtually maintenance-free when new but can present problems in an older boat when faded colours, cracks, splits and delamination may all require preventative maintenance. More traditional wooden built dinghies may require a great deal of time and money by comparison, but these tend to appeal to the kind of sailor who actively enjoys the upkeep of his boat and regards it as a source of pride.

Insurance

In a litigious society, third party insurance is vital for dinghy owners and mandatory for most racing. Comprehensive cover, which insures against theft, fire or serious damage, is wise.

Clubs

The costs of belonging to a sailing or yacht club vary enormously, as do the associated costs of boat storage. One advantage of belonging to a club with active fleets is that they are good outlets for second-hand equipment, whether buying or selling.

Other costs

These may include launching fees, harbour dues and winter storage.

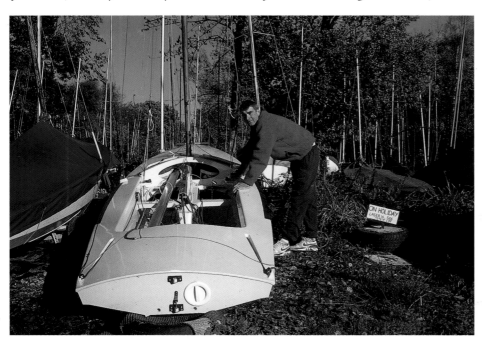

ABOVE **Where are you going to keep it? A dinghy needs secure storage both in and out of the sailing season. This is often provided by a sailing club boat park.**

Sailing schools

Sailing schools in general are governed by national sailing authorities. They are highly organized when it comes to teaching both children and adults and generally make a pretty good job of what they set out to do. As a rule, sailing schools should guarantee that all tuition is done safely, and at an all-inclusive price, which should include the necessary equipment and clothing.

Courses should be run according to detailed principles laid down in national authority logbooks, and the time span is important. A weekend beginner's course may be adequate time enough for adults to enjoy casual sailing, but depending on the area's general climate may not necessarily allow for unsuitable weather conditions. The time span may also be too short a period for children to discover an interest in the sport. A five- or six-day course, by contrast, can become a real group adventure as well as improving the odds on good weather. Time spent on the

ABOVE **Learning to sail in a sailing school should involve a carefully structured course, which provides the right mixture of knowledge, safety and fun under good supervision – preferably in the sun.**

water is what counts when learning to sail and, with luck, a week at a sailing school can provide as much as 25 hours of quality sailing time, which is the

equivalent of a great many weekends of occasional summer sailing, ample time enough to learn the basics.

During a sailing course, students will have the opportunity to overcome various hurdles placed in their way, such as learning to rig up, get afloat, sail the boat upwind and downwind, tack, gybe, try capsizing and then progress beyond. They learn at their own pace, but if the school knows its job that pace will be fast, the course will be fun, and should clearly be experienced as a holiday.

Teaching children

If parents know little or nothing about sailing, it obviously makes good sense to send the children to a school.

Sailing school induction for children should be run according to the detailed principles laid down in logbooks, such as the International Optimist Logbook or the RYA Young Sailors Logbook, whose requirements are shown here.

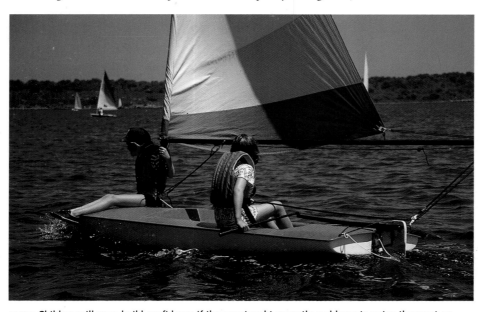

ABOVE **Children will soon build confidence if they are taught correctly and learn to enjoy the sport on their own. It is best for parents in general to leave the teaching to qualified instructors.**

Instructor qualifications

National sailing authorities require that their sailing instructors are qualified to a certain level. The basic level required by the Royal Yachting Association in Britain states that an RYA Instructor must:

- Register with the RYA.
- Hold a valid RYA Powerboat Level 2 certificate – this includes safe powerboat driving skills and the use of kill cords to eliminate any danger from propellers.
- Hold a valid first-aid certificate.
- Pass a pre-entry assessment sailing

test which includes sailing without a rudder, sailing backwards, man overboard drill and coming alongside, using the Wayfarer in difficult, windy conditions.

- Complete a five-day training course plus a one-day assessment administered by an external RYA coach assessor.

In addition, any instructor must have the rapport and communication skills to get on with the students, keep them in order and pass on a love of sailing.

International Optimist Logbook

Includes personal details, boat details (if you own one), awards divided into five grades (covering practical technique and theory) and the Coastal Bar, major racing achievements, a complete equipment breakdown and diagram of the Optimist, detailed syllabus for passing each grade with space for certificates, tips and diagrams, and suggested further reading.

Grade 1 This should be within the reach of most beginners after a six-day course.

Grade 2 Usually reached after about 12 days' instruction.

Grade 3 You need to be a confident and experienced sailor.

Coastal Bar To achieve this you must learn to sail in tidal waters. A minimum of 20 hours' sailing experience is required to achieve this level.

Grade 4 You should be racing regularly at club level and occasional open meetings.

Grade 5 To make this grade you should be racing regularly in open meetings.

RYA Young Sailors Logbook

This is a detailed booklet that includes an introduction and instructions aimed at parents, a summary of all the requirements for the awards, a personal logbook, and a record of achievement. It divides the RYA Young Sailors Scheme into a total of nine

different awards with a clear progression from novice to expert:

Start Sailing Stage 1, 2 and 3 certificates.
Advanced Sailing Blue, white and red badges.
Racing Blue, white and red badges.

TOP **The International Optimist is the classic children's single-handed dinghy, and enjoys highly competitive fleet racing worldwide.**

LEFT **Children learn rapidly when blessed with enthusiastic instructors. Helmets are one solution to save small heads from getting hurt by the boom.**

LEFT **Three teenagers get to grips with a gennaker hoist at dinghy school.**

boats at any one time. This is all part of the fun, as children enjoy roaring around with the instructors as much as sailing.

Once they are on the water, children will do what they are told without asking instructors why, and soon develop an automatic and instinctual reaction to things such as moving the tiller. On the whole children pick up the basic skills much faster than adults.

Safety first

When sailing, safety is of course a primary consideration. A specific safety problem for everyone is getting banged on the head by the boom. Schools are obliged to take a child to the local casualty department (emergency room) if there is any sign of concussion. Some schools have solved this by providing children with lightweight helmets, a good idea but not necessarily the most ideal. They can also give the wrong impression that sailing is a dangerous sport. A better solution being used by schools recently is customized dinghies featuring padded booms and high clews that eliminate the dangers of head injury.

How much do children learn?

The popular image of a sailing school is that you spend the whole of the first day in a classroom learning about sailing theory before you are allowed anywhere near the water. Apart from being boring this simply does not work with children. If they have never been sailing before there is no way they will understand the theory of it, and the first priority for any sailing school that knows its business should be to get the children on the water

as soon as possible and make sure they stay on the water, which is the ultimate classroom, throughout the course.

The ideal should be to have a dinghy such as an Optimist for each child, with two instructors teaching 10 children (minimum 1:5 ratio) from two rescue boats. If the wind is more than Force 2 the children may start to find things difficult, so then the instructors can use half the number of Optimists to let half the children take a breather in the rescue

LEFT **Young sailors can have a lot of fun, and gain important experience, by going offshore in small cruisers, which may also offer the opportunity to live on board.**

Teaching Adults

Adults, juniors and children tend to learn very differently in terms of what they accept as worthwhile, how quickly they assimilate information, the amount of hardship they will put up with and the kind of experiences they enjoy. This means that adults should always be taught dinghy sailing in separate groups from youngsters. They tend to benefit from more dedicated tuition which can be given in large, stable dinghies of which the Wayfarer is a favourite. This allows the instructor to sail with up to three students while they learn the rudiments of handling a boat as quickly and safely as possible. The instructor can then move to an accompanying safety boat when the confidence and sailing skills of the students has increased to the point where they feel comfortable enough to take physical charge of the boat.

Beyond the basic introductory levels (Adult level 1 and 2 on the RYA syllabus) adults should learn in groups of similar ability so students can progress at the same pace. Intermediate level tuition (Adult level 3) should extend beyond the basic skills of sailing in order to improve both knowledge and techniques, which is often best done by incorporating elementary racing into a five- to six-day course.

The next stages of Racing and Advanced Sailing (Adult levels 4&5) are both recommended as full six-day courses. Even if you have no desire to compete, learning to race is particularly useful for sharpening your boat handling skills and making quick assessments of on-water situations. Tactics, boat tuning, roll tacking and fast manoeuvres are all covered and a single-hander such as the Laser 1 is ideal for adult tuition. An Advanced Sailing course requires the highest level of sailing skills and is only recommended to students with real commitment and who have several years of experience. The course is designed to test sailing abilities to the limit and can only be assessed in strong winds when all boat manoeuvres must be performed to the highest standards, including specialist skills such as sailing backwards and sailing without a rudder.

LEFT **Learning to sail on a holiday in a warm climate brings all the advantages of a relaxed environment combined with predictable warm waters and reliable, mellow winds.**

Short course tuition can also be a real benefit for learning specific skills such as trapezing, spinnaker and/or gennaker techniques, as well as catamaran sailing. These are ideally run with a small group, and with suitable equipment and good winds should enable fast progress over no more than a weekend.

Learning yacht sailing

Cruising skills are also well served by a professional syllabus. The RYA National Cruising Scheme for instance ranges from a basic introductory Competent Crew five-day course, which is largely practical and aims to provide sufficient knowledge of basic seamanship for a novice to become a useful crew member. The course syllabus includes: understanding sea terms and boat parts; sail handling; rope work; fire precautions; man overboard; emergency equipment; manners and customs on board; flag etiquette; rules of the road; loading and rowing a dinghy; basic meteorology; dealing with seasickness; helmsmanship; sailing and general duties on board.

Beyond that, the next stages are Day Skipper, which is divided between shore based and practical to provide enough ability to skipper a small yacht in familiar waters by day. Coastal Skipper is also shore based and practical, and should provide the ability to skipper a yacht on coastal passages by day and night, while the very top qualification of Yachtmaster Ocean is, as its name implies, sufficient to skipper a yacht across oceans.

ABOVE **Theory is a vital part of any sailing course, covering subjects such as sailing dynamics, the effects of wind and weather, tides, first aid and safety.**

Dinghy construction

There is a massive choice of dinghy and catamaran classes, with construction and components that vary from the very simple, as found on classes such as the Topper, to the downright complex on boats at the top of the performance range such as a 49er. However, all classes regardless of size and performance will share some of the principal features.

Wooden boats

Boats with wooden hulls have been almost completely superseded by modern plastics, and they are now a rarity reserved for traditionalists. Carvel and clinker are alternative methods of horizontal planked construction, with carvel planks laid flush to a frame while clinker planks overlap. Clinker, which was once widely used on small rowing boats, enjoyed a period of great popularity for racing classes such as the National 12 and Merlin Rocket, until it lost popularity to fibreglass. Clinker is still used to build the occasional modern traditional class such as the Salcombe Yawl.

Fairey Marine pioneered the art of moulding sheets of laminated wood around a frame to provide a lightweight skin, using techniques that they originally developed to build aeroplanes. Famous classes built in this way included the

ABOVE **The 49er uses a modern sandwich laminate to provide the optimum mix of light weight and rigidity in a severely stressed platform, which has to cope with both waves and an exceptionally powerful rig.**

Firefly, Finn and Flying Dutchman, all of which were Olympic classes. This building technique has been completely superseded by modern plastics.

The simplest and cheapest wood construction used sheets of laminated marine plywood to give a box-like shape, and was extremely popular with many of

the new generation post-war dinghies such as the Optimist, OK, Enterprise and GP14. The Mirror, for many years one of the most popular small dinghies in the world, helped pioneer the home-built technique. It was constructed with plywood panels held together by stitches of wire and fibreglass tape.

ABOVE **The International Cadet class for children was one of the first postwar designs with a simple plywood box shape and flat pram bow.**

ABOVE **Labour of love: a wooden boat can look very beautiful, but requires a considerable amount of care if it is to stay that way.**

ABOVE **The Salcombe Yawl is a modern racing class based on a traditional design, which still uses clinker planking in its all-wood construction.**

ABOVE **A fibreglass yacht requires rather more maintenance than a small dinghy, with an annual application of anti-fouling paint below the waterline and possible use of varnished fittings.**

Fibreglass boats

GRP (glass reinforced plastic) began to replace wood for dinghy building in the 1960s. Despite years of development, construction principles have remained the same.

Sheets of woven glass fibres are laid in (or sometimes on) a hull or deck mould, and layers are built up to the required thickness. The fibreglass sheets are laminated by brushing or spraying on a liquid catalyst, which is usually a polyester (sometimes called Vinylester) resin. When the resin cures, the fibreglass sheets provide a hard-skinned hull, which can be removed from the mould with the help of a release agent. Hull rigidity is usually formed by using plywood frames, and a gelcoat (polyester paint finish) is used to give a smooth outer and inner finish to the hull. The deck may be plywood, but on a modern dinghy it is more likely to be moulded fibreglass as well, and features such as the thwart and centreboard case made from additional moulds.

The attractions of fibreglass are threefold. First, it is economic to set up a production line using the same mould or set of moulds, which will guarantee a virtually identical series of mouldings. Secondly, the skills required to produce mouldings are likely to be considerably less than those needed to build a wooden boat and the raw materials are much

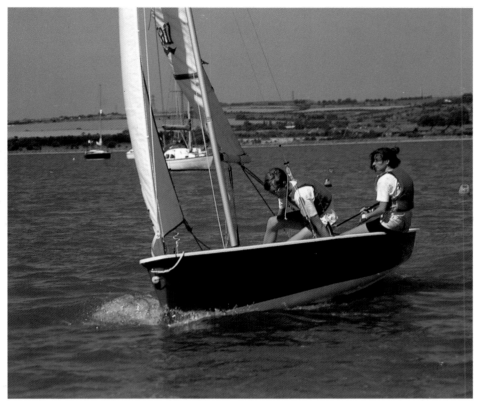

ABOVE **Modern fibreglass dinghies put fun and function first with an easy-to-clean hull and deck that requires minimal maintenance over the first few years.**

cheaper. Finally, fibreglass requires virtually no upkeep. It does not need the rubbing down, painting and varnishing that wooden dinghies used to require annually, but it does need cleaning, and over the years the gelcoat may be prone to cracking and fading and will then need painting to restore its appearance.

Serious problems on older fibreglass boats may include: osmosis (bubbles forming on the hull when the skin delaminates); the hull soaking up water between laminates and putting on weight; and the seams between hull and deck coming apart. However, fibreglass remains the number one choice for dinghy construction, and modern materials and techniques help to ensure that the long-term problems that afflict many earlier boats have become less prevalent.

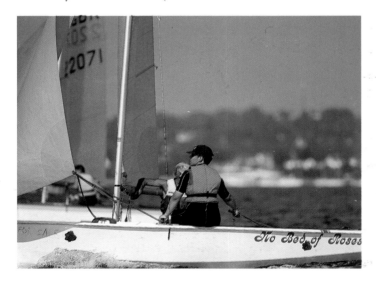

LEFT **The effects of salt, sun and dragging up the beach will degrade fibreglass over a number of years. Once you get to the stage of having to paint the hull, the advantages become less obvious.**

ABOVE **The Laser Pico has a rotomoulded and foam sandwich hull, which makes it rigid, giving better performance. It has become a favourite with sailing schools and holiday operators.**

ABOVE **The Dart 16 has rotomoulded hulls that combine high volume, light weight and durability.**

Plastic boats

Rotomoulded plastic hulls were developed for the mass production of simple dinghy hull and deck shapes, at the same time as the boom in windsurfing technology. The first and best known rotomoulded dinghy is the polypropylene Topper, while other more recent designs include the Pico and Dart 16 catamaran moulded in Techrothene, a polypropylene variation that is combined with a plastic foam sandwich.

The principal advantage of roto-moulding is that it is one of the most economic means of ensuring high volume production using a material that is highly durable (though prone to scratching) for beach use. However, initial tooling costs are very high, which restricts rotomoulding to a very small number of strongly marketed classes, and the skin material is likely to be too flexible and/or too heavy for a really high performance.

Advanced laminate boats

Basic fibreglass technique has led on to a variety of materials and skills that can provide greater rigidity combined with a much lighter weight. These requirements are reserved for the high performance end of the dinghy market where cutting edge construction is likely to feature foam sandwich and advanced laminates.

Foam sandwich construction utilizes a layer of superlight foam, such as Airex, sandwiched between two fibreglass skins. This makes it possible to produce thicker, more rigid hull walls at considerably lighter weight than pure fibreglass. The building technique is considerably more advanced and more time consuming, which tends to add significantly to the cost. With older boats there is also the possibility of the sandwich delaminating, and the foam deteriorating and soaking up water, all of which may spell the end of the road for an old (or not so old) hull.

Foam sandwich may also be used in conjunction with more advanced materials than basic polyester with fibreglass. Epoxy resin produces a stiffer and stronger moulding than polyester, but is more expensive and difficult to work with,

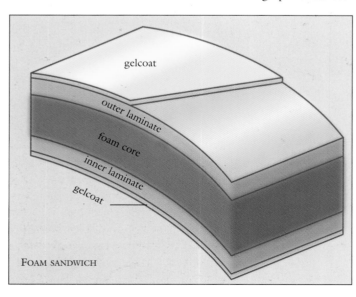

gelcoat

outer laminate

foam core

inner laminate

gelcoat

FOAM SANDWICH

LEFT **A typical section of foam sandwich. Hull walls can be made much thicker with this, and therefore more rigid, while the superlight foam filling ensures that they also remain light.**

RIGHT **Aluminium tubing is a popular material for racks, and can also be incorporated to stiffen up the hull with a space frame structure.**

ABOVE **Advanced sandwich construction, which makes use of epoxy and carbon, is favoured by large-scale, high-performance boats where weight is at a premium. This is a big catamaran under construction at Multiplast in France.**

and the critical curing times may require intensive techniques such as vacuum bagging to suck out excess air or hot oven curing to ensure a consistent finish. More resin equals more weight, so pre-preg fibre is impregnated with exactly the correct amount of epoxy resin for the optimum strength/weight ratio before it is oven baked.

Fibreglass comes in a variety of specifications, and may be replaced by a higher performance woven material, of which black carbon cloth is most widely used. Carbon can only be laminated with epoxy resin and has the potential to

produce the lightest, stiffest boats of all. There is a considerable price penalty in both materials and construction technique, which ensures that carbon is mainly reserved as a reinforcing material in critical hull areas.

Extra hull reinforcement may be provided by a tubular space frame that gives lateral support. This allows heavy deck areas to be removed, increasing working space for the crew and cutting down weight. Aluminium is the favoured material as there are likely to be too many complex joins for effective use of carbon.

High performance dinghies such as the Laser 4000 and .eps feature wings that increase righting moment and can provide a weight equalization system – this is used on the widest setting for the lightest crews and narrowest setting for the heaviest crews. Favoured materials for wings are foam filled fibreglass, which provide a solid rack (Laser.eps), or aluminium tube, which may have nylon mesh that you can both sit on and trapeze off (Laser 4000). The possible disadvantages of wings include increased weight, and catching a wing end in the water, which can lead to capsizing when the boat heels too far.

ABOVE **A large, modern sportsboat such as the Mumm is an all-out racer that demands sophisticated construction.**

LEFT **The Laser.eps uses foam filled fibreglass wings to allow the crew to exert more leverage. The wings require maximum rigidity and minimum weight for top performance.**

Foils

Centreboard, daggerboard and rudder foils have to be rigid with maximum resistance to sideways pressure, though some twist in the tip may be built into the design to help promote lift to windward.

Foils generally need to be as light as possible for ease of use and high performance. The exception is a ballasted centreboard, which is weighted to keep the boat stable while sailing or at a mooring. Ballasted centreboards are mainly found on traditional pre-war dinghies, with a cast iron plate weighing as much as 50kg (110lb) and requiring a drum winch to lift it.

Laminated plywood This is the simplest material for a foil. This type of foil can be relatively light, but is likely to be prone to flexing and impact damage, while the constraints of the material are likely to limit it to a basic foil shape with parallel rather than tapered sides, which will inhibit performance.

THE DINGHY

mast

mainsail

forestay

kicking strap

jib

boom

shroud

mainsheet

tiller

bow

stern

hull

rudder

centreboard

foredeck

tiller extension

sidedeck

LEFT **This shows a typical two-man dinghy that is easily handled and does not require a high level of sailing expertise. It has most of the basic common features of the majority of dinghy designs.**

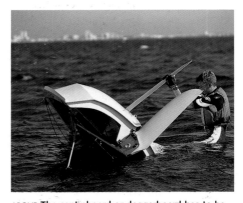

ABOVE **The centreboard or daggerboard has to be strong enough to withstand one or both crew using it as a righting lever during a capsize.**

ABOVE **Rudder foils are prone to impact damage if the tips hit the bottom. Most sailors have to make simple repairs at the end of a season.**

Moulded plastic This is the most price-effective foil material for mass-produced dinghies such as the Topper and Pico. The foil can be moulded in any shape using a strong and durable material, but is likely to be too heavy for really high performance sailing.

Solid fibreglass This is moulded round an internal frame and is a popular choice for an overall improvement in weight and rigidity characteristics. Refinements on this system may use more exotic materials such as self-skinning epoxy foam that expands inside the outer skin to produce a super-light, super-rigid core to help ensure the foil will not bend or break on impact. At the top of the scale in price, performance and beauty, glass sheathed wood-laminate foils are hand built and shaped on a one-off basis using a variety of materials.

Hiking aids

Dinghy sailors hook their feet under webbing straps so they can hike over the side and use their weight to hold the boat upright. Over a period of more than a few minutes the experience may range from moderately enjoyable to downright

painful, depending on the ergonomics of the boat and the fitness and dynamism of the crew.

A more efficient alternative is to stand out from the boat, a technique pioneered by Sir Peter Scott in the 1930s. The modern variation uses a trapeze wire, which is attached to the mast next to the shrouds, and has a handle and ring to hook on to with the free end secured to the boat by an elastic shockcord.

ABOVE **The skipper has his feet hooked under the straps for hiking, while the crew stands out on trapeze, and both working to hold the boat down**

Masts

Aluminium masts Classes such as the Topper and Laser have a very simple mast made up of two parallel sided, sealed (to prevent water ingress during a capsize) aluminium tubes with a round section. These are sleeved together and it is vital to ensure that the sleeved area is free of sand or grit, and to take the mast apart regularly to ensure the two halves do not fuse together. The mast is supported at the base and at the deck of the boat, but is otherwise self-supporting and requires no forestay or shrouds. The mainsail is pulled over the mast using a luff sock, similar to the system used on windsurfers. *Pros*: Low cost, easy storage and roof racking, with very little to go wrong. *Cons* Relatively heavy, with unsophisticated bend characteristics.

A more refined alternative is a one-piece, oval section, tapered, aluminium mast. The taper at the top is designed to provide bend characteristics that match the curved luff of the mainsail, and the lighter weight reduces pitching moment. An aluminium mast should ideally be sealed to prevent sinking and inversion during a capsize, but using internal

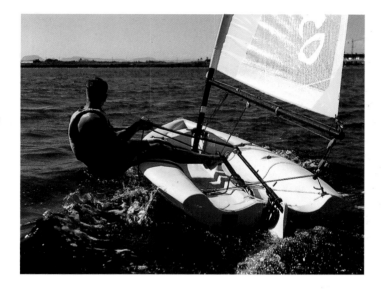

LEFT **The Pico has a simple, unstayed aluminium mast that is cheap and highly functional. The sail can be stowed by wrapping it round the mast.**

halyards to reduce wind drag may prevent this. In some cases a compromise is possible, using a foam-filled top section to provide sufficient buoyancy. *Pros* Good performance and weight characteristics are possible, though tapered aluminium masts come in all sizes and shapes, so this varies. *Cons* Tends to be complex and heavy.

Carbon masts These offer the greatest performance potential in terms of light weight, strength and resilience, and the best available bend characteristics. Carbon is equally suitable for both fully supported masts (forestay, shrouds and spreaders) and unsupported use as on windsurfers, and can be combined with a glued aluminium or plastic track and riveted fittings. A lower cost compromise is a carbon top mast, which combines a carbon top section with an aluminium bottom section. *Pros* Lightest possible weight makes rigging and righting easy, and reduces pitching moment. Precise bend characteristics can be built into carbon to provide potential top performance. *Cons* The most expensive option at present, but price differences will fall and carbon masts will gain in popularity.

Catamarans tend to have masts with a wide oval section that look like a tear drop when viewed from the top. The mast rotates at the base to keep in line with the mainsail, and plays an aerodynamic role as a part of the sail when the catamaran sails at high speeds. Due to its shape, a catamaran mast will bend sideways with little or no movement fore and aft, and doesn't require any spreaders because the shrouds are spread over a wide base.

Carbon masts are gaining in popularity for catamaran use due to their much lighter weight, while extreme high performance catamarans have for many years experimented with full-sized wing masts – these may completely supplant the conventional sail in terms of performance, but are impractical for regular use.

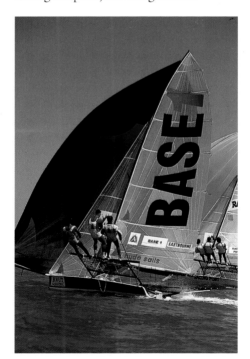

ABOVE **This skiff's masthead gennaker and powerful mainsail relies on the lightweight strength and resilient, pliable characteristics of its carbon mast.**

ABOVE **The 470 has a tapered aluminium mast for high performance. The support from shrouds and spreaders can make the mast relatively complex.**

Booms

On the majority of dinghy classes the boom is an aluminium tube whose sophistication matches that of the mast. A carbon boom is the luxury, lightweight choice for high performance.

The boom is attached to the mast by a gooseneck, which allows it to swing freely from side to side in a near 180 degree horizontal arc to the limit imposed by the shrouds. The gooseneck will also allow the boom to swing in a vertical arc. When sailing, the boom is held up by the pull of the mainsail and held down by the combined forces of mainsheet and kicking strap.

Until the 1990s most dinghy booms featured a slot for a bolt rope in the foot of the mainsail. On modern dinghies this has been superseded by a loose-footed mainsail simply held at the tack and clew.

While aluminium is the traditional material for spinnaker poles, carbon has become a popular alternative for gennaker poles due to its superior stiffness and weight characteristics.

ABOVE **The bolt rope, which is built into the luff of the mainsail needs to be guided carefully up the mast slot. The Dart 16 catamaran shown here has no boom and therefore relies on a loose footed mainsail, which is secured by the tack at the mast and clew by the mainsheet.**

RIGHT **Shrouds and spreaders are used to support the mast and control how far it bends sideways. Sail controls such as the mainsheet, downhaul and kicker tension also affect the degree of mast bend. A great deal of extra stress is created by sailing with a gennaker, a feature of the Laser 3000.**

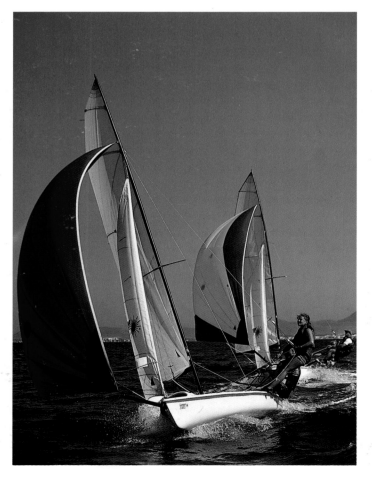

Shrouds and spreaders

A tapered aluminium or carbon mast, which supports both mainsail and jib, will usually need to be upheld by a wire forestay at the front and wire shrouds at the sides. Shrouds are generally made from 3mm (⅛in) wire, and may be covered in plastic to help prevent wear when the mainsail is let out against the leeward shroud on a downwind course.

An una-rig dinghy has only a mainsail and may not require shrouds or forestay despite its bendy mast. The Finn and Europe, both Olympic classes, are typical examples. Some boats such as the Laser.eps feature a mini-shroud system that only supports the bottom of the mast.

Spreaders are used to increase the angle at which the shrouds join the mast in order to give greater side-support. Due to the width of the platform, spreaders are not used on catamarans.

The length of both forestay and shrouds should be adjustable using chainplates. This enables the mast to be raked forward and back to tune the boat's handling characteristics.

Mainsails and jibs

The mainsail is the main powerhouse of the boat, and is usually held to the mast by a bolt rope, which is pulled vertically up the mast slot by the main halyard. Problems maintaining sufficient luff tension led to a period when locks at the top of the mast became popular, but the advent of 2:1 halyard systems featuring non-stretch braids (synthetic woven lines) such as Dyneema (Spectra) made the halyard lock unnecessary.

The mainsail roach (the outer edge beyond a simple triangle shape, see diagram right) must be supported by battens. The old style of wooden battens have been completely supplanted by modern, superlight, tapered, laminate fibreglass battens, which allow precise flexing characteristics to be incorporated. Catamarans and some high performance

RIGHT **All modern dinghies have similar features. Note the large roach shown here, which must be supported by full length battens.**

dinghies such as the 49er and International Canoe feature full-length battens that run from mast to luff, emphasising the aerodynamic concept of a wing style sail to maximise high speed sailing. Fibreglass battens that are moulded in a round section may give a better stiffness to weight ratio for this application.

The role of the jib is primarily to help drive the boat upwind, while the size of the slot between jib and mainsail needs to be carefully adjusted for optimum performance.

The luff of the jib is traditionally attached to the forestay with small plastic hanks, or cloth snaps, which replaced the brass hanks of long ago. Aerodynamically sophisticated alternatives include a

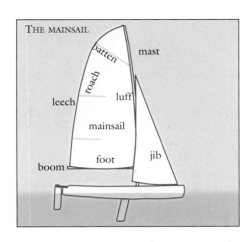

THE MAINSAIL

zippered luff, which closes over the forestay and is often found on high performance catamarans. However, most modern dinghies have dispensed with any attachment to the forestay. They rely instead on non-stretch halyards to provide sufficient luff tension, which are combined with a luff wire that gives enough strength to dispense with the forestay altogether.

Roller systems are a useful feature for jibs, allowing them to be furled for storage onshore or when sailing with a gennaker or spinnaker.

Sail materials

Woven polyester replaced cotton as the leading sail material in the 1950s and, in terms of numbers of sails produced, seems likely to continue as the most popular material. Dacron™ is the best known brand name. In some aspects of performance, however, woven polyester sails have been left far behind by sails made from laminate materials of which the best known brand name is Mylar™.

The main advantage of woven polyester is that it is tough and hard wearing over a long period of time, as well as being relatively cheap. Apart from being on the

LEFT **Most catamarans use a fully battened mainsail, which acts like a rigid foil when set on a rotating mast with an elliptical section. This type of mast is aero-dynamically extremely efficient for high speed sailing, but considerably heavier than a normal dinghy mast.**

RIGHT **The Laser.eps has a novel system that features "mini shrouds", which support the lightweight carbon mast on three sides at boom height.**

ABOVE **The Hobie 17 uses a radial cut mainsail combined with full length battens, that help create a rigid wing effect. Note the furler, which is a slick method of stowing the jib away.**

BELOW **High performance racers like the 29er opt for laminate sails which combine light weight with maximum stability, and also look smart.**

RIGHT **Dinghies for regular use, such as the Sport 14, are most likely to use hard-wearing woven polyester sails with traditional horizontal panels.**

heavy side, the major disadvantage is that it is prone to stretching. Woven polyester is a woven cloth in which the fibre yarns snake or crimp over and under each other. Under tension the crimp will pull straight, which is why there will always be a small amount of stretch in a woven polyester sail. The warp fibres run down the cloth, and have to bend round the fill fibres, which run across the cloth. The fill fibres therefore have less crimp (less potential stretch), so the cloth stretches less across the fill than down the warp. This makes woven polyester most suitable for traditional cross-cut sails where the joins between the sail panels are virtually horizontal with most of the load across the cloth.

The amount of stretch in a woven polyester sail should not be exaggerated. In most circumstances it is likely to be invisible to the eye, and a woven polyester sail will provide maximum durability combined with excellent performance for most dinghy uses. The exception is dinghy classes which are looking for ultimate performances. In these classes it is common to combine a laminate mainsail with a woven polyester jib since the flogging of a jib can soon destroy a laminate.

In terms of ultimate performance, woven polyester has steadily been overtaken by the use of plastic laminate materials, of which the best known is Mylar™. The laminate can be used in a number of ways, but the basic principle is that two sheets of clear plastic form the outside of a sandwich, which is filled with a flat lattice scrim made of polyester, kevlar or carbon fibres. Everything is then bonded together to produce sail panels that are glued together, and the use of conventional stitching is reserved for reinforcement at the corners. Variations on this formula include the use of hybrid laminates for cruising, which combine woven polyester with a rigid scrim.

The final result is a sail cloth that is considerably lighter and more stable than woven polyester. Laminate sail material will not distort when hit by a gust, and can be used to create radial cut sails where the predicted load that radiates from the corners will travel along the length of cloth. The result is a highly efficient sail that looks smarter than woven polyester, but the downside is that laminate sails are

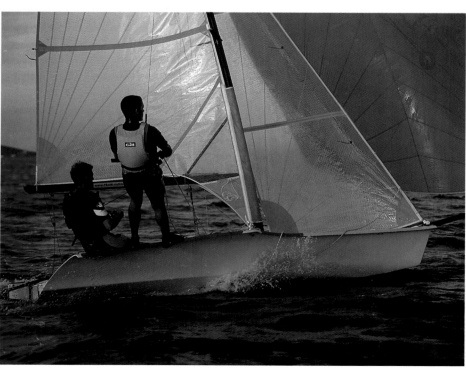

more expensive. Most importantly they are likely to be considerably less durable as well as suffering from UV degradation in strong sunlight. This will lead to cracks in the plastic and a less than aesthetically pleasing sail. However, development in laminate materials is so rapid that these problems may soon be overcome.

Spinnakers and gennakers

The spinnaker is the traditional downwind sail, cut very full and primarily suitable for running downwind. It is supported by a pole or boom, which must be hoisted on the windward side and makes hoists, drops and gybes a relatively complex affair. A spinnaker can be launched from a bag or chute and will tend to collapse and pull sideways if the wind comes on the beam (from the side).

The gennaker is a modern downwind sail that seems set to supersede the spinnaker. It is much simpler to use.

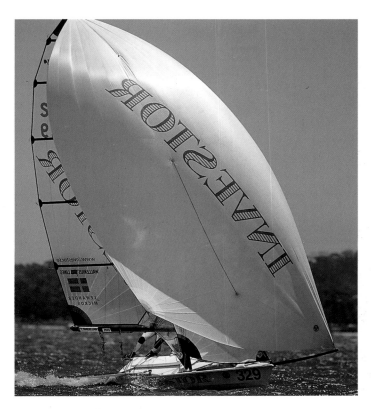

LEFT **The 49er opts for a huge gennaker to maximize its reaching performance. Gennakers – usually rather smaller than the one shown here – are generally fairly simple to control. They lack the complexity of a spinnaker, and can be treated like a massively oversized jib set with a loose luff.**

BELOW LEFT **The 470 has a traditional spinnaker to aid downwind performance. It may look easy, but spinnakers can take a lot of knowledge to control.**

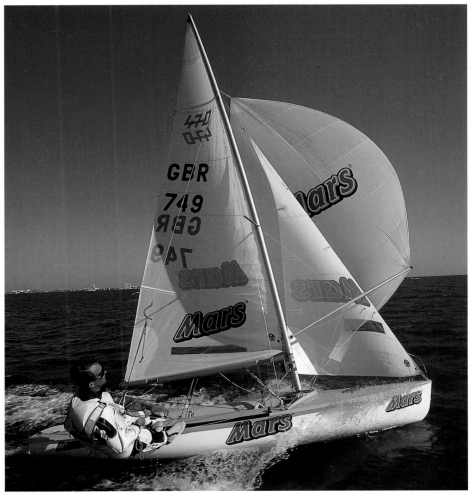

The gennaker is like an oversize, over-full jib with a very loose luff, and is designed exclusively for broad reaching. This has generated a new style of fast sailing in which sailors tack downwind to optimize their speed, aiming to keep the boat planing while bearing away on the apparent wind to sail as deep downwind as possible.

Gennakers are cut much flatter than spinnakers in order to promote fast reaching, and are not at all suitable for sailing straight downwind. They are supported at the tack by a bowsprit, which is launched at the same time as the gennaker is hoisted from its bag or chute, and have a single continuous sheet, which makes hoists, drops and gybes comparatively easy.

Spinnakers and gennakers need to be as light as possible so that they pull easily and stay filled with minimal support. The favoured material is woven nylon or polyester cloth. Both have a light weight to tear strength ratio combined with excellent stretch stability and zero porosity – for obvious reasons it is important that the sail does not hold water when stored in its bag or chute.

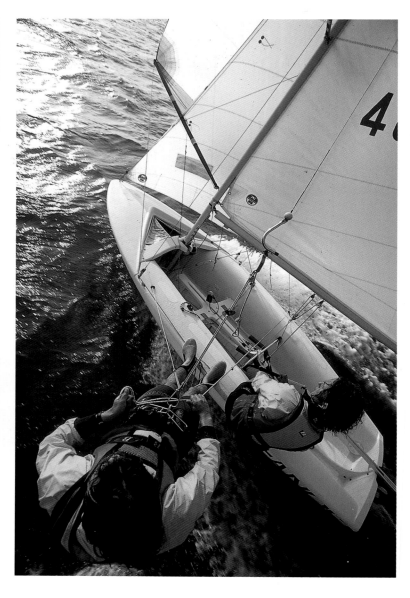

ABOVE **The RS300 single-hander has an uncluttered cockpit with all sail controls in easy reach of the front hand for easy adjustment on either tack while the sailor concentrates on hiking and steering.**

RIGHT **The layout of control lines needs to be made as simple as possible. The complexity of sail controls relates directly to the number of sails, and a spinnaker-driven boat is the most complex.**

Sail controls

The mainsail is built with a pre-determined amount of camber and luff curve that must be matched to the natural bending characteristics of the mast. Sail controls are used to adjust the depth and position of the camber with the outhaul simply flattening the camber of the foot of the sail, while the downhaul and/or kicking strap both flatten and pull the camber forward for sailing upwind and better control in stronger winds.

Mainsheet This is used to control the angle of the attack of the mainsail.

Centre mainsheet Favoured by most dinghy classes, despite some obvious disadvantages: it clutters up the boat and

as it is closer to the mast it requires more sheeting movement and has higher loadings than a transom mainsheet. This requires a multi-purchase sheeting system with extra blocks and extra expense.

The most obvious advantage of a centre mainsheet is that the sheet won't lasso the back of the boat every time you tack or gybe, or worse still lasso other boats during a race. A less obvious advantage is that many sailors prefer to handle the boat with their sheet hand held forwards, in particular when tacking.

When centre mainsheets first appeared they were mainly used with a full length traveller. However, apart from use on

catamarans, the traveller has been replaced by a much simpler strop or hoop, and the role of the traveller has been superseded by sail development and sailing technique, which makes use of maximum kicking strap tension.

Transom mounted mainsheet Found on the Topper and Laser 1, this is altogether a simpler system, which gives greater power for less sheeting purchase than the centre mainsheet. However, it frequently suffers from the lasso effect, catching round the transom or rudder stock when you tack, and is otherwise not fashionable.

The loading on the mainsheet will determine the number and complexity of blocks being used. This may range from a

Many modern dinghies feature an open transom, which immediately drains water from the boat, but makes a transom mounted mainsheet impractical. The crew can adjust the sail controls from both side decks.

simple 2:1 purchase of the most basic single sheave blocks on a Topper, to a heavily loaded 16:1 purchase on a Tornado catamaran with complex twin block systems that allow the sheet to be led through eight sheaves to a high load auto-ratchet jammer.

All blocks should feature low friction, precision machined components, which can flourish in a marine environment. Acetal (plastic), stainless steel and

LEFT **The NACRA 6.0 features a multi-purchase mainsheet led to a traveller, which runs the full length of the aft beam, allowing the mainsail to be let out, but still sheeted in, when sailing offwind at speed.**

anodized alloy are favoured materials. The most efficient blocks have sheaves mounted on ball bearings for smooth running under load. Most mainsheet systems require an on/off auto-ratchet, which will lock the sheet while giving the crew up to 14:1 holding power for use with the mainsheet, jib sheets or spinnaker and gennaker sheets.

Downhaul and/or cunningham This control is used to increase luff tension, flattening the camber of the sail and bringing the draught (draft) forward to maintain control in stronger winds. On all but the smallest dinghies it relies on a multi-purchase system to maximise control.

Kicking strap or boom vang This system forms a triangle that links the underside of the boom to the base of the mast. It holds the boom down at a constant angle, and is used to tighten the leech and control power in the mainsail using a multi-purchase system. The alternative **GNAV** was pioneered by Laser as an upside-down vang. It has a rod-on-roller mechanism mounted above the boom, which provides extremely powerful luff tension control, as well as opening up the area below the boom for much better crew movement.

LEFT **With three sails on a gennaker-driven boat it is vital that all controls are easy to use and identify, and within easy reach. The RS200 provides a lesson in control ergonomics.**

LEFT **The downhaul plays a major role in mainsail control on a high performance dinghy or catamaran. A multi-purpose system is needed to exert maximum leech tension.**

Cleats

Four main types of cleat, produced in glass filled nylon, anodized aluminium or stainless steel, are used for sheet controls. **Cam cleats** feature two, spring-loaded, swivelling jaws, which lock on the rope or line. The cam cleat is the most sophisticated cleat design, combining maximum holding power with easy rope entry and exit while under load with minimum rope wear. The cam cleat is the number one choice for mainsheet and jib sheets. It may also be used in smaller sizes for secondary uses with high loading such as the spinnaker/gennaker halyard, where a combination jamming fairlead is sometimes used.

Open cleats are based on the traditional style of cleat where the rope is criss-crossed over a horn. Available in a number of different designs, but only suitable for securing ropes that are not under load. It is superseded for dinghy use by the Clamcleat and V cleat.

The outhaul stretches the foot of the mainsail and is usually led along the boom. It plays a secondary role to the downhaul/cunningham and kicking strap when flattening and moving the flow in the mainsail, and on some boats may be left in a fixed position.

Controls for the jib are generally kept to a minimum. The angle of attack is adjusted by jib sheets on either side of the boat, led through fairleads or blocks (ratchet optional for high loadings) to cleats where they can be locked off. On some dinghies and catamarans it is possible to adjust the lead block fore and aft or sideways to flatten the luff or foot, as well as fine tuning the angle of attack.

RIGHT **The outhaul is led to the end of the boom. Note the loose footed mainsail that has superseded the use of a bolt rope led through a slot in the boom. When used with modern, stable sail materials it is an equally effective solution to controlling the foot of the sail, and one that allows lower manufacturing costs and makes rigging just that bit faster.**

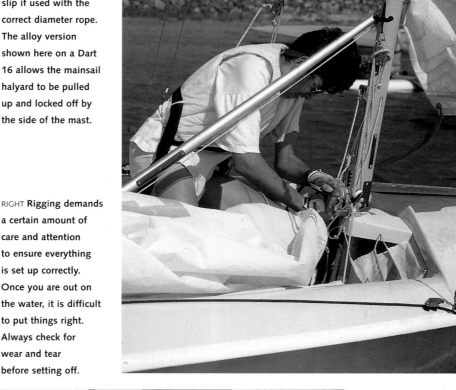

LEFT **The Clamcleat is a simple and clever design which will not slip if used with the correct diameter rope. The alloy version shown here on a Dart 16 allows the mainsail halyard to be pulled up and locked off by the side of the mast.**

V cleats offer the simplest solution to very low load application for small diameter ropes such as the outhaul on a Topper dinghy.

Clamcleats are a refinement of the V cleat and offer a more precise lead, better grip and more efficient entry and exit for small diameter ropes while under load. They are particularly suitable for in-line, mast-mounted applications such as halyards and downhauls.

RIGHT **Rigging demands a certain amount of care and attention to ensure everything is set up correctly. Once you are out on the water, it is difficult to put things right. Always check for wear and tear before setting off.**

LEFT **The role of cleats in high performance sailing is to catch and hold a control line with a fail-safe grip, and immediately free the line when required. This provides the right kind of back-up for sailing on the edge, such as allowing this catamaran to perform wildthing (the lifting of one hull) while sailing fast downwind, a manoeuvre that requires nerve and firm control.**

What to wear

Part of the fun of sailing a small open boat is being exposed to the elements. In the early days enthusiasts had to make do with the most basic protective garments, but modern high-performance clothing has transformed the sport and made sailing a pastime that can be enjoyed year-round in most corners of the world.

DRYSUITS

The modern drysuit is a descendant of the all-enveloping diver suit with a brass helmet and is the first choice for committed dinghy sailors who have to cope with cold water. Sailing ceases to be fun if you get cold and, worn with a thermal fleece base layer, a drysuit provides the best protection available. It is designed to keep all the water out and has the following prime benefits:

- Jumping in and out of a drysuit, particularly one with a front entry zip (zipper), is quick and easy when compared to the horrible, soggy hassle that often has to be endured when struggling in and out of a wetsuit.
- Unlike a wetsuit, a precise fit isn't necessary or even desirable. A drysuit should be big enough to allow easy movement but not so big that it flaps and gets in the way. A drysuit is also excellent for growing children and will accommodate at least three years' growth.
- A good quality drysuit may be expensive, but it is a hard-wearing item that will last over several seasons. The stretchy latex rubber of the neck, wrist and ankle seals or socks will eventually tear or perish, but can be replaced with a proprietary do-it-yourself kit. Tears in the main fabric of the suit can be patched, and if the suit eventually leaks it can be returned to the manufacturer for re-proofing.

HOW TO PUT ON A DRYSUIT

1 Slide the foot gently into the foot of the suit, ensuring that you do not snag the rubber ankle seal on anything.

2 Pull the rubber seal up over the ankle. Dusting your foot with talcum powder makes this easier and is kinder on the seal.

3 The seal guard is made of stretchy latex rubber that will ensure minimum entry of water at that point.

4 Before attempting to put the top of your drysuit on, remove your watch and any other items that may snag the wrist seal.

5 Next, slide the suit over your head, stretching the rubber around the neck so that your head can fit through.

6 When you have put your hand into the sleeve of the drysuit, ensure that the rubber seal around your wrist fits properly.

7 The diagonal front zip means that the whole suit can be done up easily without needing any outside assistance.

8 The seal around the neck and flap over the zip means that you should remain well protected against the elements.

9 A well-fitting drysuit, although it can be expensive, is well worth the investment for the comfort it gives you.

Choosing a drysuit

The lighter the material the easier it is to wear, but it is no good having a drysuit that is prone to tearing and there must be a compromise with durability. Favoured drysuit materials tend to feature PVC (vinyl)/polyurethane coated nylon fabrics in the 115g (4oz) weight range.

The areas that are in most contact with the boat, mainly the seat and knees, need to be heavily reinforced. If you spend a lot of time sliding around on your seat, a trapeze harness or hiking pants will provide extra protection.

When trying on a drysuit, remember to bend and stretch in all possible directions to ensure the suit really is the right size for you.

Seal guards These are like reinforced cuffs, offer valuable protection against inadvertently snagging the wrist or ankle seals, and if made of neoprene may give some thermal advantage.

Storm collar This adjustable collar around the neck has a measurable effect on limiting heat loss.

Internal braces These help to keep the drysuit sitting correctly on your body and can be invaluable if you overheat and want to "drop the top" for onshore activities such as rigging in the dinghy park.

Diagonal front zip This means you can get in and out of the drysuit without an extra pair of hands. The more traditional style of drysuit zip is aligned horizontally across the shoulders, and may be preferred by trapeze crews if a front zip clutters up their harness. The more heavy duty the zip, the more robust the zip handle or puller needs to be. If the handle comes off in your hands, you'll have to use wire or rope as an emergency handle!

Drysuit variations

Breathable drysuits for dinghy sailors have been developed from drysuits for offshore sailors where the no-sweat concept is of particular importance when suits are being worn for long periods. These are likely to be the most expensive drysuits available and the concept will only work properly if your other clothing allows the suit to breathe. This makes it

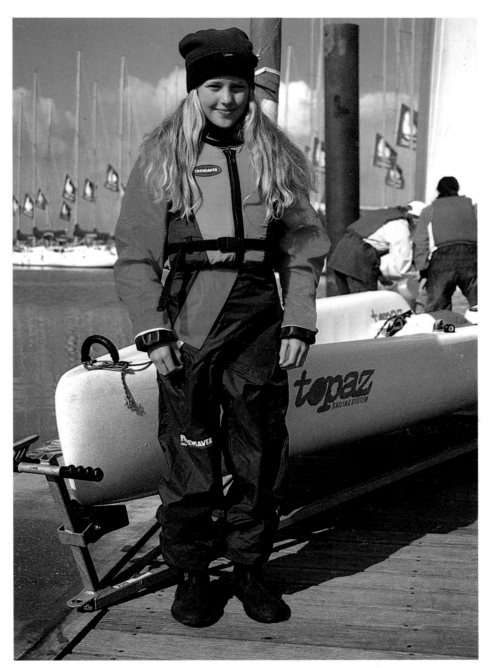

ABOVE **The drysuit is recommended for children sailing in colder weather. It is comfortable, easy to wear and should provide many years of use for an extended family.**

imperative to wear performance-based thermal underwear, which draws perspiration away from the skin without retaining any moisture. It is also important to realize that any part of the drysuit that is covered – for instance by a buoyancy aid and trapeze harness – will not be free to breathe correctly. In general terms, the more physically demanding your style of sailing is, the more desirable a breathable drysuit becomes.

Most drysuits offer a choice between ankle seals or integral socks in the same latex material. Both have their pros and cons. Wearing ankle seals makes it easier to get in and out of dinghy shoes, and gives you the option of being able to walk around the dinghy park in bare feet. Latex socks can be worn with neoprene boots and are the best choice for sailing in water at freezing winter temperatures. Slipping your feet in and out of a latex sock is also much easier than dealing with an ankle seal, but the unprotected sock is very vulnerable to being damaged by a rough surface such as shingle or concrete.

Variations on the conventional drysuit also include the two-piece drysuit, which joins at the waist with two pieces of latex rolled together to create a perfect seal. This dispenses with the need for a zip (zipper), and means you can also wear the top on its own with a wetsuit or shorts.

Another variation is the combi-suit, which combines a loose drysuit-style top with a tight wetsuit-style bottom. This gives a trimmer fit and may provide better thermal protection.

Drysuit care

A drysuit is an expensive garment and care and a small amount of maintenance will be repaid.

Latex seals are one size, which means they often need to be cut down to achieve a comfortable fit. Take great care when you do this because there is no going back if you cut too far. Use very sharp scissors and cut slowly and carefully round one ring at a time before trying each seal for comfort. Remember that the neck seal in particular will stretch when you are using the suit on the water. A perfect seal must be tight enough to keep out the water without choking you at the same time.

Be as gentle as possible when pushing the various parts of your body through the seals. Give the seals a regular dusting with talcum powder to keep them supple and prevent them going sticky, which happens when the chlorine residue from the manufacturing process wears off. Remember that a ring or watch can easily snag and tear a latex seal.

Check your boat over for anything like split pins, screw ends or frayed wire, which could snag and tear a drysuit. At the very least, wrap them with tape.

Clean and lubricate the zip regularly. Rub candle wax on both sides of a metal zip, and very briefly melt the wax into the teeth with a hair dryer. Never allow salt residue to build up on the teeth.

Do not store the suit while it is still wet. Wash it out in fresh water and allow

it to dry completely. Be sure to lubricate the seals with a proprietary solution before storing. A drysuit is best stored out of full light on a plastic hanger. Drysuits

are easily damaged by overexposure to direct sunlight or heat. Leaving a drysuit on the rear shelf of your car is never a good idea.

FEATURES OF THE DRYSUIT

1 Some drysuits have zips across the back. This creates less clutter when wearing a harness, but you will need help opening and closing the zip.

2 Once zipped up, the dry suit will be full of air, so squat down to force the air out of the legs.

3 Pull the neck seal open to let all the air out and deflate the drysuit round your body.

4 Stretch to make sure you have a good fit and can move easily in the suit.

5 Be very careful of snagging latex socks on rough ground. A good way to get dinghy boots on is to fill them with water first.

WETSUITS

The neoprene wetsuit is the popular choice for keeping warm and comfortable when dinghy sailing in all but the hottest sea and air conditions. The principle is that the neoprene traps a thin layer of water, which warms up to the temperature of your body. This is fine so long as the wetsuit is a perfect fit and doesn't let any more cold water flush through that layer.

A close-fitting wetsuit is therefore critical to warmth and comfort and, when buying off the rack, it is important to differentiate between male and female suits and accept that suits for children will only work for as long as they fit correctly. An option is to buy a made-to-measure wetsuit provided by specialist manufacturers.

Choosing a wetsuit

The tight fit of a wetsuit means that the neoprene must stretch in all the right places to provide maximum freedom of movement. In this respect modern neoprenes are far lighter and more supple than their predecessors, and laminate materials such as woven titanium can allow thinner, and therefore lighter and more supple, neoprene to maintain the same body heat. In general, the thicker the neoprene the warmer, heavier and bulkier the suit will be, and the current

ABOVE **Perfectly fitted wetsuits are generally favoured for the kind of performance summer sailing in which a drysuit would simply overheat.**

norm is to have a 5mm ($\frac{3}{16}$in) body and 5mm ($\frac{3}{16}$in) legs used in conjunction with flexible 3mm ($\frac{1}{8}$in) arms for the coldest sailing conditions, while a 3mm ($\frac{1}{8}$in) body should suffice for summer use.

The system used to hold the neoprene panels of a wetsuit together will have a major impact on how much water can flush through. The cheapest, most basic form of stitching is the mechanical overlock, which punctures the neoprene with hundreds of tiny holes that will allow water through. This may be acceptable for a short summer suit, but is no good for serious cold weather sailing. By contrast, flatlock and blindstitching use a stitch that only pierces one side of the edge of the panel, which is also bonded and taped with neoprene glue to produce a virtually failsafe watertight join.

Neoprene is usually lined with lycra on the inside (single lined) to make it easy to pull on and off your body. It may also be lined on the outside (double lined), which increases both abrasion and tear resistance, but is thought to reduce the thermal

effectiveness of the neoprene as the lycra holds cold water on the outside of the suit instead of running straight off a plain neoprene surface. The compromise solution is to have strategically placed double-lined panels in a predominantly single lined suit, providing a hard wearing surface where needed, and the added advantage of incorporating bright primary colours.

ABOVE **Modern wetsuits combine single or double lined neoprene in different thicknesses to ensure a warm body with flexible limbs.**

LEFT **The steamer style wetsuit creates its own closed weather system, but the fit must be body hugging to keep cold water ingress to a minimum.**

The right fit

A good fit at the neck, wrists and ankles is vital to prevent cold water flushing through the suit, while the zip (zipper), which normally runs straight up the spine, should feature some kind of water barrier such as two overlapping neoprene flaps or a single C-Flap that folds over. An alternative solution is to have no zip at all, which has become possible with the most modern flexible neoprenes, and is the direction in which wetsuit development seems likely to go. It is considerably easier to get in and out of a wetsuit with ankle zips, but they can be expensive and they do let water flush through. When trying on a wetsuit, remember to bend and stretch in all directions to ensure it is both tight fitting and comfortable.

Reinforcement

Whether a wetsuit is single or double lined, knee pad reinforcement, which is built into the suit, is vital for any style of sailing that involves the crew going down on their knees, for instance on the mesh trampoline of a catamaran or on the deck of a high-performance gennaker-driven monohull. Depending on your style of sailing, a trapeze harness or hiking shorts may also be necessary to protect the seat.

Steamers

The steamer was first used by surfers who needed a warm, watertight wetsuit, which allowed them to sit in cold water and wait for waves for long periods. Modern steamers are one-piece, full-length suits featuring watertight seams and watertight or fully protected zips. A super-flexible neoprene suit may have no zip at all.

Long john and bolero

The long john is a traditional style of armless, one-piece suit, which can be slipped on without a zip and is therefore very easy and cheap to manufacture. It can be worn in conjunction with a bolero-style neoprene jacket, but this tends to be a poor thermal solution and a loose-fitting dry top with a watertight seal at the waist should provide better flexibility and warmth.

FEATURES OF THE WETSUIT ....

Knee reinforcement is vital for any high performance dinghy in which the crew may have to kneel to launch and retrieve the gennaker.

Most wetsuits have a zip, which is pulled vertically up the back. Care must be taken to ensure that neoprene flaps behind the zip fold in correctly to keep water out.

Convertibles

The convertible is a full-length suit, which has to a large extent outdated the traditional long john and bolero. It has removable single-lined neoprene sleeves, which can be peeled off in seconds to create a short sleeve/bare arm suit for warmer days. The concept works well, making a 3mm (⅛ in) convertible the ideal summer companion to a 5mm (³⁄₁₆in) winter steamer in your wardrobe.

A steamer may be suitable for three or four seasons' use, depending on the thickness of the neoprene, but will overheat in warmer weather.

Short sleeves give much greater upper body freedom for summer sailing, while long legs help protect knees and shins from the hard edges and non-slip surfaces of a modern performance dinghy.

ABOVE **The convertible wetsuit is a clever answer to the overheating problem – pull off the sleeves and enjoy the breeze. The concept can effectively add another season.**

ABOVE **The shortie is for the warmest weather, when it will help protect your body from the ravages of salt and sun as well as providing a barrier to wind chill.**

Shorties

For warm sailing conditions, a short sleeve, knee-length wetsuit allows maximum agility while heat loss from the central body core is still protected by 3mm (⅛in) neoprene.

Rash vests

The seams of a wetsuit can chafe against bare skin, which is why some sailors choose to wear a nylon rash vest as an accessory. Rash vests are also available in thermal material to provide extra insulation.

Wetsuit care

A quality wetsuit will last for many years provided a few basic care and maintenance principles are adhered to:

- Always wash the wetsuit inside and out in clean, fresh water after use, ensuring that salt does not build up on the zip.
- Allow the suit to dry, and then store in a cool, dark place on a plastic hanger.
- Do not leave the suit folded or lying around in a crumpled heap for long periods of time.
- When not in use do not leave the suit exposed to sunlight.
- Make a regular inspection for damage to the neoprene or frayed stitching. Single-lined neoprene is prone to small tears, which are easily repaired with super-glue.

It is worth remembering that since the wetsuit is worn next to your body, personal hygiene should be a general consideration. Some people tend to assume that being in and out of water automatically cleanses the wetsuit. This is not at all true, and a neglected or maltreated wetsuit can easily become a bacteria-ridden garment.

LEFT **Made out of flexible, super-stretch neoprene material, wetsuits are a sailor's favourite item of choice for use in the modern action-packed style of dinghy sailing and racing, which requires plenty of continual body movement to and fro.**

ABOVE **One-piece (centre) or two-piece (right) dinghy suits can be more comfortable and easier to wear than a wetsuit. Braces (left) help keep trousers in position.**

DINGHY SUITS AND OTHER EQUIPMENT

The dinghy suit affords sufficient protection for any type of open boat sailing where the crew needs to stay warm and dry from wind, spray and rain, but does not expect to fall in, capsize, or spend time in the water when launching or retrieving. Most dinghy suits are made in proofed nylon and feature a separate smock with a tight-fitting neoprene waistband and velcro-adjustable wrist and neck closure, which is worn over chest-high trousers with an adjustable ankle closure or, more unusually, a pair of matching dinghy shorts.

Features to look out for include reinforced knees and seat for longevity, a short zip (zipper) at the neck of the smock, full length zip on the trousers to make them easy to get on and off, and one or more pockets. The fit should be loose, light and comfortable allowing thermal layers to be built up underneath. Breathable outer materials are available at the top end of most ranges. One-piece dinghy suits are also available and are likely to be lighter and more comfortable to wear at the expense of being a single garment.

Dry tops

The dry top bridges the gap between the dinghy smock and drysuit, using latex seals at the neck and wrists plus a deep, neoprene waistband to create a fully waterproof top that can effectively be worn with dinghy trousers, a long john or a convertible-style wetsuit.

Thermal underclothing

In cold weather, thermal underwear should always be worn beneath drysuits and dinghy suits. Using stretch fleece materials that are light and quick drying when wet, such as Polartec, enables layers of internal warmth to be built up with minimal bulk. When used with a breathable outer suit they can draw perspiration away from the body so that sweat can be dissipated rather than trapped on the surface of the skin where it becomes cold and leaves the wearer feeling clammy and wet.

For general use, the most user-friendly base layer tends to be thermal trousers or salopettes worn with a matching, long-sleeved thermal zip-top polo- or turtle-neck jersey. One-piece thermal suits may offer marginally better thermal protection.

Boots and shoes

Sailing a dinghy barefoot is seldom a good idea, as there are fittings that can bruise or cut your feet, bare skin won't grip as well as rubber, and there may be something sharp and unpleasant when you come ashore and put your feet over the side.

For all-round use, the dinghy boot combines a neoprene sock, to provide warmth and comfort, with a hard-wearing rubber sole, plus extensive PVC (vinyl) rubber reinforcement at the heel and over the top of the foot to allow for tucking the boot under footstraps and hiking out. The traditional height is high enough to give complete protection to the ankle bones, with zips or laces for easy access. A pull-on boot with neither will be cheaper as well as more thermally efficient, but can be a pain to put on (fill it with water or use talcum powder) and pull off.

The optional choice for warm water sailing is a slip-on rubber or neoprene shoe such as the Okespor Beachsurf. These shoes are light and comfortable, grip like limpets, and are much cheaper than boots – they can also fall off your foot at inopportune moments such as during a capsize.

ABOVE **Neoprene boots have a tendency for unpleasant odour after a period of time. Wash them in fresh water and air regularly. To clean them properly, use a little soap or soak them in a solution of sterilizing tablets.**

ABOVE **Thermal base layers are available in different weights and for various degrees of cold. From left to right: short-sleeved top; long Johns and long-sleeved top; and a thick one piece suit.**

LEFT **Neoprene provides wind-stopping warmth to all-seasons gloves in a variety of styles, but cut-off fingers ensure that small diameter control lines are easier to handle.**

RIGHT **Modern high-performance sailing requires clothing that controls body warmth during periods of relative physical inactivity interspersed with furious activity.**

Gloves

Modern dinghies have a battery of synthetic ropes and control lines, which can be hard on the hands, particularly heaving on a downhaul or taking the strain of the gennaker sheet when a slip could cause a serious burn. For this reason gloves are now widely worn in all seasons.

Summer gloves consist of a reinforced palm made in a synthetic leather material, which can cope with being wet and won't harden when dry (popular materials include Amara and NASH), combined with lightweight mesh backs, which let spray drain through, velcro wrist straps for a precise fit, and the option of short fingers so that relevant ropes can be picked out more easily. Synthetic DIY knitted gloves covered with a PVC lattice provide a lower cost alternative that works as well, even if they don't have the same style rating.

Dinghy gloves for winter pose more of a problem. A glove that is both warm and waterproof tends to be bulky and lack feel. It is no doubt only a matter of time before a winter glove that really works becomes available, but in the absence of anything better most sailors opt for a wet solution, which combines Amara style palms for grip and feel with 3mm (⅛in) double-lined neoprene backing for warmth.

Headwear

An unprotected head is a major source of heat loss in cold weather, which is easily and very effectively protected by a beanie-style hat made in a quick drying thermal material. With the right fit these hats are extremely resilient, offering basic protection against knocks by the boom, and they generally stay in place even during a capsize.

For more extreme cold weather conditions it may help to resort to a neoprene hood or balaclava, but they tend to inhibit hearing and are not particularly pleasant to wear.

Hiking shorts

A long, hard hike off the deck of a small performance dinghy like a Laser or Optimist can be tough and uncomfortable. The role of hiking shorts, similar to cycling shorts, is to provide a soft layer between you and the deck. Made with a combination of mesh, neoprene, straps and padding they may look bizarre but they do the job well and should be very hard wearing.

Knee pads

These are yet another extra that make the modern dinghy sailor look like a medieval knight dressing up for battle. They are necessary on the type of high performance dinghies and catamarans where the crew have to drop to their knees, as when stowing the gennaker in its bag, and therefore need all the extra knee protection that materials such as neoprene and kevlar reinforcement provide.

LEFT **Variations on all-seasons headgear. The peaked cap will help keep the sun off your face but has no thermal properties; the "bush ranger" hat looks good, but stands a good chance of going over the side; balaclavas in fleece or neoprene are the best choice for keeping cold winds out, but not particularly comfortable to wear.**

Buoyancy aids

The buoyancy aid is considered the most vital item in a dinghy sailor's wardrobe. It is only designed to provide sufficient (50 Newton) buoyancy in the water to float a fully conscious person, and should not be confused with a full lifejacket, which is a much bulkier item that has considerably greater (inflatable) buoyancy and is designed to roll an unconscious person on to their back so they can continue breathing. The bottom line is that if you knock yourself out and fall face down in the water, you will continue to float face down when wearing a buoyancy aid. However, this type of accident rarely happens in dinghy sailing and usually there is someone to provide an immediate rescue.

A modern, vest-style buoyancy aid is the top choice for dinghy sailors because it is lightweight and compact, providing maximum freedom of movement in the boat and in the water. Padding provides extra thermal insulation and protection against the kind of knocks and bashes that can occur in a fast-moving capsize.

ABOVE **Capsize is all part of the fun of dinghy sailing. A good buoyancy aid will ensure that you can enjoy the experience in a relaxed frame of mind.**

ABOVE **The waistcoat style buoyancy aid (left) is simple to wear and provides good protection. The buoyancy aid (right) that slips on like a vest, allows freedom of movement with a harness.**

Price will to some extent depend on the type of foam used. PE (polyethylene) foam is both lighter and cheaper, but is layered in sheets that will degrade in time. PVC (vinyl) foam is heavier and more expensive, but will last much longer and provides better thermal insulation.

Always be sure and check that the buoyancy aid fits with your wetsuit or drysuit. Ensure that it is a close, comfortable fit, which allows unrestricted arm movement and will not ride up if you go down in the water. If you intend to sail wearing a trapeze harness, it is important to ensure as well that the buoyancy aid leaves the hook area unobstructed.

Trapeze harnesses

The number one feature to look for in a trapeze harness is comfort. Do not buy a harness unless you can give it a dry land test. A precise fit, which moulds to the body, is vital and, although there is nothing that can simulate the reality of trapezing on the water, you should at least seek answers to these four questions when selecting a harness to buy:

- Is the harness quick and easy to get in and out of, with failsafe buckles that are simple and fast to adjust?
- Is it comfortable and user-friendly when worn with your wetsuit/drysuit and buoyancy aid?
- Does it still feel good when you're bending and stretching?
- How does it feel hanging off a line and what is the pull like on your hips and groin area?

Harness styles

The most popular style of harness is the Nappy, which features a full back with padded straps, padded waist flaps either side, and a padded crutch strap that passes between the legs. An alternative style replaces the nappy element with twin thigh straps that need to be well padded as they pass either side of the groin.

Back support has always been considered vital to help maintain a straight-out stance in a harness, but the newer skiff-style of sailing requires more of a sit-up stance plus maximum upper body mobility. Therefore for short course racing many skiff sailors favour the windsurfer type of harness that has no upper back support at all. Lower back support can still be provided by padded foam inserts and hip tensioning points.

An aluminium spreader bar spreads the load across the hips and prevents crushing. Adjustable hook height is a useful feature as some people require extra lumbar support, which means they like to wear the hook higher.

Shoulder, hip and thigh straps should feature a quick and easy adjustment system using velcro or buckles. When sailing, the ends of webbing straps must be tidied away so they do not interfere with the hook.

Trapeze sailing tends to involve a lot of sliding in and out on your bottom. A tough reinforcement material such as Cordura is vital for durability in the seat area. Custom made-to-measure harnesses that provide a virtually perfect fit, are available from specialist manufacturers.

ABOVE **The harness should give full support tailored to the individual. Size is chosen to give a close fit round the hips and tuning the shoulder and leg straps ensure that the harness stays put.**

Sailing bags

A large sailing bag is a vital accessory for stowing all of your dinghy sailing kit. It is important to get the right size for your personal requirements, and the best bags should have the following features:

- Built in hard-wearing, water-resistant fabric, with a reinforced waterproof base that will cope with wet changing room floors or dinghy decks.
- Separate wet and dry compartments.
- Large cargo pockets for small extras.
- Heavy duty zips (zippers) all round.
- Shoulder and hand straps.
- A built-in name tag so that the bag won't go missing.

ABOVE **It is worth investing in a top quality sailing bag that is tough and water resistant.**

ABOVE **Daring young men on the flying trapeze. It looks good, but a trapeze harness must be as comfortable as possible to actually enjoy trapezing over long periods of time.**

Sunglasses for sailing

The combination of blue sea and white water provides a brilliant reflective surface for the sun, which can make sailing both trying and tiring without sunglasses. It is also potentially dangerous, since the effects of ultraviolet (UV) light on a person's eyes are cumulative throughout their lifetime. When choosing sunglasses for sailing, consider the following:

- Good quality sunglasses should block out both UVA and UVB sunlight to at least 99 per cent.
- For dinghy and small boat sailing it is vital that sunglasses fit comfortably and securely and stay in position come what may. The wrap-around, face-hugging style tends to be more secure and has the advantage of having no protuberances to catch on a flailing rope or line. A good security back-up for an expensive pair of sunglasses is an adjustable eyewear retainer.
- The main disadvantage of wrap-around sunglasses is that they tend to reduce the field of vision.
- Top quality lenses and frames for sailing should be virtually unbreakable, and manufacturers should provide a repair service.
- If you wear corrective lenses, check the availability of prescription sunglass lenses or consider using daily disposable contact lenses with sunglasses.
- Investing in the best will reduce potential eyestrain.

BELOW **You can simulate the feel of a trapeze harness on dry land, and ensure that the fit is right and the straps provide the necessary support.**

How a sailboat moves

At its simplest, wind pushes a sail from behind, which is known as running downwind. Sailing a few degrees either side of downwind was the only direction in which the old-fashioned square-riggers could go, and if the wind was blowing in the wrong direction they would simply have to wait days or weeks for it to change. Thankfully the modern style of Bermudan rig came along to change all that, and now sailboats can sail in almost any direction with the obvious exception of straight into the wind; the more sophisticated and performance-oriented the sailboat, the closer to the wind it will be able to go.

The ability to sail towards the wind rather than just away from it is achieved by the airfoil effect of modern sails. Wind flowing over the sails is composed of a moving mass of air particles that separates when it hits the front or leading edge of the sail. From there it accelerates around both sides, following the curved shape of the sail to produce positive high pressure on the windward side (the side the wind is blowing on to) and negative low pressure on the leeward side (the side the wind is

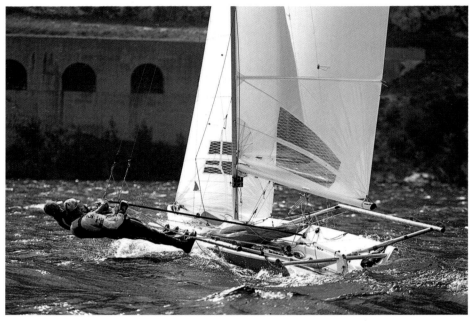

ABOVE **With sails pulled hard in, a modern sailboat can sail towards the direction the wind is coming from. The sails and daggerboard provide a lift to windward.**

blowing away from). The difference between this positive and negative pressure creates the aerodynamic force that sucks the sail forwards and drives the boat along, generating sufficient force to overcome the natural resistance of water

against the lower part of the hull as well as air resistance against the top of the hull, sails, rigging, fittings and crew.

Sail camber and incidence

The cross-sectional shape of a sail will help determine its performance. The degree of curvature (camber) must be correctly aligned with the apparent wind (the angle of incidence) to produce maximum drive. The optimum angle of incidence is widely held to be at 15 degrees between the chord (an imaginary straight line connecting both ends of the sail) and the apparent wind. If the angle of incidence is greater, airflow will detach from the leeward side creating turbulence and reducing drive. If the angle of incidence is smaller, the sail will stall as positive air flow ceases to flow over the windward side.

The amount of camber and its position in the sail will greatly effect performance characteristics. All modern

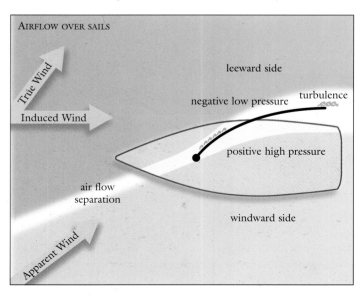

AIRFLOW OVER SAILS

True Wind

Induced Wind

Apparent Wind

leeward side

negative low pressure   turbulence

positive high pressure

air flow separation

windward side

LEFT **Airflow over sails separates on to the windward (high pressure) and leeward (low pressure) sides, and turbulence is created at the leading and trailing edges. The sails must always be adjusted to make maximum use of the speed and direction of the apparent wind.**

high performance dinghies provide adjustment systems to alter luff (leading edge) and foot tension, which will maximize or minimize camber as well as changing the position of maximum camber fore and aft from the midpoint of the sail.

True wind and apparent wind

The wind's force in a sail is concentrated in an area known as the centre of effort (CE) while the outer area of the sail plays a secondary role in keeping the power of the wind under control. This concept can be directly experienced by windsurfers who hold up the rig and can effectively feel the centre of effort pulling between their hands.

Windsurfers also have the most direct experience of the difference between true wind and apparent wind, a concept that is particularly important with all types of high performance dinghy and keelboat sailing, particularly skiff-style, gennaker-driven dinghies and catamarans.

True wind is the real wind. In terms of speed and direction it is the wind experienced by a stationary observer.

Apparent wind is the wind experienced by any moving object. For instance, if a cyclist is cycling at 16kph (10mph) directly into an oncoming wind, which has

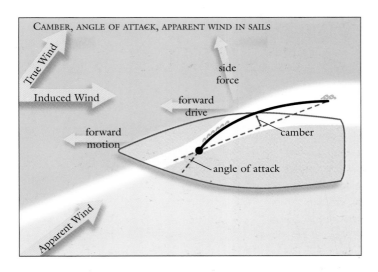

CAMBER, ANGLE OF ATTACK, APPARENT WIND IN SAILS

True Wind

Induced Wind

side force

forward drive

forward motion

camber

angle of attack

Apparent Wind

LEFT **The main sheet or jib sheet is the primary control used to control the angle of incidence or angle of attack, which is adjusting the position of the sail relative to airflow. Adjusting the deepest point or camber is equivalent to tuning the sail to maximize performance.**

a true speed of 16kph (10mph), the apparent wind he has to contend with will total 32kph (20mph). Conversely, if the cyclist is cycling in exactly the same direction as the wind, and both are moving at 16kph (10mph), the apparent wind will be zero. The speed of true wind and apparent wind will never be the same when a boat is moving. Apparent wind is at its lightest when a boat is travelling in exactly the same direction (running dead downwind) as true wind, and becomes progressively stronger as a boat sails closer to the wind. This phenomenon also has a marked effect on the difference in temperature when sailing downwind and upwind.

The direction of true and apparent wind will only be the same when a boat is travelling in the same direction (running dead downwind). On any other course the apparent wind will come from further forward (the direction the boat is heading towards) than the true wind. This is the induced direction of the wind as a result of the boat's forward progress. The greater the speed of the boat, the more the direction of the wind will move forward, which is why the fastest sail-powered craft for their size – windsurfers and catamarans – must always have their sails pulled hard in when they are sailing at speed in order to maximize the apparent wind.

ABOVE **Rapid forward movement transforms the true wind into apparent wind. This is the wind the sailor actually sails in, and may be stronger and from a different direction than on dry land.**

ABOVE **As a boat accelerates, the direction of the apparent wind changes and comes from further ahead. To keep up speed, the helmsman must steer away from the wind.**

Slipping sideways (leeway)

Because of their design, sails cannot achieve a pure forward force. Instead, most of the force is sideways, and becomes progressively more as a boat sails closer to the wind. The sideways force must be converted into forward speed instead of driving the boat sideways or blowing it on to its side. This is largely achieved by the use of a centreboard or daggerboard to provide leeward resistance, combined with minimizing hull and air resistance to allow the boat to move forwards and the crew's skills to keep the boat upright.

Centreboards and daggerboards

While displacement yachts have a fixed keel to prevent them being blown sideways, dinghies are fitted with a centreboard or daggerboard foil which prevents side-slip and also helps lift the boat to windward when it is being driven hard. Both are housed within a case inside the boat – a centreboard swivels through

90 degrees to its down position while a daggerboard drops vertically.

The centreboard is a neater system and has the major benefit of kicking back without damage if the boat hits the bottom. The daggerboard is a simpler system and cheaper to manufacture, and

can be made in a longer, narrow foil shape to optimize both lateral resistance and lift to windward. However, a long, fixed foil can cause serious problems when sailing at speed in shallow water because it is difficult to lift this type of daggerboard quickly.

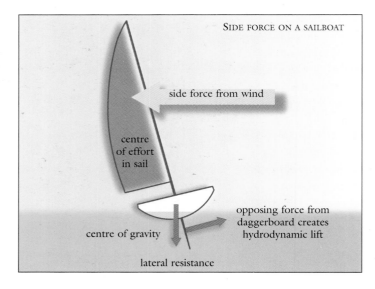

SIDE FORCE ON A SAILBOAT

side force from wind

centre of effort in sail

centre of gravity

opposing force from daggerboard creates hydrodynamic lift

lateral resistance

LEFT **The side forces on a sailboat act on the rig, sails and hull, which are pushed one way, while the centreboard, daggerboard or keel provides a counter balance. It helps to transform the sideways movement into forward movement, as well as providing resistance against the sailboat heeling.**

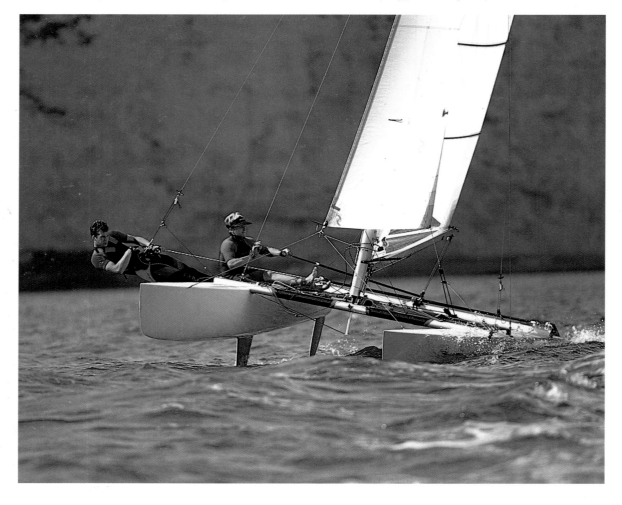

RIGHT **A catamaran has a smaller surface area in contact with the water and a wide platform that provides sufficient leverage to carry an over-size rig. The Tornado shown here is wider than any racing catamaran of a similar size. The disadvantage of such a large catamaran is that in most countries its platform has to be dismantled or tipped on its side to be able to transport it legally.**

A centreboard or daggerboard foil will work with the rudder foil to maximize leeward resistance. The shape and area of the foil is critical to performance, which will depend on the length to thickness ratio, the position of maximum thickness and the radius of the leading edge.

Hull and air resistance

These are related to the speed and course of a boat, the wind speed and direction, and water conditions. Resistance due to friction under the boat is known as skin friction, and is created by individual layers of water passing beneath the boat. The solution is to reduce the amount of boat in contact with the water (wetted surface area) to a minimum, which is first achieved by design and second by the crew trimming the boat correctly.

Resistance due to the shape of the hull (form resistance) is mainly caused by hitting waves, plus the turbulence created by the imperfect shapes of bows, stern and centreboard or daggerboard and rudder foils. Form resistance decreases in proportion to the weight of the boat, and

ABOVE **All modern dinghies need to be sailed virtually flat on the water to minimize friction and optimize performance. A slight degree of heel, as shown here, is almost inevitable.**

ABOVE **Once a dinghy is allowed to heel over, its underwater shape changes and form resistance increases dramatically. At the same time its foils cease to function as efficiently.**

is the factor that prevents displacement boats such as heavy keelboats from accelerating beyond a specific point.

However, with the kind of planing hulls found on most dinghies, resistance stops increasing once the boat rises off its bow wave, leaves its stern wave behind and begins planing. A displacement boat will create a single wave, from bow to stern, from which it cannot escape, but planing boats can break out of that wave and plane over the waves. This is a sensation akin to skimming over the sea, which feels like a great leap forward. It is the fastest form of sailing on a monohull or windsurfer, but the speed of the pencil-slim hulls of a catamaran is due to the combination of minimum wetted area with maximum sail area.

Means of reducing form resistance include: producing a boat to minimum weight at the design stage, sailing with minimum weight, trimming the boat correctly both fore and aft and sideways, and ensuring the stern does not drag and create turbulence, which may also be created by an incorrectly profiled rudder.

Resistance due to heeling of the boat increases in form resistance in direct

relation to the angle of heel. The solution is to sail dinghies absolutely flat at all times, while most yachts should be sailed as upright as the given conditions will possibly allow.

Resistance due to leeway (induced drag) builds up turbulence on the leeward side of the boat as form resistance increases. This can be cured by sailing the boat as flat as possible, ensuring the centreboard is fully down, and driving the boat forwards, which is a specific skill.

Wind resistance on hull, rigging and anything else that stands out is most apparent when sailing close to the wind. The solution is to make the outline of a boat as clean as possible, using internal halyards, which do not break up airflow round the sail, combined with minimalist rigging and no unnecessary protuberances. Wind resistance caused by the physical bulk of the crew is likely to be minimal, and it is more important for the crew to sit in the right place to trim the boat correctly.

Resistance caused by sailing through rough water is best solved by technique to keep the boat driving and prevent it stalling on waves.

ABOVE Wind resistance on mast and rigging can be kept to a minimum by using the simplest possible fittings, as on this catamaran mast.

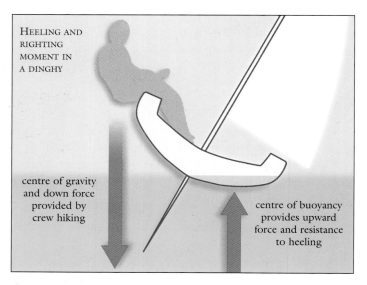

HEELING AND RIGHTING MOMENT IN A DINGHY

centre of gravity and down force provided by crew hiking

centre of buoyancy provides upward force and resistance to heeling

LEFT The heeling and righting moment of a dinghy is determined by the crew acting as the centre of gravity, while the centre of buoyancy lifts the opposite side of the hull. The more the boat is allowed to heel, the less responsive it will be to the down force exerted by the crew.

Keeping upright

All sailboats are designed to be sailed virtually upright, particularly dinghies that have nearly flat bottoms, to maximize their planing ability.

Unlike a yacht, which has a fixed keel weighted (ballasted) with lead, the centreboard of a modern dinghy is not ballasted and totally relies on the skills of the crew to keep the boat sailing upright. How easy or difficult this is will depend on the stability of the hull and the power of the rig. A sturdy, wide-bottomed cruising dinghy with a modest rig such as the Wayfarer will be slow to heel over and easy to control. An ultimate high performance dinghy such as the 49er combines a superlight, minimum wetted surface area hull with a powerful rig that its crew can control using racks and trapezes for maximum leverage. It therefore demands lightning responses and the very best technique to keep it upright.

The skills used by a crew to keep a dinghy upright are a combination of depowering the sails as necessary and using weight to counteract the pull in the sails. This is achieved by using their own centre of gravity as a lever that pulls against the boat's centre of buoyancy, which is directly related to its wetted surface area. The power of that lever is increased by hanging over the side of the boat (hiking) or standing out using a trapeze.

When a dinghy heels over a number of things happen: the angle of the centreboard allows greater side-slip, the angle of the rudder foil can lead to loss of control with the foil leaving the water in extreme cases. As the wetted surface area increases it creates extra drag and prevents effective planing. This change in the wetted surface outline can lead to loss of control. The sails become less efficient and drive is reduced. The righting effect of the crew is diminished as their centre of gravity lifts towards the centreline of the boat. Once a dinghy heels beyond a certain angle its centre of gravity (the crew) will pass over its centre of buoyancy (the wetted surface area). At this point its natural righting moment is transformed into positive heeling moment as the weight of the rig helps pull the boat over into unavoidable capsize.

ABOVE Hiking or trapezing is the lever that helps keep a performance dinghy upright. Hiking on a Laser can be an extremely physical pastime that demands determination.

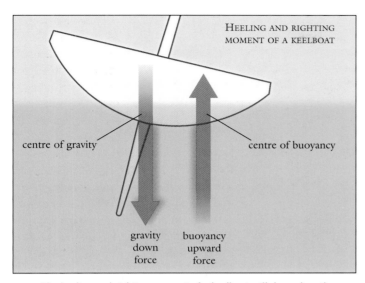

ABOVE The heeling and righting moment of a keelboat will depend on the position of the centre of gravity. This is much lower than in a dinghy and will depend on the length and relative weight of the fully ballasted keel.

ABOVE Getting all the crew to sit up on the windward (weather) deck of a yacht will help keep it upright, but the effect is slight when compared to a crew hiking out on a dinghy. Sitting outside the guardrails is not allowed.

The behaviour of a keelboat is different since its centre of gravity, principally the weight of the yacht itself – is much lower down and will remain lower than the centre of buoyancy which is within the yacht. The righting arm between the centre of gravity and centre of buoyancy actually gets longer as the angle of heel increases, which means that the yacht's resistance to heeling increases. So while a yacht may be blown almost flat, there will be minimal heeling moment induced by the sails, and the ballasted keel will soon bring her back upright, albeit with her bow slewing into the wind. There are exceptions. If a yacht is held down by an out of control spinnaker or knocked down by waves, its cockpit could fill with water. This has caused a few sinkings, but it is a rare occurrence limited mainly to small, open keelboats racing on inshore waters or yachts caught in extreme conditions. These can occur in confused waters on a coastal shelf after a storm, as in the open wilds of the southern oceans where well publicized capsizes have been the result of racing yachts losing their keel.

LEFT In normal conditions a yacht will not capsize, since the righting arm between the centre of buoyancy and centre of gravity gets longer as the yacht heels further, while the effect of wind on the sails is reduced. This means that a yacht can only be capsized by a wave, or an accumulation of waves, in very extreme weather conditions.

Where and when to sail

Dinghy sailing probably qualifies as a risk sport, although the risks are so minimal for those who take care that fatalities or serious injuries are extremely rare. However one should always have great respect for the elements of wind and water, particularly when sailing near a coast.

Safe locations

When starting out, the ultimate safe sailing location would probably be a fresh water lake or reservoir of no more than 1 km (1.6 miles) diameter, with an even depth, warm water, a regular, steady wind of Force 4 maximum, a club to sail from

and non-stop rescue cover. Look for a gently shelving beach or easily accessible pontoons or launch ramps from which to launch. There should not be any overhead powerlines in the locality, no obstructions such as moored boats, no swimmers and absolutely no powered craft except for rescue boats in case of emergency.

The shoreline

The suitability of where you launch and land on the shoreline will depend on its composition and location, how you launch and how it is affected by the prevailing wind. A gently shelving launch ramp with

a hard surface is ideal if you have a trolley, but beware of any slippery areas. Grass or soft sand is fine to launch from if you don't mind dragging the boat, otherwise you may need a trolley with oversize wheels. Shingle makes for hard work when it comes to pulling a boat up. It can also be unforgiving on your feet and even worse on the smooth, shiny bottom of your dinghy.

Launching or landing on mud is to be avoided at all costs. It is most often found in harbours and estuaries that dry out at low water, and can grab your feet and act like glue. Apart from being very messy,

LEFT **With an easily accessible shoreline and no difficult tides to deal with, a lake or reservoir may often be more user-friendly to beginners, with the added bonus that fresh water does not sting like sea water.**

ABOVE **Choose level ground to rig up on. Try not to disturb sunbathers or people having a picnic, and beware of all overhead lines.**

it can also be potentially dangerous if a boat and its occupants get stuck in the mud and are unable to extricate themselves.

Steeply shelving beaches can cause a lot of problems as well. First, the angle of the beach may make it difficult to manage and control the boat on the way down, followed by a struggle to pull it back up. Secondly, you will soon find yourself in deep water, which is difficult when launching and landing. Thirdly, if there is an onshore wind, a steeply shelving beach will encourage waves to build up and crash, and cause heavy undertows that follow.

Lee shores

A lee shore (a shoreline that the wind is blowing on to) was a terrifying prospect for all the old square-rigged ships. It was a lee shore in Ireland that became the wrecking ground for the Spanish Armada. Their captains often found themselves in an impossible position, blown on to inhospitable lee shores with no ability to sail upwind and escape the danger. To this day a lee shore in strong winds can still be extremely dangerous for modern yachts sailing offshore, as was demonstrated by the loss of the famous racing yacht *Morning Cloud* (owned by the former British Prime Minister, Edward Heath) together with two of her crew off the south coast of England in 1974.

ABOVE **When launching, make sure the water is deep enough to get the rudder down, but not so deep that the crew struggles to hold on to the boat.**

By contrast a lee shore can be a positive advantage for dinghy sailors and deserves a five star rating for most windsurfers (who spend a lot of time drifting downwind when they are learning). A U-shaped bay with the wind blowing across becomes an ideal location to sail in if it provides a lee shore for a capsized boat to drift down on rather than being blown out to the open sea. This assumes that the shoreline is easy to land on, and is not being battered by waves.

Crowded water and shores

It is a fact of modern life that all popular pastimes attract crowds, and sailing is no exception to the rule. Always be aware of beach users and swimmers when launching and landing. In an ideal situation swimmers and dinghies should be separated by lanes, but there are times when swimmers will still cross your path and get in the way. Furthermore, they probably do not realize that they are causing an obstruction, and have little idea

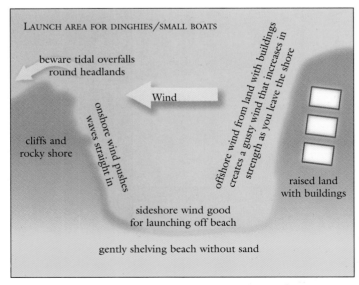

ABOVE **A sideshore wind is generally favoured for launching and landing. Both offshore and inshore winds require care and consideration.**

ABOVE **Keep clear of other boats when launching or landing. Take your turn, help others and, if necessary, tell people what you are going to do.**

RIGHT **The Topper is easy to launch owing to its light weight and a shallow hull moulded in extremely tough polypropylene. Touching the bottom should cause few problems.**

that the dinghy you are sailing may be difficult to manoeuvre and unpredictable in waves. Take extreme care in these situations, particularly with children, and consider giving a friendly call to the swimmers to clear the way.

Be thoughtful and considerate towards other boat users. There is plenty of pushing and shoving in real life, and no need to follow such behaviour when pursuing a pastime. When launching or landing wait your turn; leave plenty of space for other boats to manoeuvre; help others and they will help you. Beware of boats that are anchored or moored close in to the shore when you are launching. Give them a wide berth and if in doubt always aim to pass downwind (or down tide if applicable) of them.

Beware of powercrafts. Power gives way to sail, but some powerboat owners are unaware or oblivious to this, go much too fast, and often have very little comprehension of the problems of manoeuvring a small sailboat. Jet-skis have a particularly bad reputation, but large powercrafts can be equally lethal.

Safety first

- Make sure that the dinghy is correctly rigged, ready to sail and properly buoyant.
- Wear buoyancy aids whenever you and any other crew members are on the water.
- Take suitable clothing for yourself and your crew. Dress up not down, and always allow for the weather worsening.
- Take a paddle in case the wind drops to a flat calm, and a spare rope in case you need to be towed.

RIGHT **Fibreglass dinhies such as the Topper Sport are heavier and more prone to scratches, and require extra care when launching or landing.**

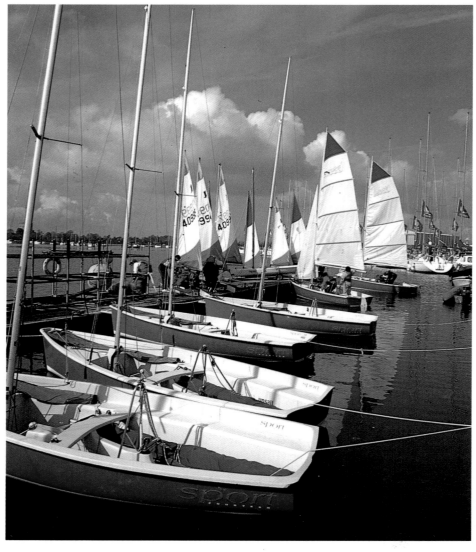

EXTREMES OF TEMPERATURE AND WEATHER

Dressing correctly for the conditions, in particular wearing an efficient drysuit with thermal underwear and protecting your head from heat loss, is essential when sailing in very cold weather.

Sailing in cold water

Exposure to water temperatures below 20°C (68°F) needs to be treated with progressive seriousness as the temperature decreases and the time increases. Very cold water below 10°C (50°F) may be experienced when sailing on freshwater lakes and reservoirs, where temperatures are potentially at their lowest in spring. This is just when many people start to sail after winter, and a sunny spring sky is all that is necessary to lull them into a false sense of security.

Hypothermia

Prolonged exposure to cold water causes hypothermia (acute heat loss) and is eventually fatal. The timescale is very short. Tests have shown that an average person in normal clothes loses consciousness after 20 minutes of floating in water of 10°C (50°F), and death usually follows. If they attempt to splash around to keep warm, the heat loss will be even faster.

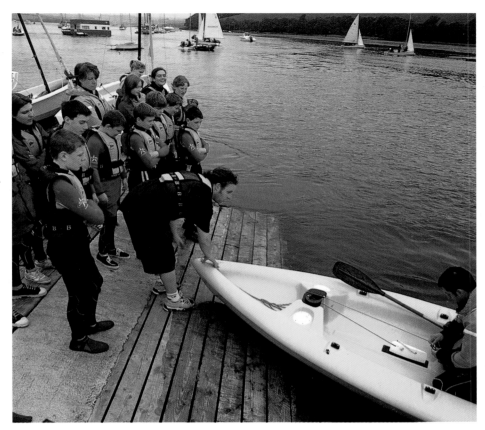

ABOVE **There can be a lot of standing around, sometimes in cold conditions, when learning. Instructors must keep a watch for any signs of the first stages of hypothermia, and be ready to take action.**

Before losing consciousness there are two phases. During the first phase, the person in the water is alert and has the will and ability to participate in his or her rescue; during the second phase, the person's will to survive is effectively lost and rescue becomes totally dependent on outside assistance.

ABOVE **A delicate balancing act is required for sailors to be able to sail to their full potential in cold water areas. Advances in clothing design tailored for cold conditions has made a tremendous difference.**

Treating hypothermia

First stage Shivering, looking cold, complaining of cold. Time to head for the shore without delay.

Second stage Lethargy, drowsiness or confusion followed by numbness, cramp, nausea, slurred speech and eventual loss of consciousness.

Action If a person complains of the cold or shows any symptoms of moving towards the second stage of hypothermia, keep them warm and get them ashore as soon as possible. Get them out of the wind and provide them with dry clothing/coverings. If their condition deteriorates or fails to improve, seek urgent medical attention.

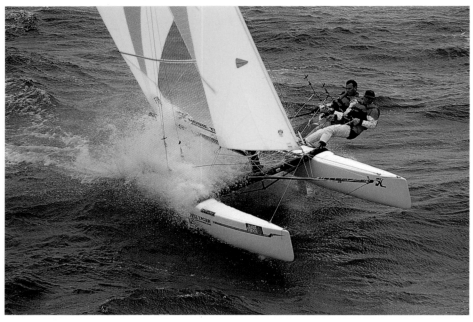

ABOVE **Catamaran sailors know they have to dress correctly to enjoy whistling along at high speeds in all weathers. The faster the boat, the more you need to dress up.**

ABOVE **Sitting in a cold shower is fine so long as the body core keeps warm. With the added effects of wind chill, a leaking drysuit or ill-fitting wetsuit could help kick-start hypothermia.**

Wind chill

It's always warmer out of the wind, and the stronger the apparent wind on a boat the more it will chill the crew. This is why catamaran sailors always need to dress for colder sailing conditions than those who sail at slow speeds. As an example, an air temperature of 20°C (68°F), rated as warm in zero wind, will become progressively cooler as the wind passes a Force 2 breeze (3–6 knots) and be rated cold at a Force 6 (27 knots). By comparison a very cold air temperature of 5°C (41°F) will become icy cold at Force 6 (27 knots).

Wind chill is dependent on what you are wearing, how much of your body is exposed, whether you are wet and your general fitness and body temperature.

Wind chill is not so important in air temperatures of 30°C (86°F) and beyond when a warm wind is guaranteed, but beware the possibility of a thunderstorm or heavy rainfall, which can make the temperature drop dramatically.

RIGHT **When sailing in hot climates the effects of wind chill may become irrelevant due to the warmth of the wind, so that sunburn combined with dehydration becomes a more pressing problem. However, if a thunderstorm occurs the temperature will lower dramatically, and hypothermia becomes a real possibility.**

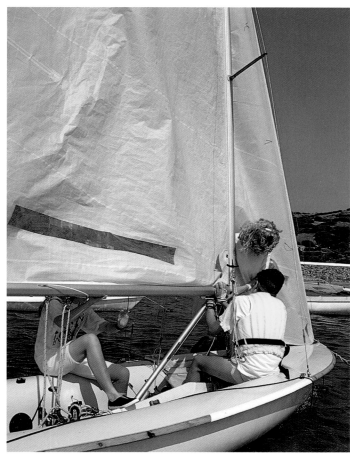

ABOVE **The cooling effects of wind and water can easily deceive about the strength of the sun. Maximum protection should be applied to prevent sunburn.**

ABOVE **The reflection of water combined with the white hull and super-structure of a dinghy or yacht provides a medium in which the effects of the hot sun are magnified. Stripping your shirt off could be hazardous.**

Beware the sun

Sailors in cold climates can seldom get enough of it, but when sailing in hot temperatures the sun needs to be treated with caution. The effect of a cooling wind can be very misleading and, when combined with the effect of strong sun reflected off the water, can lead to severe sunburn, which is exacerbated by the drying effect of a salty sea. Sailors are always advised to use sun block (SPF 15 or higher) on exposed body parts in strong sunlight, and if they burn easily to ensure that their body is suitably covered with lightweight protection and to wear a hat.

A secondary effect of strong sun is dehydration. It is easy to ignore or even not to notice the effects of drying out while sailing, until symptoms, which include a parched mouth and a muzzy, tired, headachy feeling, become apparent. The best cure is prevention, making sure to drink plenty of liquid and regularly to ward off the onset of dehydration. Plain water is as good as anything and on most dinghies you can store it quite easily in large plastic bottles.

If dehydration does begin to get to you, the first thing to do is to seek protection from the sun. Head for the shore and shade, or take refuge behind or even under a lowered sail.

LEFT **The proliferation of skin cancer has struck a chord in countries such as Australia where the sun ethic is being tempered by the need to avoid full exposure.**

Lost in the fog?

A sea fog or sea fret is a common phenomenon in early summer at the start and end of the day. It relies on the heat of the land to burn off as the morning progresses, but frustratingly fog may linger on the coastal stretch where the warm land meets the cold sea. Fog should be avoided at all costs for the following reasons:

- There will be zero or very little wind at all.
- It will be cold, clammy and unpleasant.
- Getting lost in fog is very easy and the chances of collision are high. Be wary of sound signals such as hooters and horns, it can be difficult to tell where they are coming from.
- You need to keep well clear of shipping lanes and out of the way of powercrafts who are relying on radar unable to detect a small boat and that are travelling too fast.
- Persistent fog has a habit of clearing, and then rolling back in to envelop the sea. It is better to wait until all fog has cleared before launching.

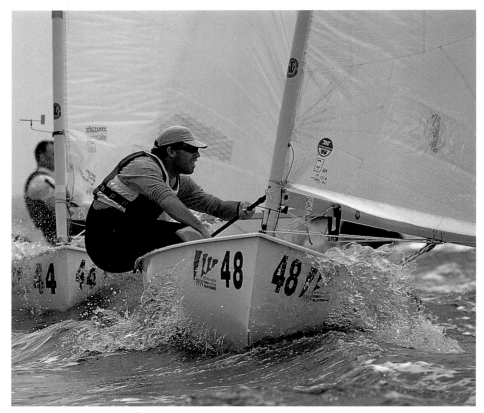

ABOVE **Murky conditions can deteriorate and if fog drops down it becomes an unnerving experience. With minimum visibility racing would certainly be cancelled.**

RIGHT **Inland lakes surrounded by high mountains can be prone to violent thunderstorms in warm weather. Be prepared for high winds, and make sure you have sufficient clothing to cope with a considerable drop in temperature.**

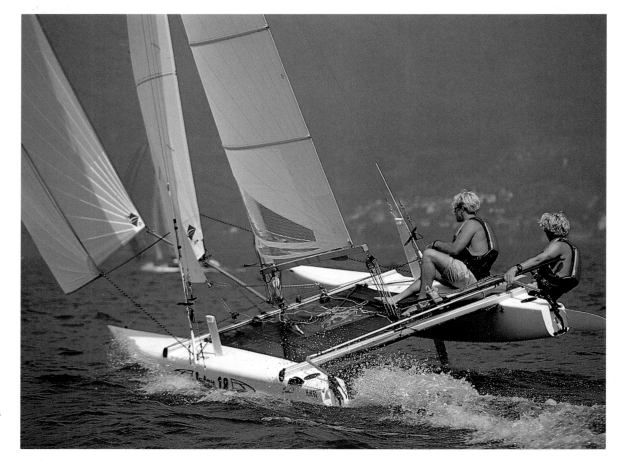

Thunderstorms and lightning

It is rare for yachts or dinghies to be struck by lightning, particularly when out on the water. All you can do is be philosophical; lightning must strike somewhere, but the chances of being injured or killed by lightning while sailing are remote.

However, being caught in a thunderstorm while sailing a small dinghy can be an unnerving experience. Following a period of humidity and light winds, there will be a sudden drop in temperature accompanied by fierce gusts of wind fanning out from the leading edges of the storm. If you are unprepared in terms of technique or clothing, capsize and hypothermia become real possibilities.

Most thunderstorms are created inland when the ground becomes overheated. A thermal low leads to falling pressure over the land and rising pressure out to sea, and as the unstable air from the thermal low shoots high into the sky it forms massive cumulonimbus clouds along with thunder and lightning.

If the thunderstorm is moving offshore against an onshore wind, it will suck up this wind and throw back a downdraught (downdraft) gale, creating violent gusts, which are often followed by heavy rain or hailstones. The effects can be most extreme on inland lakes surrounded by high mountains, with downdraughts of Force 6 (27 knots) or more tearing into the surface of the lake and kicking up a violent sea. Some Italian and Swiss lakes

in Europe are so prone to this phenomenon that storm warning lights and flags are on regular stand-by.

The most obvious sign of an impending thunderstorm is a heavy and oppressive feeling in the air, while on land everything, in particular the birds, appears to go silent. The first rolls of thunder can be heard up to about 16km (10 miles) away and, if the thunder is clearly coming your way, you can reckon that the usual rate of progress is about 19kph (12mph). This allows only a modest time to prepare yourself by putting on waterproof and windproof clothing, or to seek shelter on land. Needless to say it is prudent to avoid standing alone on the shoreline, and keep well away from solitary trees.

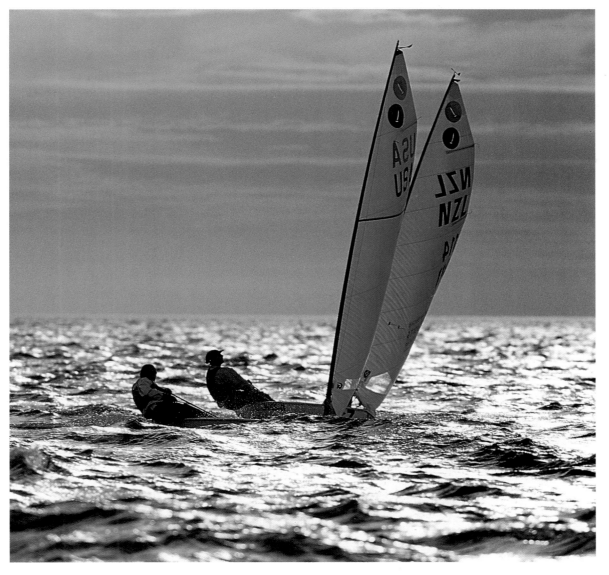

LEFT **Never sail too far offshore or out of sight of land in a dinghy. The wind may increase beyond your capabilities or drop to nothing and leave you stranded, or its direction may transform what was to be a fast reach home into a slow, cold and very wet upwind grind.**

Dinghy sailing probably qualifies as a risk sport, although the risks are so minimal for those who take care that fatalities or serious injuries are extremely rare. However one should always have great respect for the elements of wind and water, particularly when sailing near a coast.

Safe locations

When starting out, the ultimate safe sailing location would probably be a fresh water lake or reservoir of no more than 1 km (1.6 miles) diameter, with an even depth, warm water, a regular, steady wind of Force 4 maximum, a club to sail from and non-stop rescue cover. Look for a gently shelving beach or easily accessible pontoons or launch ramps from which to launch. There should not be any overhead powerlines in the locality, no obstructions such as moored boats, no swimmers and absolutely no powered craft except for rescue boats in case of emergency.

The shoreline

The suitability of where you launch and land on the shoreline will depend on its composition and location, how you launch and how it is affected by the prevailing wind. A gently shelving launch ramp with a hard surface is ideal if you have a trolley, but beware of any slippery areas. Grass or soft sand is fine to launch from if you don't mind dragging the boat, otherwise you may need a trolley with oversize wheels. Shingle makes for hard work when it comes to pulling a boat up. It can also be unforgiving on your feet and even worse on the smooth, shiny bottom of your dinghy.

Launching or landing on mud is to be avoided at all costs. It is most often found in harbours and estuaries that dry out at low water, and can grab your feet and act like glue. Apart from being very messy, it can also be potentially dangerous if a boat and its occupants get stuck in the mud and are unable to extricate themselves.

Steeply shelving beaches can cause a lot of problems as well. First, the angle of the beach may make it difficult to manage and control the boat on the way down, followed by a struggle to pull it back up.

ABOVE **This Enterprise with hoisted mainsail and jib is being launched in crowded surroundings that require extra vigilance. Once off its launching trolley the boat can easily become a handful should the wind speed suddenly increase.**

LEFT **It is always necessary to have a fairly accurate idea of wind speed and direction before you leave the shore. Most sailing clubs will have anemometers (wind speed indicators) for this purpose. Otherwise, if in doubt, you can always consult with other sailors.**

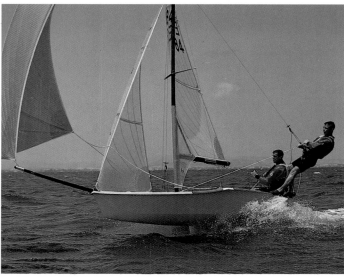

LEFT **Launching on a sideshore wind will allow the crew of this 29er to sail on a reach straight out from the beach and back in again. This boat is the high performance small sister to the Olympic 49er, and is particularly suitable for teenage crews.**

conditions and start to capsize, your boat will be driven further offshore where the wind gets progressively stronger and your difficulties increase.

Lulls and gusts

These are caused by rising and sinking air on days when cumulus clouds indicate an unstable wind pattern. Because the gusts come straight from above they will veer (turn clockwise) in a direction more closely aligned with the isobars. The gust may last for a few minutes, followed by a lull when the wind backs to its original direction. The difference in the wind shift direction is an important tactical consideration in all yacht racing, and no more so than in dinghy races inland, which are often decided on playing the wind shifts.

Wind speed

On a weather map closely spaced isobars generally indicate strong winds, while wide spacing mean light winds. If the gap between the isobars halves, the wind speed will double.

The perfect sailing breeze will depend on ability. Beginners will prefer a light wind, but not so light that it is difficult to assess where the wind is blowing from or keep the boat moving. For most beginners winds between Force 1 and 3 (1–10 knots) wind should be suitable. Those with more experience will enjoy sailing in stronger winds. Force 3–4 (7–16 knots) represents perfect sailing conditions for most dinghies, though catamarans and windsurfers perform best when the wind is even stronger. Force 5–6 (17–27 knots) becomes considerably more demanding, but should be viewed in the context of the sailing location. Low air temperatures, cold water and the effect of tides and waves are likely to make such winds considerably more challenging than when sailing close to the shore in a warm, tideless location.

There are plenty of tall tales told by dinghy sailors of braving Force 8 (30–40 knots) winds, but most are down to exaggeration. Despite Force 6 (22–27 knots) being described by Admiral Beaufort as merely a strong breeze it is in effect very windy. Beyond Force 6

ABOVE **Wind shifts play a major role in deciding tactical success in dinghy racing. They become particularly important in classes such as the Laser, which can be tacked with minimal loss of speed.**

conditions become extremely unpleasant and controlling a dinghy can become a matter of survival.

Summer winds

Seabreezes are created by the sun warming up the land ahead of the comparatively cold sea, and are mainly a coastal, summer phenomenon that will continue to blow no more than 48km (30 miles) inland. They are most effective when the change from cold night to hot day is reliable and pronounced, but will not work if the land is shrouded by cloud. A typical seabreeze

location is the eastern Mediterranean where the afternoon summer wind turns on like clockwork on most days.

A regular coastal pattern is for the seabreeze to gradually cancel out the effect of any night wind that has been blowing offshore. A period of calm and irregular wind ensues, before the seabreeze is established in the early afternoon and provides a steady onshore wind of Force 4 (10–15 knots); perfect for summer sailing. The seabreeze will then die away to a calm as the land starts to cool in the early evening.

ABOVE **Piles of cumulus clouds indicate a weather pattern with frequent gusts and lulls creating wind shifts. The timing of the gusts can be critical when racing.**

Lakes that are surrounded by mountains can also be affected by summer winds. A well known example is Lake Garda, a popular sailing location in northern Italy that benefits from this. There, the normal pattern is for a fairly light mountain wind (named the Ora on Lake Garda) to blow from the mountains during the night and early morning, and be replaced by a much stronger valley wind (the Vento on Lake Garda), which blows in the opposite direction from the lake towards the sunny side of the mountains. This will blow from midday to late afternoon, and is at its strongest at the leeward (onshore) end of the lake (the Torbole on Lake Garda).

ABOVE **Waiting for the wind. The summer seabreeze is a delightful phenomenon, which relies on a marked difference in night and daytime temperatures. These Dart 18 catamarans are ready to start racing with the afternoon wind.**

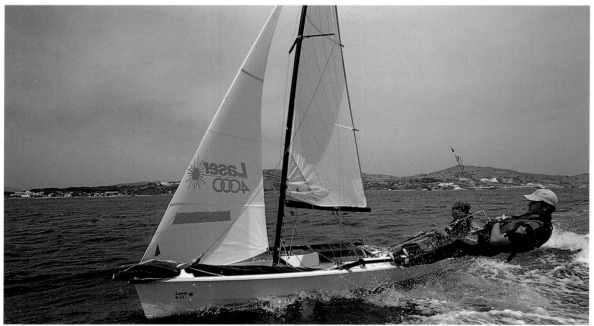

ABOVE **Lakes or coastal waters which are surrounded by high mountains can experience strong thermal winds. These often turn on like clockwork, but are never 100 per cent reliable.**

LEFT **Beware the end of the summer seabreeze. By late afternoon the wind will start to die again, so make the most of it while the wind is up.**

Admiral Beaufort's scale of wind force

Distances over the sea are measured in nautical miles (1 nautical mile equals 1,853.27 metres, 2,025 yards or 1.15 statute miles), and wind speed is measured in nautical miles per hour or knots. These knots are divided into wind forces, which describe the speed of the wind. This system, invented by Admiral Beaufort in the 18th century, is still in use today with modern updates, describing likely conditions both inland and on the open ocean. Conditions on protected coastal waters will generally be less marked, but in some instances may be more extreme if there is a tidal influence.

Force	Description	Velocity
0	**Calm**	**Less than 1 knot (less than 1kph)**
	Smoke rises vertically.	
	Sea like a mirror.	
1	**Light air**	**1–3 knots (1–5 kph/1–3 mph)**
	Direction of wind shown by smoke drift, but not by wind vanes.	
	Ripples like fish scales form on the sea.	
2	**Light breeze**	**4–6 knots (6–12 kph/4–7 mph)**
	Wind felt on face. Leaves rustle. Ordinary vane moved by wind.	
	Small wavelets, still short but more pronounced.	
3	**Gentle breeze**	**7–10 knots (12–19 kph/8–12 mph)**
	Leaves and small twigs in constant motion. Wind extends light flags.	
	Large wavelets. Crests beginning to break.	
4	**Moderate breeze**	**11–16 knots (20–29 kph/13–18 mph)**
	Raises dust and loose paper. Small branches are moved.	
	Small waves become longer. Fairly frequent white foam crests.	
5	**Fresh breeze**	**17–21 knots (30–39 kph/19–24 mph)**
	Small trees in leaf begin to sway. Crest wavelets form on inland waters.	
	Moderate waves taking more pronounced long form. Many white foam crests. Chance of spray.	
6	**Strong breeze**	**22–27 knots (40–50 kph/25–31 mph)**
	Large branches in motion. Whistling heard in telegraph wires. Umbrellas used with difficulty.	
	Large waves begin to form. White foam crests are more extensive. Probably some spray.	
7	**Near gale**	**28–33 knots (51–61 kph/32–38 mph)**
	Whole trees in motion. Inconvenience walking against the wind.	
	Sea heaps up and white foam from breaking waves begins to be blown in streaks along the direction of the wind.	
8	**Gale**	**34–40 knots (62–74 kph/39–46 mph)**
	Breaks branches off trees. Impedes progress.	
	Moderately high waves of greater length. Edges of crests begin to break into spindrift.	
9	**Strong gale**	**41–47 knots (75–87 kph/47–54 mph)**
	Slight structural damage such as chimney pots and slates blown away.	
	High waves. Dense streaks of foam along the direction of the wind. Crests of waves begin to topple, tumble and roll over. Spray may affect visibility.	
10	**Storm**	**48–55 knots (88–101 kph/55–63 mph)**
	Seldom experienced inland. Trees uprooted. Considerable structural damage occurs.	
	Very high waves with long overhanging crests. The resulting foam is blown in dense white streaks along the direction of the wind.	
11	**Violent storm**	**56–63 knots (102–117 kph/64–73mph)**
	Widespread damage.	
	Exceptionally high waves sometimes concealing small and medium ships. Sea completely covered with long white patches of foam. Edges of wave crests blown into froth. Poor visibility.	
12	**Hurricane**	**64+ knots (118+ kph/73+ mph)**
	Widespread damage.	
	Air filled with foam and spray. Sea white with driving spray. Visibility bad.	

UNDERSTANDING WAVES

Waves come in all types and sizes. They can either increase power on the water, or seriously tax a sailor's skills.

Ground swell waves These are generated by far off storms and can travel thousands of miles across an ocean, steadily growing in size. They approach a coastline in long, even and well-spaced parallel lines, until they hit shallow water and break. Ground swell is only experienced on open waters, and is most relevant to offshore yachts.

Wind swell waves These are wind-blown waves created by local conditions, which travel at about three-quarters of the speed of the wind. They are unlikely to get bigger than 1.5m (5ft) high, and tend to break in shallower water close to the beach. Wind swell is directly relevant to small boat sailing. The behaviour of wind swell waves will depend on the wind, tides, shoreline and other obstructions. It will also depend on the angle at which wind swell meets ground swell. If wind swell is blowing across ground swell, it can produce confused waves. If wind swell flows with or against ground swell, it can create occasional oversize waves.

Wave height The height of a wave is proportional to its length. A wave that is 7m (23ft) long can be no more than 1m

ABOVE **Playing the waves is an important skill when racing dinghies, which accelerate rapidly on wave faces. Avoiding ploughing into the back of the next wave is just as important.**

(3ft) high. When it exceeds this height as it is pushed up by contact with the bottom in shallow water, it will break.

Refraction This is a phenomenon that turns waves in towards the shoreline and helps create a wave current that runs one way along the beach.

Rip This is a surface current where water that comes into land with the waves is allowed to flow back out to sea. A rip can

be a fast-moving outgoing piece of water between incoming waves, and is potentially dangerous. When closely spaced waves prevent the water landing on the beach from returning to the sea via rip currents, there will be an outgoing undercurrent known as the undertow that runs seaward beneath the incoming surface water. When waves break on steeply shelving beaches at high tide an undertow can be extremely powerful.

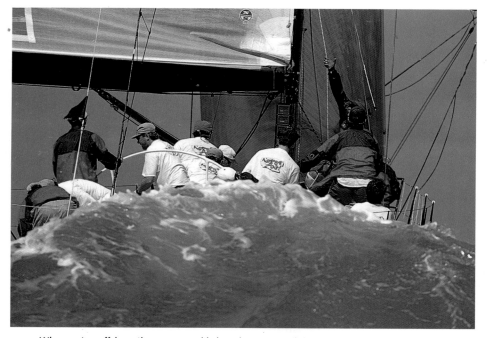

ABOVE **When racing offshore the waves are likely to become much bigger, and may become confused and dangerous when wind swell and ground swell cross one another.**

Wave height international scale

The height of the face of a wave is measured by doubling the height of the back of the wave.

Code	Sea	Height
0	Calm	0m (0ft)
1	Rippled	0–0.2m (0–½ft)
2	Good	0.2–0.5m (½–1½ft)
3	Slight	0.5–1.25m (1½–4ft)
4	Moderate	1.25–2.5m (4–8ft)
5	Rough	2.5–4m (8–13ft)
6	Very rough	4–6m (13–20ft)
7	High	6–9m (20–30ft)
8	Very high	9–14m (30–46ft)
9	Huge	14m+ (46ft+)

UNDERSTANDING TIDES

With the exception of seas such as the Mediterranean, which are surrounded by land, most seas are influenced by the tide, which is directly related to the gravitational pull of the moon. The tide ebbs (flows away), turns and then floods (comes back again) in a regular cycle. How long this process takes depends on geographical location. There are three major types of tide.

Diurnal tides Mainly confined to the Tropics where they experience just one high and one low tide per lunar day. The tidal range (the difference in height between high tide and low tide) is usually small.

Semi-diurnal tides These are experienced on the Atlantic shoreline and round much of the European coast. The tide cycle takes approximately 12½ hours between successive high or low tides. For instance, if high tide (also called high water or HW) is at 6 a.m., low tide (low water or LW) will be shortly after midday with the next high tide following at 6.30 p.m. From then on the times of high or low tide will be about 50 minutes later every day.

Mixed tides Experienced along the Pacific coast of North America and on much of the Australian shoreline. These areas also

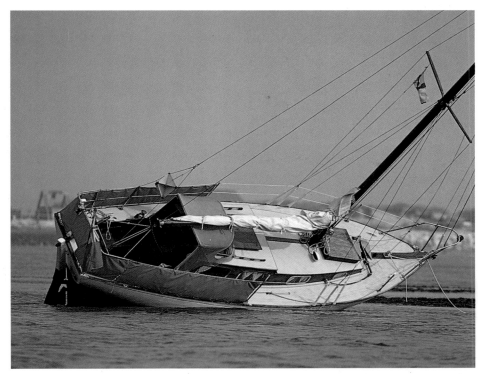

ABOVE **Be prepared! The difference between high and low tide can be extreme, with yachts left stranded and open sea replaced by a huge expanse of sand or mud at low tide.**

have two high and two low tides in a full lunar day, but there are noticeable differences in height between the first high and low and the second high and low, which becomes higher high water (HHW) and lower low water (LLW).

Tidal flow

Tides are measured in vertical height using feet or metres, and the difference between high and low tide is known as the range. The greatest range is experienced during the period known as spring tides. This is when the gravitational pull of the sun and the moon coincides, and is usually experienced around the time of a new moon and a full moon. In between this phase the range of the tide dwindles, with the smallest range experienced during a period known as neap tides, when the moon is in its first or last quarter. The timing is never precise; the spring tide with the greatest range may take place from one to three days after a new moon or a full moon. This phenomenon is also true of the neap tide, with the smallest range following the first and last quarter of the moon.

Tidal currents relate to the flow of the tide and the direction in which it is heading. The rate of flow is not consistent. As the tide approaches low or high water the current slackens before ceasing during a period known as slack water. This is when the tide turns from flood to ebb or vice versa.

ABOVE **Tidal flow will have a marked effect on racing tactics, with the most tide usually in deep water channels and the least tide in shallow water close inshore.**

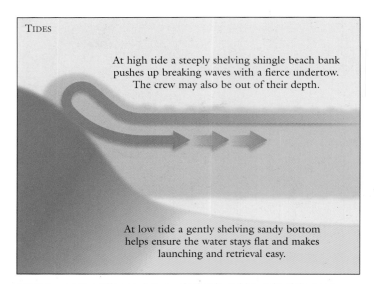

TIDES

At high tide a steeply shelving shingle beach bank pushes up breaking waves with a fierce undertow. The crew may also be out of their depth.

At low tide a gently shelving sandy bottom helps ensure the water stays flat and makes launching and retrieval easy.

ABOVE **Beware the difference between high tide and low tide. If the beach shelves steeply at high tide, it may create large crashing waves and a fierce undertow, which makes landing dangerous and may roll the boat.**

ABOVE **Knowledge of the state of the tide is vital when racing, particularly when the course is near to the shoreline where yachts will venture into shallow water to minimize the effects of tidal flow.**

The twelfths rule

To determine how far or fast the tide has risen or dropped at any given time the normal method is to use an approximate system known as the twelfths rule. The twelfths rule divides the tidal range into twelve, and in the first hour after high or low water the tide falls or rises by one-twelfth. This is the period when the tide flow is slowest. In the second hour it falls or rises a further two-twelfths. In both the third and fourth hours it falls or rises a further three-twelfths. This is the period when the tide flows fastest, beween half and three-quarter tide. In the fifth hour it falls or rises a further two-twelfths as the tidal flow begins to slow. In the final sixth hour the tide once again falls or rises by one-twelfth in the approach to slack water. This is the period when the tide flow is once again slowest.

The times and heights of tides can be found by consulting the relevant tide tables, which are widely published, sold by all good boat shops, and are on display at sailing clubs.

Tides and launching

Understanding tidal heights and times is important when launching in a tidal area. You should know in advance what happens at the opposite end of the tide. If you don't you might, for example, launch

at high tide, land at low tide, and discover you have to drag the boat two miles over flat, soggy sand to get back to your start point, or discover that the rapidly dropping tide has brought rocks, reefs, wrecks or groins within striking distance of your centreboard.

You might, on the other hand, launch at low tide in a light onshore wind, then return in a much increased wind to

discover that the incoming tide has advanced from the gently shelving beach where you launched to the steeply shelving shingle at the top of the pile. The sudden change in the angle of the bottom increases the force of the waves which crash down on the shingle. The only way home is to sail straight through the surf and up the shingle; you'll survive the experience, but damage your boat.

ABOVE **High performance boats such as the 49er are likely to be least affected by tides, but the crew must still beware of being pushed into or away from a racing mark when their boat slows down.**

ABOVE **A shingle beach could turn into a nightmare if the wind turns onshore and the tide comes right up. As well as consulting charts and tide tables, local knowledge is required for safe sailing.**

Obstructions

Check for submerged and semi-submerged obstructions before you sail. These may range from the most obvious reefs and rocks through to wrecks, sand banks and sea defences, such as groins. Problems are most likely to occur when these obstructions cover and uncover at different states of the tide, and something that wasn't there an hour earlier suddenly meets your precious daggerboard with a sickening impact.

Tidal acceleration

The behaviour of the tide can be affected by land configuration. A narrow channel will concentrate and accelerate the tidal flow, which will be fastest in the deepest area. In extreme cases the current may flow at 10 knots or more, making it impossible to sail against the current and potentially dangerous to sail through it. A headland or closely spaced islands may also concentrate and accelerate the tidal flow, particularly when combined with a shelf of shoal water. This can accelerate the tidal flow so violently that it becomes a race, producing an unpleasant series of closely spaced waves, which are at their most chaotic and violent when the directions of wind and tide are opposed. The headland may also feature a mass of underwater rocks, which produce equally violent overfalls. Further problems can occur when a headland produces a reverse eddy that sends the tidal flow back in the wrong direction as it rebounds off the next part of the coast.

The direction and strength of the wind can also have a marked effect on tides. Strong winds combined with low barometric pressure can play havoc with tide heights and times, but of more concern to sailors is the effect of wind against tide. When the wind blows in the same direction as the tide it will calm the waves and make for a smooth passage. However, when the tide turns and flows against the wind, the combination of strong wind and fast flow can push up an ugly series of tightly packed waves. In such conditions sailing against the tide is likely to be a long and unpleasant process, while sailing with the tide could resemble a scary roller-coaster ride.

Capsize

This is probably the most common form of trouble for dinghy sailors. Some boats are generally easy to right after a capsize while others are more difficult. All capsizes sap the energy of the crew due to the physical exertion required to get into a position to pull the boat upright and climb back on board. Depending on the sailing location, there can also be the added effect of being in cold water, which saps energy even further. Multiple capsizes cause a lot of problems, particularly when associated with problems such as the crew becoming separated from the boat and having to swim to make contact or the boat coming up and flipping over through a full 180 degrees. Each capsize progressively saps strength as the crew enters a vicious circle in which the attempted recovery gets harder every time.

Don't leave the boat. A capsized dinghy is easily spotted and provides the crew with something to hang on to and, depending on the type of dinghy, they may even be able to get some protection from the wind and water. Leaving the boat and swimming for land is normally a recipe for disaster but there could be rare instances when it proves the best course of action. Otherwise, always stay put.

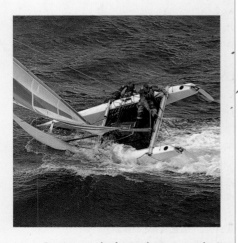

ABOVE **Capsizes can be fun, as long as you don't do them too often. A huge amount of energy can be lost through physical exertion combined with the effects of too much cold water.**

Safety measures

The sport of dinghy sailing is as safe as you choose to make it. For sure there are many potential hazards, but these can generally be avoided if you think ahead, take care and accept that you have embarked on a process of continuous education. Accidents may happen and emergencies may occur, but the well prepared sailor will always be able to minimize the damage through a process of common sense and knowledge.

The following safety measures will help ensure that you still have fun while practising safe sailing:

- Never sail on your own until you are suitably experienced. It is also best to never sail alone in a solitary area. If possible, only sail in an area where there is a rescue boat on call.
- Tell someone when you are going, and when you expect to be back.
- Never risk sailing after sunset. Always aim to return to the shore in plenty of time and don't wait until you get tired.

- Always check that there are no overhead powerlines when you are launching or sailing. Touching one with any part of the mast can easily result in fatality.
- Get a weather forecast and assess the strength and direction of the wind before you launch. Don't overestimate your abilities. If the conditions don't look right for you, leave it for another day.
- Consult charts and tide tables when launching in a tidal area. Make sure you know where and when the tides and currents are flowing.
- Avoid any fast flowing tidal race, and ensure that you find out about underwater obstructions such as rocks and sand banks, which may be covered at high water.
- Offshore winds must be treated with the greatest respect.
- Always keep clear of shipping lanes and commercial vessels.
- Learn the Rules of the Road and abide

by them (see Basic Sailing Rules), but don't assume that everyone will possess the same knowledge as you have.
- Never sail in a dinghy too far offshore or out of sight of land. In France it is a legal requirement for dinghy sailors to stay within two miles of a suitable point of refuge on the coast. However, two miles is considerably further than we would recommend to any dinghy sailor without specific safety support. Be sure to check the local sailing regulations wherever you are.
- Beware the effects of cold and tiredness. They are cumulative, particularly if you capsize. Consider heading home after the first capsize, and if you start to capsize consistently make every effort to get to the nearest land without delay. If necessary sail under jib alone or accept outside assistance.
- Drink plenty of liquids when sailing on a hot day. The effects of dehydration are marked.

LEFT **So much to play for and so much to go wrong. The combination of strong wind, cold air, powerful waves, strong tides and freezing water is a potential killer. However, armed with sufficient knowledge, common sense, the right equipment and an appreciation of personal safety, a sailor can turn all those negatives to a positive experience and have a great time.**

INSURANCE

As sailing areas become more crowded and attract too many inexperienced people, the risk of collision grows. Hitting and injuring a swimmer or running into another boat and causing damage could result in litigation, and it is vital to ensure that at the very least you have sufficient cover for third party liability.

In some cases a household insurance policy will provide adequate cover, but it may be preferable to seek out a specialized dinghy insurance policy that will operate on a number of levels with premiums tailored to the value of the dinghy and associated equipment. The most important aspects of a specialist policy might include:

Third party liability The most vital component, with a comparatively cheap premium as a stand-alone policy. The amount of cover is tailored to satisfy all legal possibilities.

Liability cover while racing This is mandatory when taking part in most organized events.

Accidental damage cover Normally subject to a policy excess. A specialist insurer should be able to evaluate the claim fairly, help arrange repairs and speed up the entire process.

Accidental cover while racing As for the previous.

ABOVE **Basic liability cover is likely to be mandatory while racing. As speed increases, so does the danger of boats becoming damaged in close-fought situations.**

Cover for theft Normally subject to a policy excess. Check that the cover is sufficient for associated equipment such as clothing, which can sometimes cost almost as much as the boat itself and is easily stolen from a sailing club changing room. Be sure to check the insurance requirements as well, which may stipulate keeping the boat in a locked compound or building.

Roadside rescue and recovery Very useful if the wheels of your trailer decide to seize up due to too much salt water, but this may be covered by your motor insurance policy.

Worldwide cover If you plan to tow your boat abroad, ensure that it has sufficient cover for the relevant countries.

Fire damage A rare occurrence with a sailing dinghy, but occasionally the result of vandalism.

Medical expenses and transfer These are useful features if you are not already covered by a household insurance. Note the maximum amount of cover being offered.

Dealing with an incident

If you are involved in an incident that is likely to lead to a claim, don't waste time and effort getting angry with the other party. Ensure that everyone is safe and that there is no imminent danger. Be as courteous and logical as the conditions permit, and make a sensible appraisal of both the incident and the damage. Record the time, date and place, take notes and, if possible, make a sketch showing details such as direction of boats, wind speed and direction and conditions on the water. Take a photo of the damage if you can.

Find witnesses to the incident and note down the relevent addresses and sail numbers/boat names for all concerned. Lastly, do not forget to exchange insurance information with the other party involved in the incident. Contact your insurance company at once and deal with sailing experts preferably. Be honest and truthful with your claims.

ABOVE **When a mass of crew are engaged in sailing a high performance boat with associated high risks, it's important to ensure that everyone is covered against accidental injury.**

Basic sailing rules

It is vital to know the rules of the road when sailing. If you don't, your attitude is akin to someone driving on the wrong side of the road. The basic right-of-way rules are comparatively simple, unlike racing rules, which can become incredibly complex and deserve a book (of which there are many) in their own right.

Port gives way to starboard Nothing could be clearer. A sailboat on starboard tack has right of way over all sailboats on port tack.

The windward boat keeps clear If two sailboats meet on the same tack, either port or starboard, the one that is to leeward (downwind) has right of way. This means that a boat that is beating to windward has right of way over a boat that is reaching or running on the same tack.

The overtaking boat keeps clear When cruising, a boat that is behind keeps clear of a boat ahead; a matter of common sense and courtesy. The rule changes somewhat in racing.

LEFT **Whether racing or cruising, the whole purpose of sailing rules is to avoid collisions and ensure that skippers and crews know how to avoid them.**

Keep to the right in a channel This applies to all powercraft and should be borne in mind by small sailboats. In some cases it may be safe and feasible for sailboats to tack from side to side in a channel, but they must leave plenty of space for all craft that need to use the main deep water area and are best advised to keep to the shallower water at the sides.

Right of way rules cover all sailing craft, but they sometimes need to be overruled by common sense. It is a courtesy to give way to a yacht that is racing when you are cruising, but not mandatory. The racing yacht has no right to force a passage if you have right of way. But, if you meet a large yacht in your small sailboat, it is often much easier for you to give way.

Don't stick rigidly to "power gives way to sail" either. There are times when it is easier for a small sailboat to give way. Some powerboat drivers show little regard or respect for sail, which could lead to tragic consequences if a sailboat insists on enforcing its rights.

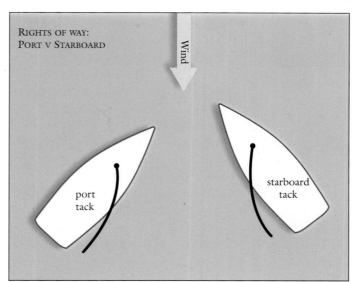

ABOVE **Port must always give way when crossing tacks. In this instance the port tack boat can either tack on to starboard, or bear away below the stern of the starboard tack boat.**

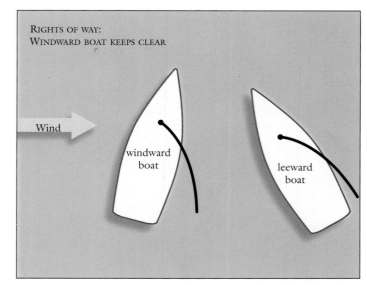

ABOVE **When boats are on the same tack, port tack in this instance, the boat that is on the side the wind is coming from must alter course to keep clear of a boat that is sailing higher.**

RIGHT **Racing rules make overtaking a more complex affair, and rely on the inside boat gaining an overlap before it reaches the turning mark.**

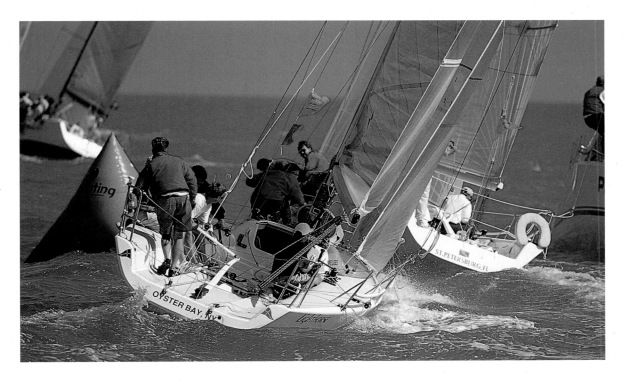

Rules definition

The use of the rules of the road depend on where your boat is positioned at the time of an incident, what it is doing, where it is going and what is in the way.
Position A boat may be clear ahead, clear astern or have an overlap. This can be determined by running an imaginary line from the stern and bow, set at right angles to the centreline of the boat. If another boat crosses either line, there is an overlap. If no boat crosses either line, your boat is either clear ahead or clear astern.
Movement Many of the rules refer to a type of movement or change of course.

• Luffing is altering course towards the wind.
• Tacking is from the moment a boat is beyond head to wind until she has borne away to a close hauled course.
• Bearing away is altering course away from the wind.

• Gybing is from the moment the foot of a boat's mainsail crosses the centreline with the wind aft, until she completes her gybe when the mainsail has filled on the other tack.

Something in the way An obstruction is any object that is large enough and close enough to require a boat to make a substantial alteration in course to pass to one side. This could include buoys and anchored vessels.

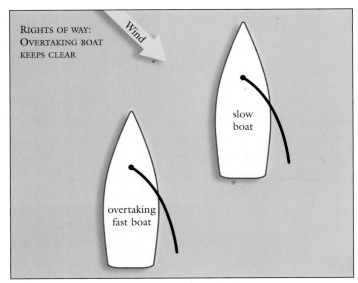

ABOVE **Overtake to either side without forcing the slower boat to alter course. You cannot barge another boat from behind. Overtaking to windward, as shown here is generally the easiest way to get past.**

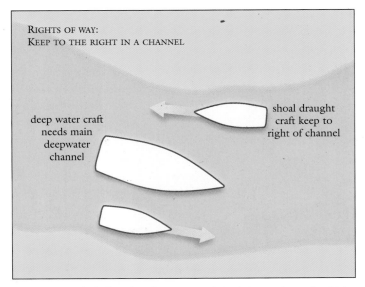

ABOVE **Boats with shallow draught must not obstruct deep water craft, which have priority in a channel. Always be courteous and sensible, and be prepared to give way to larger craft whether under sail or power.**

Points of sailing

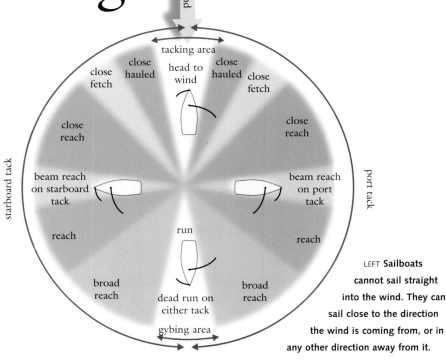

The angle between a sailboat's heading and the true wind is referred to as points of sailing. The points of sailing can be divided into three main categories: running, reaching and sailing upwind – with various subcategories within them.

Running

A dead run describes sailing with the wind blowing from behind, when the true angle of the wind exactly matches the heading of the boat. In reality a boat will seldom stay perfectly aligned to a following wind, nor is it desirable, as the dead run can be a very unstable point of sailing. Maximum wind pressure on one side of the sails, combined with minimal rig-induced stability when a boat sails through waves, leads to poor forward drive as well.

It is most efficient to let the mainsail out at 90 degrees to the centreline, but on many dinghies this is impossible as the leeward shroud gets in the way. With an unstayed or mini-shroud rig, letting the sail right out can make the boat very unstable: power increases in the top of the sail, the boat rolls to windward, and a

LEFT **Sailboats cannot sail straight into the wind. They can sail close to the direction the wind is coming from, or in any other direction away from it.**

regular rolling motion is created that can lead to a death roll, in which the boat capsizes, usually to windward.

On a run the mainsail will tend to obscure or blanket the jib and steal its wind. This can be solved by goose-winging the jib (going wing on wing), which means holding it out on the other side, but it will not pull consistently until you bear away and sail by the lee.

Sailing by the lee is sailing with the wind blowing onto the leeward side of the stern while near to dead downwind. Get it just right and the boat will be better powered with the jib pulling hard. Bear away too far, usually due to a lull in the wind or an untimely wave, and the wind will catch the back of the mainsail, force it into an unwanted gybe, and all too easily lead to immediate capsize.

Reaching

A reach is sailing with the wind blowing across the boat. This ranges from a broad reach (wind from behind), through a beam reach (wind straight in from the side) to a close reach (wind from ahead).

From a dead run the tiller can either be pushed away to luff on to a broad reach on the same tack, or pulled in to gybe (change tack downwind) on to the opposite run, and from there luff onto (head up to) a broad reach. On a broad reach the wind blows at an angle of around 45 degrees over the transom. This is potentially the fastest point of sailing in

Downward variations

To optimize performance, a sailboat may make rapid changes to its point of sailing, particularly when sailing downwind. For instance the direct course may be a beam reach, but when a gust hits, the boat bears away on to a broad reach to keep control. If however the wind drops, it luffs on to a close reach to accelerate wind over the sails and build up speed. These changes may be combined with the use of waves, steering the boat to make it sail downhill on the faces while avoiding sailing uphill on the back of waves.

ABOVE **Running with the wind behind is a relaxed form of sailing in light air conditions that allows the boat to travel in a virtual straight line.**

Sail sheeting angles

The point of sailing does not always dictate the sheeting angle of the sails, which also depend on the speed of the boat and consequent angle of the apparent wind. On a dinghy with slow or modest performance, apparent wind will not differ greatly from true wind, and the sails will be conventionally sheeted to match the wind angle. However, on a high performance sailboat – windsurfer, catamaran or skiff-style monohull – the apparent wind will get closer to the centreline of the boat as speed increases. The sails have to be sheeted to match the apparent wind, and so are pulled hard in for almost all points of sailing.

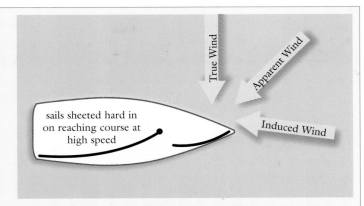

ABOVE **When sailing at speed the apparent wind direction can be very different from the true wind direction and sails need to be sheeted hard in.**

a strong wind in which the rig produces maximum power combined with minimum side-pressure.

Luffing (pushing the tiller away) from a broad reach changes the course to a beam reach, with the wind blowing at about right angles to the boat. The sails will be sheeted further in to accommodate the change in wind angle, and side-pressure increases so speed through the water will be slower, but still remain rapid.

Luffing from a beam reach changes the course to a close reach, with the wind blowing at around 45 degrees over the bows. The sails will be sheeted even further in, and greater side-pressure slows the boat still further.

Sailing upwind

Luffing from a close reach leads to a point of sailing known as a close fetch when the boat is sailing towards the wind, but not so critically close as for close hauled or beating. Luff a little further, and a close hauled or beating course is as close as you

can sail to the wind – at best about 30 degrees away from the true wind direction. The object is to point the boat as high as possible towards the wind, known as pointing, without the sails luffing and losing power, which is indicated when the telltales (see Basic Manoeuvring) start to lift on the windward side of both mainsail and jib.

To sail to an area that is directly upwind, a sailboat must sail to windward on alternate tacks (this is known as beating). Changing tacks avoids the head-to-wind or no-go zone where the wind blows from bow to stern directly down the centreline.

ABOVE **When beating upwind the wind comes from ahead and it is on this point of sailing that the boat is most likely to heel over.**

BELOW **On a reaching course the wind comes from the side and the crew may need to balance the boat to prevent it from heeling over.**

Which tack?

- Port tack (red) is when the wind blows on to the port (left) side of the boat and sails. This is the windward side that you normally sit on.
- Starboard tack (green) is when the wind blows on to the starboard (right) side of the boat and sails.

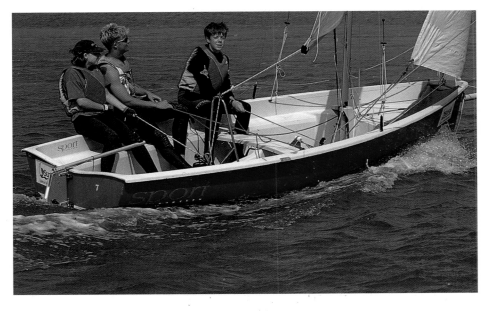

Sail care and maintenance

Direct, strong sunlight is your worst enemy. It will degrade all sail materials, especially Mylar™ style laminates and windows, the most vulnerable. Sails should always be stored out of the sun and never near direct heat. Always keep laminate sails away from solvents such as fuel and cleaning agents that can dissolve the glue and cause separation.

Avoid flogging

Try to prevent sails flogging (hard flapping in the wind), which will degrade the material, especially laminates. A flogging sail may also damage anything around it – a clew hitting someone in the face can knock a tooth out. Never dry a sail by leaving it to flap like a flag in the boat park. Allow it to dry where there will be minimal movement. Avoid letting the jib flog while launching, landing or waiting on a start line. It is better to back the jib if you don't want it powered up. If you have a roller, always roll the jib away. Learn to sheet the jib in quickly and efficiently when tacking. If the spinnaker or gennaker starts to flog repeatedly, it means your ability doesn't match the conditions. Avoid explosive refillings, drop it and stow away.

Go easy on the tension

On a high performance woven polyester sail it's common to put a lot of weight on the downhaul or cunningham to increase luff tension, take out the stretch and move draught forward. A more stable laminate sail should require considerably less luff tension to get the same effect. Pull the downhaul or cunningham until any horizontal wrinkles disappear, then don't pull any more or you could damage the sail.

Tears and repairs

Small tears can be temporarily taped over with sailmakers' tape, but the tear should be professionally repaired as soon as possible. Never sail with a torn spinnaker or you'll find a new meaning to the word ripstop. Laminate sails are prone to impact damage. If you capsize, try to avoid falling into the sail and never do so feet-first or head first.

Avoid rough contact

Try to keep the mainsail pulled back off the leeward shroud and spreader when running downwind. This will leave unsightly marks on the sail and will start to rub through

ABOVE **Letting a sail flog in the wind is not the best way to care for it as it will degrade the material.**

the outer surface of the cloth. Plastic-coated shrouds give some protection.

Never drag a sail over a hard surface like a concrete slipway. Avoid rolling or folding a sail away on a rough surface. Check the boat for any sharp or rough edges that sails may catch on. The relatively fragile material of a spinnaker or gennaker is vulnerable to snagging on untaped cotter pins, screw threads or hooks, while the foot of the jib may get damaged by dragging across the deck when you tack.

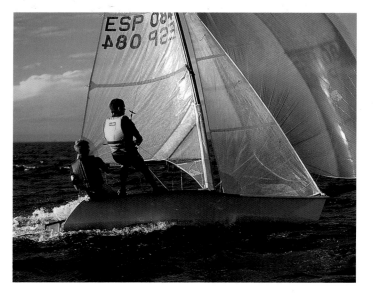

LEFT **The laminate sails are all pumped up on a 29er. They look great and give brilliant performance, but need a certain level of care and attention, even more so in a sunny climate.**

ABOVE **Salt is the enemy. It scratches and holds moisture that will damage your sails, so wash it off after every outing.**

Wash sails regularly

Sails don't like the corrosive crystals of salt, which may cause long-term damage if allowed to build up on the cloth. So if you sail on the sea, give your sails a regular hose down with fresh water.

Dry them well

Always let sails dry thoroughly before you put them away, and never leave a wet sail in a bag. Given time a damp environment will promote mildew, which can be difficult to remove from the cloth, and dark colours on a nylon spinnaker or gennaker can bleed into lighter colours.

Check the corners

The head, tack and clew have to cope with high loadings on high performance dinghy sails. Check that all reinforcement, plates, cringles and stitching are intact before you put sails away, if not, take them to the sailmaker for repairs.

Free up the battens

Let the tension off battens before putting sails away. Depending on the way the sail is cut you may be able to leave the battens in, but battens that obstruct a nice tight roll or fold must be removed. Check

ABOVE **The traditional way to pack a woven polyester sail is to "flake" it in zig-zag folds. Try to avoid permanent creases by not folding along the same lines every time.**

the batten end pockets for wear and abrasion, and send the sail to a sailmaker if reinforcement is required.

Roll them up

Never stuff a sail into a bag. The exception is a spinnaker or gennaker which, due to its light material, can be stored in a loose bundle. The traditional method of storing woven polyester sails is to fold them from head to foot, holding the luff and leech to make horizontal creases, which are folded

ABOVE **All laminate sails should be rolled. Use a plastic pipe if there aren't any full length battens to support the sail, and remove battens as necessary.**

in a concertina pattern. Don't fold along the same creases every time, or the creases may become permanent. Laminate sails must be rolled into a tube as any creases can crack the laminate. If you have the right sausage-shaped bags this is the easiest and most efficient way to store sails, whether laminate or woven polyester. You may also find it convenient to roll the mainsail around the boom, or to roll the sails around the length of a plastic drainpipe, and remove when necessary.

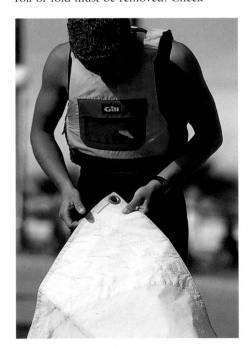

ABOVE **Sails get a lot of stress. Make a regular check of the head, tack and clew for any signs of wear or fatigue.**

ABOVE **Battens have a nasty habit of wearing holes in the ends of their pockets. Make sure it is not happening to your sails.**

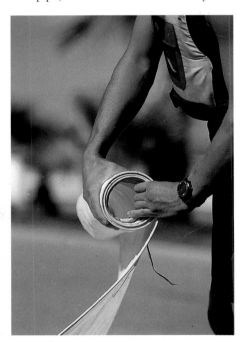

ABOVE **It's often easiest to roll the jib, whether laminate or woven polyester. Roll it around the luff wire, starting at the head.**

Boat maintenance

If you sail on salt water make a regular practice of washing your boat with fresh water. This will help keep the boat looking good for longer, and ensure that everything works by flushing salt out of spars and fittings.

Household cleaning products, such as washing-up liquid, can be used to clean a fibreglass or plastic boat quite adequately, but beware of leaving an undesirable super-slip finish on the deck and in the cockpit. If in doubt, it's worth paying the price of proprietary boat cleaners, which include specially packaged shampoos, polishes and rubbing compounds to burnish the hull plus aluminium cleaners for spars and fittings.

Laying up

When laying up a boat for a long period such as a winter lay-off, take time to ensure it will not deteriorate.
Ensure that you do the following:
- Wash everything down thoroughly with fresh water.
- Remove all ropes and lines that may retain moisture.
- Check over all blocks, cleats and other fittings. If you have washed them regularly in fresh water, they should stay in perfect working order. Be wary of using any lubricants that may lead to slipping lines.

ABOVE **Salt degrades everything, so wash it off the bottom of your boat.**

ABOVE **High performance sailing depends on reliability; and that depends on taking care of your equipment.**

- Remove all hatch covers and bungs to promote circulation of air.
- Leave the boat fully supported so that air can circulate under the hull. The trolley or trailer should be ideal for this.
- If possible store the boat under cover. If the boat has to be left outside, make sure it has an effective cover that drains water off and raise the bow so any water that gets inside will run out from the transom.
- Spars should be supported so they are horizontal to the ground, but never lying on the ground. Inspect shrouds and forestay, and replace any broken wires. Inspect rivets, and if any need replacing use Chromite paste to prevent corrosion between aluminium and stainless surfaces.

ABOVE **Boats take in water. Make sure it gets regularly drained and dried out, and arrange to leave the hatch covers off when the boat is laid up and out of use.**

ABOVE **Control lines will abrade and eventually break under stress. Check and replace them on a regular basis.**

Foil repairs

Denting foils, particularly in the bottom and leading edge, is very common. Most dent repairs can be accomplished by using a proprietary gelcoat of the correct colour. Only if the dent is on a large scale will fibreglass need to be added. The best way to repair the damage is to:
- Thoroughly wash and dry the repair area.
- Grind out the dent to solid material.
- Mask the repair area.
- Pour liquid gelcoat into the hole, and build up layers as necessary.
- Once the gelcoat has cured, rub the surface to a smooth finish with wet and dry sandpaper.

ABOVE **Rig fittings can suffer from corrosion and stress damage. It is vital that shrouds do not fail, so check both the terminals and shroud wires themselves.**

Fibreglass hull and deck repairs

A small surface dent in the hull is primarily a cosmetic problem, which can be repaired with the right colour gelcoat. If a dent goes right through the boat:

- Thoroughly wash and dry the repair area.
- Grind out the damage to solid material, cutting back and chamfering the edges.
- Lay in fibreglass and resin, and build this up to about 2mm(¹⁄₁₆in) below the surface of the hull.
- Dab on the right colour gelcoat with a brush, building up two or three layers until it is above the surface.
- Rub the gelcoat flat and smooth with wet and dry sandpaper.

- To completely disguise the repair area, dab on a final layer of gelcoat with an extensive overlap, and rub down to an acceptable finish.

If there is damage to a foam sandwich, contour foam can be moulded to any size or shape and inserted between fibreglass layers during the repair.

Gelcoat fade

Exposure to UV sunlight causes the colour of a fibreglass gelcoat to fade over a number of years, and the surface eventually breaks down to a powdery appearance. Polishing with wax may delay this, but if the appearance worries you the only real solution is to paint the hull with proprietary fibreglass paint. It is vital that all release agents from the original moulding process and any build-up of grease are removed by using a fibreglass cleaner before starting.

Polypropylene repairs

In the unlikely event of holing the hull or deck of a boat made from polypropylene or a derivative, a special gun is required, which places the repair outside do-it-yourself abilities.

Avoid dragging polypropylene boats as the resulting scratches can only effectively be removed by professional repair.

Polypropylene boats with dark decks are prone to fading. There is no solution, beyond ensuring your boat is protected from strong sunlight. Use a cover or store it indoors when possible.

Time well spent

- All do-it-yourself repair and refurbishment jobs require time, care and patience. Allow as much as 80 per cent of total job time for preparation. This is the key to a successful finish.
- Gelcoats, resins, catalysts, solvents and fibreglass are volatile materials that all need careful and precise handling. Read the instructions right through before starting to use them, and pay particular attention to personal safety such as ventilation and protection from splashes.

REPAIRING A HULL ....

1 Preparation is 80 per cent of the job. Leave enough time to make it perfect.

2 Cut out all the damage and make sure it is totally dry before going further.

3 Endless burnishing of the gelcoat is the key to a perfect finish.

Dinghy Sailing
Techniques

All sailing techniques start from a set of basic principles that govern the skills required to utilize the wind. At their most basic, the skills of sailing towards the wind and away from the wind are very simple, but that statement relies on perfect conditions, flat water, a steady breeze and no obstacles. Real sailing is seldom like that, the wind yo-yos up and down, waves form, tides run and other boats get in the way. Neither are sailing boats so simple that you just steer and pull a piece of string. The desire for improved performance is natural, and with it comes the potential for more complex rig and sail controls, such as those used on the Olympic 49er, where maximum power set on a superlight platform has to be controlled.

The message is that sailing technique is an exceptionally wide-ranging subject that can be learnt at all levels. It can also be learnt quickly, but there is nothing like practice combined with experience to ensure that the lessons are learnt well.

Rigging, knots and preparation

All dinghies are rigged using the same basic principles, but there is likely to be an enormous leap in complexity between an unstayed single-hander and a three-sail, skiff-style dinghy.

Unstayed single-handers

The Pico, Topper and Laser are typical of very simple una-rig dinghies, which are great for solo sailing but can also be enjoyed with a crew on board. In all three cases the mast is made of parallel aluminium tube, and is sleeved in two halves to make storage and rigging as easy as possible. The sail has a luff tube, which fits over the mast like a sock, and sail controls consist solely of a downhaul, outhaul, kicking strap and mainsheet.

BELOW **The traditional butterfly-shape cleat is still often used to secure halyards. Start with a full turn followed by a half turn and a final locking turn. Never use a locking turn if you need to let a line off in a hurry.**

The result is a small dinghy that is simple, efficient and very easy to put together. The lack of sophisticated rigging and sail controls, however, means that the shape of the sail cannot be very effectively dictated by the crew, which leads to a consequent relative downturn in performance with increased winds.

Time taken to rig 10 minutes
User-friendliness 10/10

Three-sail dinghies

A three-sail rig, such as an RS200, or Laser 3000 generally requires full support for the mast in the form of shrouds, a forestay or reinforced jib luff wire, and possibly spreaders. Consequently it is much more complex both to set up and use, but enables an experienced crew to shape the sails to combine maximum performance and control in the prevailing conditions with more ease. With the addition of a spinnaker or gennaker, the amount of rope required to act as sheets and control lines

becomes even more complex, which is a very good reason why everything should be colour coded.

Time taken to rig 40 minutes plus
User-friendliness Becomes easier with greater familiarity

Always uncleat the sheet

Never leave a mainsheet (or jib sheet) cleated on dry land. If you need to leave a boat unattended with the mainsail up, ensure all sail controls are let right off. If possible unclip the outhaul or disengage the clew so the mainsail is not attached to the mainsheet or boom. Better still, and for complete peace of mind, drop the mainsail altogether and stow it neatly inside the boat with the mainsail halyard secured or removed.

SECURING ROUND A CLEAT

JAM CLEATS

LEFT **Most halyard and control ropes on modern dinghies are locked securely with a mixture of jam and clam cleats. Pull the rope through the cleat under load and it will lock automatically, but the angle and diameter of the rope must be correct to securely jam it. To let the rope off pull it in a fraction tighter while at the same time lifting it away from the locking jaws.**

SHEET BEND

LEFT **The sheet bend is neither strong nor secure, but this said is part of every sailor's basic repertoire. It is principally designed to attach two lines of different diameter, but is also simpler and more effective than a reef knot when attaching lines with different characteristics.**

REEF KNOT

LEFT **The reef knot can only be used to attach two identical lines. Beware of getting the ends the wrong way round, or of using a reef knot on small diameter lines, which can pull very tight and become difficult to undo. In this instance a sheet bend provides superior performance.**

RIGGING A DINGHY WITH AN UNSTAYED MAST ....

1 Slot the two halves of the mast together, then slide the luff tube of the sail onto the mast before pushing in with the sail furled.

2 Clean sand or dirt off the mast base before pushing it down, and ensure the mast is held firmly in position by the deck lock.

3 Attach the boom fitting to the mast. On a Topper or Laser Pico this is a plastic jaw that simply clips around the mast.

4 Secure the end of the mainsheet to the transom, and lead it up so it runs through the block on the outer end of the boom.

5 Pull the mainsheet through the blocks. The sequence will depend on the boat, with small differences between Pico and Topper.

6 Lead the inner end of the mainsheet through the main central block, and secure the end with a figure-of-eight knot.

7 Unfurl the mainsail. This should be done with the bows of the boat pointing into the wind, to prevent it from blowing over.

8 Pull the clew of the mainsail out to the end of the boom, and attach it to the boom outhaul line, which can then be tensioned.

9 Attach the downhaul to the tack of the sail and pull down to remove wrinkles. Then attach kicking strap between mast and boom.

10 When attaching the rudder ensure the tiller passes under the mainsheet strop. This is much easier to do on dry land.

11 Drop the rudder on to the pintles and ensure it is locked on and will not fall off in a capsize. Lift the blade before launching.

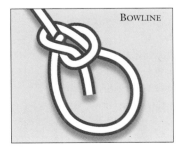

BOWLINE

LEFT **The bowline is possibly the most useful knot in sailing. It can take as much load as a rope is designed for without pulling into a hard lump and is therefore always easy to undo. Ideal for all uses when a rope is under load, such as securing mainsheet and gennaker sheets.**

FIGURE-OF-EIGHT

LEFT **The figure-of-eight is the sailors' top stop knot, used to prevent jib and mainsheet ends from pulling out through fairleads and blocks. It is also relatively easy to undo, unlike the overhand knot, when used with a modern soft rope or control line.**

RIGGING A THREE-SAIL DINGHY

1 On modern dinghies halyards are secured with a simple loop system that has replaced the use of fiddly shackles.

2 A plastic ball is enough to lock the halyard to the head of the sail, and is easy to undo when it comes to de-rigging.

3 When hoisting the mainsail, ensure the boat points into wind and all battens are tensioned. One crew feeds the bolt rope, while the other hoists the sail.

4 The mast slot should be a tight fit. If the bolt rope jams in the slot, ease the halyard off enough to clear the jam.

5 The inner end of the boom is pushed on to a gooseneck pin. The kicking strap is secured to the base of the mast and underside of the boom.

6 When hoisting the jib, attach the tack and sheets first and ensure that the head of the sail is kept clear of the spreaders.

7 On modern boats a simple loop knot tied halfway along the soft, thick sheet will be adequate to secure it to the clew of the jib.

8 You can tie the ends of the jib sheet together, so the crew can always grab an active sheet. This helps when making fast tacks.

9 It's wise to make sure that everything works while still on dry land. Make sure all sheets and control lines are secured yet run free.

10 Check that bungs and hatch covers are properly closed or you may sink the boat.

11 Ensure that the rudder retaining clip clicks shut, or it may drop off (and sink) during a capsize.

Raising the mast

Also known as stepping the mast, this procedure can be done by one or two people. Before you start, lay the mast lengthways along the boat, and sort out halyards, shrouds (and trapeze wires if fitted) to ensure they are not tangled, then attach the lower ends of each shroud to the shroud adjuster plates on either side of the boat.

Except on small, light single-handers such as the Optimist, Topper or Pico, two people are needed to raise the mast. One stands in the boat astride the centreboard case and lifts the mast, while the helper guides the mast heel into the mast step.

Depending on the type of boat, the mast is stepped into the bottom of the boat (keel stepped), or onto the foredeck (deck stepped). The helper then pulls the mast upright with the forestay, which is then attached to the bow fitting. Some performance dinghies have no forestay, which requires an alternative means of pulling/holding the mast up, such as the gennaker halyard.

Before you raise a mast or wheel a dinghy along the ground, check for overhead powerlines. Although rare, fatal accidents have occurred through this oversight.

RIGGING A THREE–SAIL DINGHY WITH A GENNAKER LAUNCH SOCK ....

1 To rig the gennaker, pull the end of the continuous halyard through the sock and tie it to the centre of the gennaker using a secure bowline knot and the loop provided.

2 Ensure sheets run outside the shrouds and round the forestay. They should be pulled tight enough to hold them up around the sides of the boat.

3 Most gennaker boats use blocks with a ratchet lock to help the crew to hold the load. Make sure the sheet is led through in the right direction.

4 The halyard must run outside everything and should be attached to the head of the gennaker with a bowline. Part hoist the sail to get a clear view for rigging.

5 Tie one end of the sheet to the clew, lead the other end through the gennaker blocks, round the outside of the boat and back to the clew.

6 Attach the tack of the gennaker to the tack line, which emerges from the end of the pole. This acts as a gennaker boom outhaul when the sail goes up.

7 Use the continuous halyard to pull the gennaker back into the sock, then relaunch to check all is well and that the sail sets on both sides of the boat.

Sail numbers

Attaching sail numbers is a fiddly job that requires care and preparation, and should never be hurried. Read the instructions with care. There are different methods of attaching numbers to a sail, but the following are good general rules:

- Prepare a clean, flat space for the area of the sail to be worked on.
- Sort the numbers into the correct order, carefully cutting them out if required.
- Lay the numbers on the sail, make sure everything is totally smooth, and mark the positions in pencil.
- Correct number spacing is vital. Numbers should start at least 75mm (3in) from the clew, and often look best when set at right angles using a batten as a guide. Allow at least 65mm (2½in) between each number.
- Do not make the mistake of putting the numbers back-to-back on either side of the sail. This makes the number impossible to read, and is illegal under ISAF racing rules. Allow at least 200mm (8in) of vertical height between the row of numbers on either side of the sail.

Launching and coming ashore

A boat is most vulnerable to damage when launching and coming ashore; banging or dragging on the ground and maybe colliding with other boats. So always think through the sequences before you start, discuss it with your crew and be patient and courteous.

LAUNCHING

Traditionally it was always considered best to hoist the mainsail and jib after the boat was launched, with the crew standing in the water and holding the forestay while the helm sorts out the sails.

The advantage of this method is that it is much easier to push or carry the boat down to the water without the wind taking control of the sails, and it can save possible damage to the hull when rigging on a trolley.

However, this method assumes that the crew can hold onto the boat in fairly flat water, which is just the right depth. If the crew is in too deep, it's too rough or the back of the boat is banging on the bottom, getting sails up on the water can be a nightmare.

Dinghies with luff tube systems, such as the Topper and Laser, can only have their sails hoisted and dropped on dry land. Many high performance dinghies

LEFT **Beware of other boats and people when launching. There may be no problems in light winds, but things can get difficult when the wind increases.**

must also have their mainsails hoisted and dropped on dry land, due to bolt rope feeds and halyard locking systems, which can be difficult to manipulate on the water. To hoist or drop the mainsail on dry land, the boat must be sitting firmly on a trolley or a soft surface such as grass, and turned to face directly into the wind to prevent it rocking from side to side. The mainsheet or boom must be disengaged from the mainsail until the boat is in the water, with sail controls such as downhaul, cunningham and kicker let right off so there is no chance of powering up the sail prior to the launch.

Guiding a rudder onto its pintles can be extremely frustrating when the boat is moving around on the water. It is usually easiest to fit and remove the rudder on

ABOVE **Rigging on the water is fine so long as the water is flat, not too windy, the boat stable, and it is easy for someone to hold on at the bow.**

dry land. Make sure that the rudder foil stays lifted and does not drag on the ground. Check that the centreboard is fully retracted or the daggerboard removed before you launch or retrieve the boat.

RIGGING ON DRY LAND

1 When rigging on dry land, ensure the boat points more or less into the wind and is stable and won't rock when sitting on its launch trolley.

2 Take care when attaching the outhaul, which will have the effect of powering the sail up on an unstayed boat like the Pico or Topper.

3 The rudder blade must be securely locked in the upright position to ensure the tip does not catch on the ground.

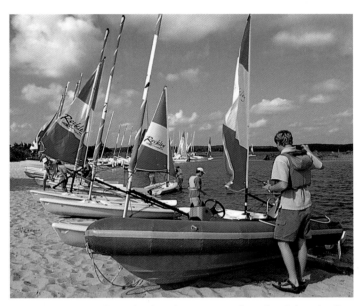

ABOVE **This is a virtually perfect launch spot operated at a beach-based sailing club, complete with a gently shelving sandy beach and rescue boat immediately to hand.**

STEEPLY SHELVING BEACH

launch area suddenly shelves

If the water is too deep, the crew rapidly gets out of depth and cannot hold boat

beach

ABOVE **Beware the steeply shelving beach! While the shoreside end of the boat may be scraping the bottom, the other end may be in very deep water for the crew.**

The best place to launch

Choose a launch spot that is clear of boats, rocks, swimmers and any other obstructions. Remember that you may have poor steerage control when you set off or come in to the beach if the centreboard or daggerboard and rudder foils have been lifted in shallow water.

● Keep well upwind of obstructions to leeward, and allow room for sideslip.

● Keep clear of breaking waves (surf) if possible. The windward end of a beach will generally have the least surf.

● With an onshore wind a gently shelving beach pushes up small waves; a steeply shelving beach pushes up big waves.

● Avoid steeply shelving launch places where you will soon be out of your depth when holding the boat in the water.

● Check that the gently shelving beach that you launch from at low tide does not become a steeply shelving mass of shingle when you return at high tide.

Getting to the water

All boats are heavy. On a gently sloping sandy beach it requires less effort to carry a boat to the nearest water and pull it round to your favoured launch spot.

If you have the mainsail hoisted and are carrying the boat or pushing it on a trolley, you must ensure the wind does not catch the sail and flip the boat. This means keeping the bows pointing more or less into the wind when you launch or retrieve. The bows are angled towards the water in an onshore wind and away from the water in an offshore wind. You obviously need to

bear off from this course to get where you want to, and how much you can do so will depend on the strength of the wind and how the boat reacts to gusts. Be prepared to spin the boat into the wind and push down on the windward side. In a sideshore wind, you may need some dry land tacks to get to and from the water, in which case it is probably better to launch where you can and pull the boat to a more suitable place.

Push the trolley into the water until it is deep enough for the boat to slide off with a shove. One crewperson should hold the boat head to wind by the forestay, while the other takes the trolley ashore and carries it above the high water mark. If you are launching single-handed, you may need to enlist help.

GETTING TO THE WATER WITH A PICO

1 Keep the boat facing downwind when you wheel it backwards. Avoid launching with the wind blowing side-on to the boat.

2 Push the trolley into the water until the hull begins to float off. The rudder blade must be fully up with the daggerboard out of its case.

3 Hold the trolley, lift the bow and push the boat away. Keep holding the bow with one hand, and the trolley handle with the other.

Launching in offshore winds

In an offshore wind the water should be flat, and the boat lie with the transom pointing out to sea. The extra depth should allow the helmsperson to lower and lock the rudder foil, ensure the mainsheet is attached and active, and put slight tension on the sail control lines preparatory to starting.

The 180 degree turn needed to sail out will require plenty of space to allow for poor initial steerage and control. The helmsperson must ensure everything is clear while choosing which tack to start on. The crew then pushes the bow away from the shore. The helm steers the boat through an arc, and the crew hops on just after the boat has started to turn out to sea. Acceleration from this beam reach position may be rapid, so the crew must get on board without delay.

On a single-handed boat the distance between mast and bow is usually small enough for the crew to stand by the front of the cockpit, get everything ready and still hold the boat head to wind.

SAILING OFF WITH A PICO

1 You don't need to push the boat in any deeper than this to get sailing.

2 When ready, move back along the boat and push down and lock the rudder.

3 Move alongside to insert the daggerboard in its case and push halfway down.

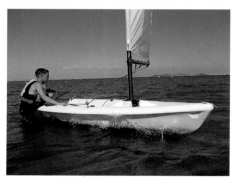

4 On the Pico you can let the bow blow downwind and hop in over the stern.

Trolley guide

Pneumatic tires make pushing a trolley much easier – the softer the surface, the bigger the tyres need to be. Ensure that they are correctly inflated throughout the sailing season.

A basic A-frame trolley has a padded cross-member between its two wheels, which is fitted with two long arms that reach forward along the sides of the hull

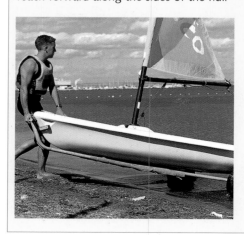

with a curved or right angle finish at the bow. It can be adapted to fit most dinghies, but the arms tend to rub the side of the boat and the load is spread over one small area of the hull, which could cause long-term damage.

A gunwale-hung trolley supports the boat beneath the deck and hull overlap. This spreads the load and completely removes pressure on the hull. The gunwale-hung trolley has to be fitted to a specific class of boat, and there is potential for scratching the sides of the boat if it is pulled on at an odd angle. In a few cases over-enthusiastic crews have split the hull/deck seam by jumping into a boat standing in a gunwale-hung trolley.

The most sophisticated twin cradle trolley supports the hull through two

LEFT **The standard A-frame trolley gives sufficient support for smaller dinghies like the Pico. Note the padding on the trolley to protect the hull along the sides.**

ABOVE **The best trolleys have supports that provide an exact fit for the bottom of the boat, and are dedicated to a specific design.**

padded cradles, which are moulded for an exact match to the hull. This dedicated design gives perfect support for the hull with minimal risk of scratching. Critics claim there is potential for a warm film of water lying between the padded cradles and hull, which will eventually penetrate the gel coat. This can be cured by using rubber slots or coarse carpet, which gives the water space to evaporate.

Launching in sideshore winds

A sideshore wind is often perfect for launching or landing, because the boat can sail out and back on an easily controlled beam reach. When setting off the boat can be held parallel to the beach. It only needs a small push from the crew to turn through 90 degrees and sail out on a reach with minimum sideslip (leeway) and maximum control. However in a side-onshore wind things may be more difficult if the boat is being being rolled from side to side by incoming waves.

Launching in onshore winds

In anything more than a light wind, launching from a lee shore in an onshore wind poses problems. Clear thinking, good communication and a carefully rehearsed plan are necessary to get away.

If the beach curves, you may be able to pull the boat round to a point where you can sail away on one tack, rather than having to tack out through waves, which is much more difficult.

There may be waves driving into the shore. While the crew struggles to keep his or her feet in deep water at the bow, the transom crashes up and down in shallow water, which prevents the rudder being fully lowered. Without the rudder fully lowered, and with the centreboard or daggerboard only partly down, the boat will suffer from a great deal of sideslip combined with poor steerage control. This cannot be cured until the water is deep enough to drop the rudder.

To get away from a lee shore, the crew should hold the boat so it is angled for the tack that leads most directly out to sea. The crew gives a push, jumps on board, lowers the centreboard or daggerboard as far as possible without grounding as the boat pitches through waves, and sheets in the jib to help accelerate and bear away. The main requirement is to get the boat moving fast to gain maximum steerage as soon as possible. If the boat stops moving it will be driven back by the waves. It is much better to sail free and fast and edge away from the shoreline, rather than attempt to point high, which will slow the boat and drive it sideways.

SAILING OFF WITH AN RS200..

1 Helm and crew ensure it is deep enough to get the rudder down. The crew gets in over the stern while the helm holds the bow of the boat.

2 The crew moves forward and gets the centre-board halfway down, while the helm moves aft to the stern and lets the bow blow downwind.

3 The helm grabs the tiller and steps in at the stern, sheeting in the mainsail while the crew sheets in the jib to help power up the boat.

4 As the boat accelerates from the shore, the helm uses his weight to level it out before sheeting in on the mainsail and sitting down inside the boat.

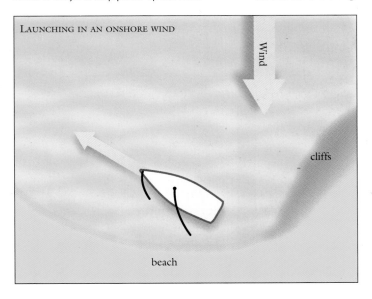

LAUNCHING IN AN ONSHORE WIND

Wind

cliffs

beach

LEFT **Do not attempt to point high when launching in an onshore wind. You need to sail free and fast, but you may have to luff into oncoming waves.**

At this stage it will be impossible to sail any higher than about 75 degrees to the wind. In a half-down position the rudder will feel very heavy and will constantly try to turn the boat towards the wind (weather helm). Do not attempt sheer physical power to overcome this, or you may tear the rudder off its pintles. Instead, make the boat bear away by heeling it to windward, moving crew weight back, and easing the mainsheet. The opposite, heel to leeward, mainsheet in, weight forward, will turn the boat to windward. As soon as the rudder can be put fully down, luffing will be controlled more easily. From then on drifting to leeward is the result of pinching to windward (pointing too high), over-sheeting the mainsheet, or not powering up the jib to help the bows bear off.

COMING ASHORE

When heading in to the beach to land, there are three essential rules: slow down, be cautious and take it easy.

Speed control

If the wind is offshore or sideshore, you can slow down the boat by depowering the sails or luffing (turning upwind). To slow to a full stop, the helmsperson must turn the boat until it is head to wind. Check for swimmers, following boats, or any other obstacle before you do this.

It may be impossible to depower the sails when coming ashore in an onshore wind. If possible, luff and drop the mainsail before entering the surf line, and from there sail straight in under jib alone.

Coming ashore in an onshore wind, the boat may pick up and accelerate on breaking surf with following waves taking control of the wide transom and slewing the boat side-on to the waves. This is a great way to have an unpleasant and very public capsize, with the boat rolling in the surf, breaking its mast, tearing its sails, and causing widespread misery.

Lifting the foils

It is bad practice to let the centreboard or daggerboard or rudder hit the bottom. At best it will put dents in a perfect smooth finish; at worst it may completely destroy a centreboard and its case. Be prepared to lift the foils in plenty of time to prevent grounding, but not so soon that you lose steerage. If the daggerboard/centreboard does touch the bottom, you will at least know it is shallow enough for the crew to jump over the side. Note though that this rule may not apply to performance craft with high aspect daggerboards.

When coming ashore in an offshore wind, a steeply shelving beach will allow you to keep the foils down until you are virtually on the beach. Don't stop or jump off too soon, or you may find yourself in deep water and unable to hold a boat that is being blown back out to sea.

Holding and retrieving

The crew should be ready to lift the centreboard or daggerboard completely when the boat has almost stopped, then

COMING ASHORE WITH A PICO

1 Luff the boat, let the mainsheet go, lift the daggerboard halfway and hop off windward side.

2 Grab the side of the boat and move forward quickly while lifting out the daggerboard.

3 Make sure the boat keeps pointing into the wind as you walk it into the shore.

COMING ASHORE WITH AN RS200

1 Coming into shore, the crew lifts the centreboard and prepares to drop over the windward side.

2 The helm balances the boat, while the crew drops in at just the right depth about hip-high.

3 The crew grabs the forestay and lets the boat swing downwind, watching for any obstacles.

4 The helm moves aft to lift and lock the rudder blade. The centreboard should be right up.

5 The helm stays in the boat or drops over the side and begins to lower the mainsail.

6 The crew fetches the trolley, which is pushed under the boat with the handle fitting tightly against the bow.

7 The boat can then be pulled up on shore safely without risk of damage to the hull.

8 Pulling up the shore can be difficult if it gets steep, and the jib should be furled if it is windy.

immediately hop over the windward side and grab the forestay. Never jump to leeward, between the beach and the boat, which can be particularly dangerous, and even fatal, in an onshore wind when waves may push and drive the boat on top of you.

In an offshore wind The boat will blow away from the beach, making retrieval easy. The helm disengages the mainsheet and frees off the primary sail controls, having ensured the rudder is fully lifted. He or she then runs ashore for the trolley while the crew holds the forestay.

In a sideshore wind The boat may be side-on to the waves, requiring a rapid retrieval with the mainsail lowered when the wind is side-onshore.

In an onshore wind The boat will be

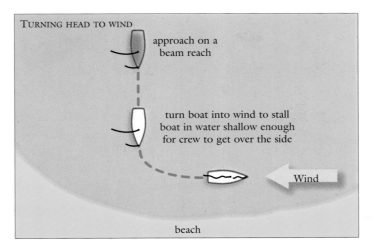

TURNING HEAD TO WIND

approach on a beam reach

turn boat into wind to stall boat in water shallow enough for crew to get over the side

Wind

beach

LEFT **You need to turn the boat head to wind to come to a halt close by the shoreline. The daggerboard or centreboard must be at least part way down for the boat to turn.**

transom-on to the beach, with the crew standing in deep water and possibly being buffeted by waves. Getting help to carry the boat out of the water and onto its

trolley may be the best option. If the boat feels heavy, it's wise to unscrew the bungs once it is out of the water in case it has taken in water.

Trailer guide

- Combi-trailers, which have a combined trailer-trolley unit are an excellent concept for those who use trailers regularly. Both trailer and trolley should be galvanised for rust protection, with efficient rollers so the trolley-borne boat can slide off and on with ease.
- Never tow a boat with the mast up, even for the shortest of distances. Lay the mast along the boat, using the crutch to lift the front with minimum overhang at the rear. Secure all shrouds and halyards with tape, and secure the mast to the boat. Beware of pulling down on unsupported areas that may kink the aluminium.
- The load should be evenly balanced. Beware of too much nose weight, which may end up steering the car.
- Use webbing straps to secure a boat to its trailer, the most effective come with ratchet adjusters. Straps should be long enough to secure to both sides of the trailer base. Beware of using ropes that can fray or cut into the gunwales. If in doubt, use small pieces of carpet for protection.

- Maximum legal dimensions for a boat trailed by a car (in Europe) are 7m (23ft) long by 2.3m (7½ft) wide, with a maximum cumulative trailer and vehicle length of 18m (59ft). Any overhangs such as the mast must be made highly visible. Maximum weight for an unbraked trailer is 750kg (1653lb), which is more than enough for most dinghies. By EU law trailer tires must have a minimum of 2mm (⅟₁₆in) tread depth over two-thirds of the width.
- Check speed limits, lane and motorway restrictions for trailers. In some countries a special driving test is mandatory to tow a trailer.
- Check wheel nuts, tire pressure, lights and fastenings before each journey. Leave enough space between trailer and car socket for turning.
- Always use a safety wire in case the tow hook fails. Always carry a fully inflated spare tyre together with a wheel brace that fits.
- Salt water eats bearings, and salty bearings love to seize up halfway down a motorway. The best rule is never launch a dinghy on its road trailer. The second best rule is never

ABOVE **Trailers range from the simple to the more complex, such as this double catamaran trailer carrying two Hurricane 5.9s.**

launch immediately after driving when the hubs are warm, the grease thin, and the bearings poorly protected. If you do get salt on the trailer, hose it down with fresh water as soon as possible.
- At the end of each season check the trailer coupling for wear and make sure it is securely attached to the trailer. If a trailer is out of use for long periods, use chocks or axle stands to take the weight off the tyres.
- Boat insurance should cover any trailer claims. You may be required to fit a wheel clamp to secure your trailer.

Basic manoeuvring

If you have never sailed before, then take the boat out on a day when the water is flat and the wind blowing at no more than Force 2 (4–6 knots). Begin by practising basic exercises such as making the boat stand still, which will help you understand how the sails work in relation to the wind, before moving on to sailing forwards on a beam reach (when the wind is blowing straight across the side of the boat). This is the easiest way to get started in sailing.

Standing still

The way that sailors conventionally make a boat stand still is by heaving-to. The boat is stalled by sheeting the jib hard in on the windward side. The jib will then blow backwards, and tend to push the bow away from the wind and drive the boat backwards. This can be counteracted by sheeting in the mainsail, which will push the bow towards the wind and drive the boat forwards.

If you sit in the middle of the boat and let go of the sails, the boat will lie side-on to the wind. It will be slowly blown to leeward (sideways), but how far and how fast will depend on wind strength and the amount of resistance put up by the centreboard or daggerboard. The mainsail will seldom blow at exactly 90 degrees across the boat, since it is usually held back by the leeward shroud or insufficient mainsheet length. The boat will therefore drive slowly forwards while being blown sideways.

This exercise works well in a light or moderate wind up to about Force 3 (7–10 knots), if it's windier the amount of leeway (sideways slip) will get progressively greater, and you may need to sit on the

ABOVE **In a light to moderate wind the RS200 makes good progress on a reach. Note how the sails are already sheeted quite hard in to allow for the wind angle of the apparent wind.**

side of the boat to balance the natural windage of the sails and rig. In addition to being an annoyance, the flapping of the sails will also destroy the sailcloth.

The RS200 (ABOVE) and Laser Pico (BELOW) are both very stable with the sails let out and with only a light wind blowing across the beam. They will move slowly sideways and forwards in this position, until the sails are sheeted in and they accelerate straight ahead.

ABOVE **The Pico is relaxed and easy to sail on a broad reach with the daggerboard two-thirds retracted. Note how the helmsperson trims the boat to keep it level without the stern dragging.**

Moving forwards

Pull in the sails until they stop flapping, and the boat will start to move forwards. If there is enough wind the boat will also begin to heel to leeward (away from the wind). This can be counteracted by moving your weight out on the windward side, or easing the sails until the boat comes back upright.

The boat must also be trimmed fore and aft so that the stern does not drag in the water. If the wind increases the extra power in the sails will start to push the bow down, and the crew will need to move their weight back in order to compensate for this.

ABOVE The RS200 heads up from a reach to a beat. Note how the crew keep the boat in perfect trim, almost flat on the water, with their weight moved forwards to lift the stern.

Rudder balance

The rudder should feel light and well balanced at all times, whether steering straight ahead, luffing up (pushing the tiller away) or bearing away (pulling the tiller in). If there is any pull on the tiller, it should be slight weather helm, where the tiller pulls slightly away from you, reflecting the boat's natural tendency to steer up towards the wind. You should however still be able to steer with just two fingers.

Something is wrong if the rudder feels heavy and the tiller keeps pulling away from you as it tries to steer the boat into the wind. This is called heavy weather helm and there are three likely causes:

- The rudder is unbalanced due to the centre of effort of the rig being too far aft. The probable solution is to lengthen the shrouds and shorten the forestay. It may also happen if you try sailing a two-sail boat to windward without the jib, which is needed to balance the boat.

- The boat is being allowed to heel too far. This gives a different shape to the boat under the water and reduces the area of rudder that is in contact with the water. Easing the sails will immediately solve the problem.
- The rudder is not fully down. People often forget to ensure the rudder is down vertically, and that it is held down securely. If it lifts a fraction, there will be immediate weather helm.

The more you push the rudder, the more you will brake the boat and slow it down. Only small rudder movements should be needed, particularly when luffing towards the wind.

Trimming sails

Both mainsail and jib need to be trimmed to the correct angle to produce maximum forward power. As you luff (head up) from a beam reach, the sails will need to be pulled in to reflect the changing apparent wind angle. The jib should be trimmed ahead of the mainsail, since it creates the slot that accelerates wind over the leeward side of the mainsail and determines how the mainsail is sheeted.

Sail trim needs to be precise. If a sail is flapping or backing (the front of the sail blowing inwards) it is likely to be too far out. If a sail is not flapping at all it is likely to be too far in (over-sheeted) with a reduction in power as the wind stalls on the trailing edge of the sail. The most precise indicators of perfect sail trim are likely to be telltales. Windward telltales start to lift if the sail is too far out or if the boat is pointing too high; leeward telltales start to lift if the sail is too far in or if the boat is sailing too low. Perfect sail trim is often indicated by a slight flutter on the leech of the jib with all the telltales flowing straight back. This should be coupled with slight backing in the front part of the mainsail where the bottom telltales are just starting to lift, indicating that the slot between main and jib is working.

TRIMMING THE JIB BY TELLTALES

1 If the leeward telltale drops you need to ease the sheet.

2 If the windward telltale drops you need to bear away.

3 When the telltales flow aft the jib is perfectly trimmed.

4 If not quite straight, then bear away or sheet in just a little.

ABOVE **With more wind the boat goes faster, so the helmsperson moves a little further aft and gets his body further outboard to balance the boat.**

ABOVE **A gust hits and the crew of the RS200 lean right out to flatten the boat. This position is physically tiring, but need only be used for short periods.**

Hiking/Sitting out

In stronger winds the heeling force created by the sails is much greater, and it is normal to hike (lean out over the side) or use a trapeze to keep the boat upright.

All performance dinghies are fitted with toe straps that allow the crew to hike, increasing righting moment by moving their centre of gravity away from the centreline of the boat. It is an effective, if tiring, means of holding the boat level.

Both crew in a two-handed boat must be able to hike in enough comfort to be able to adjust sail controls, steer the boat and concentrate on sailing.

The Laser 1 is a typical example of a boat that may be excellent in many respects, but is desperately uncomfortable to hike over long periods. This is due to wide, flat side-decks and narrow gunwales providing minimal ergonomic advantages for the crew.

It was only in the 1990s that dinghy designers began to wake up to the fact that with carefully sculpted decks and correctly positioned toe straps it would be possible to hike in relative ease. However, crews with different length legs will always pose a problem for perfect ergonomic design, and the fact remains that hiking over a long period is a tough pastime that requires physical training and a relentless mind-over-matter attitude.

Rights of way

- Port tack always gives way to starboard tack.
- Windward boat keeps clear. If three boats are all on the same tack, the boat sailing upwind has right of way over the boat on a beam reach, which in turn has right of way over the boat on a run.

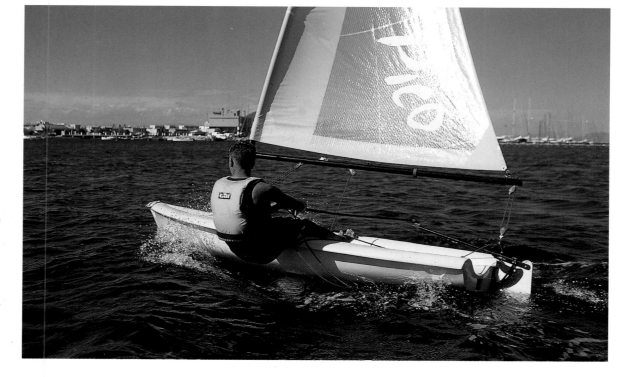

RIGHT **Sailing upwind in a moderate breeze. Note the relaxed stance with both feet close together under the footstraps and the helmsperson looking ahead. The excellent ergonomics on the Laser Pico allow this position to be comfortably maintained for long periods.**

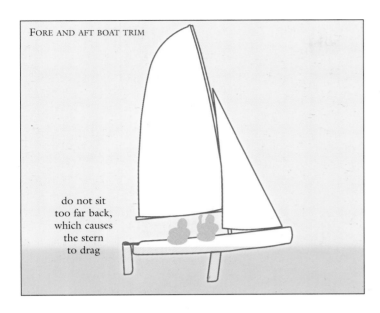

FORE AND AFT BOAT TRIM

do not sit
too far back,
which causes
the stern
to drag

LEFT **Sailing upwind the crew must ensure the stern does not drag in the water – they need to keep their weight forward to drive in the bow. This also increases the boat's waterline length and its resistance to leeway.**

SAILING UPWIND

Knowing how to sail towards the wind is an essential skill for sailing a modern boat.

Basic skills

Sailing upwind (to windward) is a precise skill. Since you are sailing towards the wind, the apparent wind is at its strongest, causing the boat to want to heel over more. The closer you sail towards the wind, the greater the effect will be. If you sail too high you will stall the boat with the sails flapping in the head-to-wind position; sail too low and you will make negligible progress to windward. Most dinghies perform best when crew weight is well forward for sailing upwind. This lifts the stern to reduce drag and increases effective waterline length giving better resistance to leeway.

Changing winds

A reach or run can be sailed in a virtual straight line on flat water, although in reality the effect of wind and waves makes a true straight line impossible. With the exception of sailing on a close fetch, sailing upwind in a straight line is neither possible nor desirable, and it is necessary to sail a course like a wavy line.

The wind is seldom constant, blowing harder one moment and lighter a few seconds later. Lulls and gusts should be balanced by the helmsperson's skill in driving the boat forward and keeping it flat on the water, rather than by the crew constantly moving their weight in and out, which is particularly tiring when hiking.

If a gust makes the boat heel, the helmsperson can steer up into the wind and luff, depowering the sails while maintaining forward momentum; this also allows the boat to sail higher upwind. A gust will often be quickly followed by a lull, and when the sails start to back and the boat begins to heel to leeward the helmsman must respond immediately by bearing away to power up the sails and bring the boat back upright.

If the wind veers, it changes to a more side-on direction. This frees the boat, allowing the helmsperson to push the tiller away and sail towards a higher point. If the wind backs, it changes to a more bows-on direction. This "heads" the boat, which means that to avoid stalling and coming head-to-wind the helmsperson must pull the tiller to bear away and sail towards a lower point. Identifying windshifts becomes vital in a race. Tacking just before a heading windshift will immediately put a boat on a better course for the windward mark.

RESPONDING TO GUSTS ON AN RS200 ....

1 Both crew watch for gusts coming from ahead. Note how the boat is trimmed with the stern lifted out of the water.

2 When the gust hits the crew hike out in unison, using their weight to maintain the same angle of heel.

SAILING OFFWIND

Steering away from the wind is more difficult than steering towards the wind, which is the way a modern sailboat naturally wants to go. Sailing offwind relies on trimming the angle of both the boat and the sails, as well as steering, to work effectively.

Bearing away

As you bear away from a beam reach to a broad reach, the sails need to be let out to allow the boat to steer off downwind; if you keep the sails sheeted hard in, the boat will constantly keep trying to turn up into the wind. Heeling moment on the sails becomes less as the apparent wind starts to blow from the stern so, unless it is windy, the crew will need to move their weight inboard.

Apparent wind decreases as you bear away downwind. (However in stronger winds the speed and angle of the apparent wind will stay constant if the boat is travelling fast enough.) With less apparent wind the boat may slow down. Leeway will also decrease when bearing off on a reach, and the boat may sail slightly faster with the centreboard or daggerboard lifted halfway.

Dead downwind

Bear away some more on to a run, and the sails should theoretically be let out so that they are at an angle near 90 degrees to the boat.

The apparent wind will decrease still further as you bear away from a broad reach to a run and sail dead downwind. If the wind increases, or the boat starts to surf on a wave, the crew will need to move their weight back. Otherwise they should trim the boat in order to prevent the stern from dragging.

Without any wind blowing from the side stability will be compromised. To balance the boat and prevent rolling, it may be best for the helmsperson to sit on

RIGHT **Bearing away from a broad reach, the sailor lets out the mainsail to allow the boat to turn. He needs to move his weight a little inboard and forward to trim the boat.**

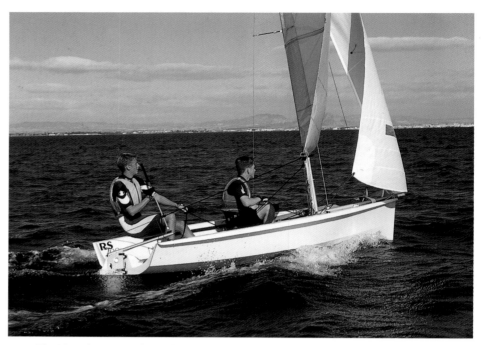

ABOVE **The RS200 bears away from a broad reach to a run. Note how full the mainsail becomes when the mainsheet is eased and the mast straightens. If the helmsperson bears away further, the jib will need to be goose-winged to the other side.**

the leeward side where he or she can hold the boom out against the shroud, while the crew sits on the leeward side and holds out the jib in a goose-winged (wing-on-wing) position.

When sailing dead downwind, a burgee or wind indicator at the top of the mast is vital to show the exact direction of the apparent wind. It is very easy to start sailing by the lee, with the wind blowing from the leeward quarter.

Sailing by the lee

This can be the most efficient way to sail goose-winged or with a spinnaker, since the mainsail will not blanket the headsail. It is a straightforward skill in light winds, which becomes more challenging as the wind gets stronger and the potential for uncontrolled rolling or unexpected and violent gybes increases. The skill is to bear away just far enough and no further to sail a few degrees by the lee, while watching

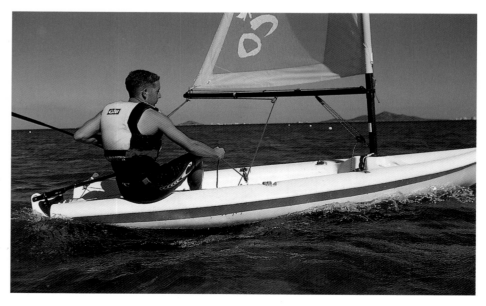

SAILING DEAD DOWNWIND ON THE PICO ....

1 Sailing dead downwind the Pico is beautifully trimmed with daggerboard lifted and boom parallel to the water.

2 A roll to windward can be corrected by pushing the tiller away to turn towards the wind and pulling the sheet in.

3 The crew can also use body weight to keep the boat even. Note how he places his feet either side of the centreline.

for gusts and windshifts, which could power up the top of the mainsail or hit it on the wrong side.

- A roll to windward can be corrected by heading up and sheeting in the sail.
- A roll to leeward can be corrected by bearing away and sheeting out the sail.
- Anti-roll corrections should be small, precise and very carefully done on waves. The idea is to eliminate the roll altogether, rather than helping build up a pendulum momentum.

Avoiding involuntary gybes

Involuntary gybes while sailing by the lee can be prevented by:

- Watching the burgee/wind indicator very closely.
- Steering very carefully, particularly on waves, to keep the boat sailing dead downwind.

- Looking for any sign of the mainsail backing. This will be most obvious on the leech near the top of the sail. The helmsperson should luff immediately but carefully to bring the wind further astern and to windward.
- Remember that the stronger the wind, the faster and more deadly an involuntary gybe will be.

When the boat gybes it is essential that the crew ducks their heads to avoid being hit by the fast-moving boom. Then, when the boom and sail come to a sudden stop as they hit the leeward shroud or run out of mainsheet the helmsperson needs to have a firm hand on the helm to steer the boat downwind, while the crew leaps up on the new windward side. Otherwise, the boat is likely to slew through 90 degrees to a beam reach position, and the momentum will create an inevitable capsize.

ABOVE AND BELOW **An uncontrolled roll can soon build to a violent momentum when sailing by the lee, as the crew of the RS200 discover.**

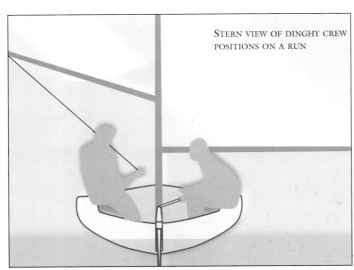

STERN VIEW OF DINGHY CREW POSITIONS ON A RUN

ABOVE **When sailing dead downwind a two-up dinghy can be balanced by the crew sitting on the windward side and the helmsperson on the leeward side.**

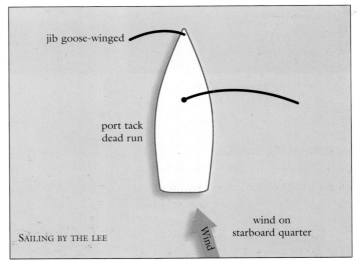

jib goose-winged

port tack dead run

SAILING BY THE LEE

Wind

wind on starboard quarter

ABOVE **Sailing by the lee the wind blows over the leeward quarter. If the boat bears away further, or rolls to windward, the wind may promote a gybe.**

Tacking

If you wish to sail directly towards the wind, you will have to sail a zig-zag course using a number of tacks. During each tack the boat will luff from close hauled to turn through the head-to-wind area (often called the no-go zone), and immediately bear away on to the new tack. A successful tack requires momentum as the sails will produce no power when they are head to wind, and if you do not bear away quickly the sails will start to blow the boat backwards. In this position the boat will stall, which is traditionally known as "getting into irons", and was a nightmare for skippers of old sailing ships.

Tack preparation

Before you tack, ensure there are no boats bearing down from behind and that you have time and space to tack and sail off without getting in anyone's way. A boat that is tacking has no rights of way over a boat sailing a course. Choosing when and where to tack is a matter of experience. A rough estimate used by dinghy sailors is that the heading on the next tack will be at about 90 degrees to your present direction. Consider that optimistic unless you know your boat well.

The boat should be upright and under control before entering the tack, and must be travelling at good speed to get through the tack. If waves are likely to stop the boat you should wait for a suitable flat patch of water.

The helmsperson prepares the crew for the tack by saying "ready about" or "prepare to tack". When the moment comes he or she gives the traditional cry of "lee-oh!" ("helm's alee!").

Tack technique

The helmsperson pushes the tiller away, but not too hard or fast or the rudder blade will act like a brake. With the sails sheeted in, the boat will naturally want to turn into the wind, and requires minimal help. The boat may heel to leeward due to turning upwind, so both crew stay on the windward side. The crew keeps the jib sheeted in until it starts to back. This will help bring the bow round on to the new tack when the boat is in the head-to-wind position. It is vital not to let the jib go too quickly. The boat will level out in the head-to-wind position, so both crew move to the middle with the boom in the centre of the boat. The helmsperson must continue to steer through the turn. If he or she allows the rudder to centre itself, the boat will stall in the head-to-wind position.

TACKING THE PICO FROM PORT TO STARBOARD ....

1 The helmsperson chooses a flat spot to tack.

2 He pushes the tiller away to steer through the wind.

3 At "head to wind" he ducks under the boom.

4 He twists his body through 180 degrees.

5 Passes the sheet to the tiller and changes hands.

6 Then sheets in hard and hikes out.

TACKING THE RS200 FROM PORT TO STARBOARD...

1 The helmsperson says "ready about!" then "lee-oh!" (helm's alee!) as he starts the tack.

2 Note how the helmsperson pushes himself across the boat as it tacks round.

3 The helmsperson is first up followed by the crew, with both sheeting in to power up the boat.

As soon as the jib has pulled the bow round on to the new tack, the crew lets go of the old sheet and pulls in rapidly on the new sheet to power up the jib. He or she may need to move smartly to the new windward side to prevent the boat heeling.

The helmsperson may need to ease the mainsheet during the tack. This may be necessary for keeping control if it is windy. However, make sure not to ease the mainsheet so far that the sail is depowered prematurely. On a fully battened sail this helps to pop or invert the battens so that they are the right way round.

LEFT **An uncontrolled roll on the Pico leads to a capsize. The helmsperson has got to the windward side too late, with the sail already powered up for the new tack.**

Changing hands

The helmsperson must change hands for tiller and mainsheet while changing sides. The normal method is to spin round through 180 degrees facing forwards while in the middle of the boat.

On many boats a centre mainsheet can be left cleated, and makes changing hands easier. As the helmsperson turns, he or she passes the tiller from the back hand to the front hand, and the sheet from the front hand to the back hand. With an uncleated centre mainsheet an alternative method is to move to the new side with the tiller held in the old hand behind your back, then bring the old mainsheet hand across the front of your body to grab the tiller and change hands. With a transom mainsheet both tiller and sheet can be held temporarily in the back hand, transferred to the front hand, and then the sheet can be handed forward. This technique will require some practice in order to ensure a smooth transition.

Finishing the tack

With his or her weight moved to the new windward side, the helmsperson bears away on the new tack and sheets in carefully to power up the boat without stalling it. It may be necessary to bear off a few degrees to build up speed, before luffing on to the proper close-hauled beating course. Do not confuse this with oversteering and bearing away too far on the new tack, which can lose valuable upwind ground.

Tacking should be like a smooth, continuous movement that can be executed almost without thought. Regular tacking drill is necessary to ensure that you can always tack when and where you want, no matter how hard the wind is blowing.

Roll-over

Changing tacks should feel like a smooth, continuous movement. It is possible to help the boat by rolling it through the tack. As the helmsperson pushes the tiller away, both crew lean out to heel the boat to windward and help accelerate it through the tack. They then move quickly to the new windward side in order to power up the sails and flatten the boat on its new course.

ABOVE **Just before the boat starts to turn, the crew lean out to roll it to windward. They need to get back in and over to the new side without delay.**

Gybing

A gybe enables you to change tacks while sailing downwind. If a boat is sailing directly downwind, and wishes to bear away, it will have to gybe. Tacking gains distance to windward as you turn upwind; gybing loses distance to windward as you turn downwind. When rounding a mark in a race you may need to gybe from a reach to a reach (requiring a full 180 degree change in direction between two beam reaches), or even from a reach to a beat.

Boats with gennakers, and catamarans are generally much faster on a reach than on a dead run. It is therefore quicker for them to sail a zig-zag course so they can reach downwind, tacking from gybe to gybe. Calculating gybing angles when tacking downwind requires experience and skill.

During a gybe the mainsail and boom describe a complete arc from full-out on one side to full-out on the other. This can create sufficient momentum to throw the boat out of control and into a capsize. A successful gybe requires a great deal of practice, particularly in strong winds.

Gybe preparation

A gybe is a fluid manoeuvre during which the boat keeps moving forwards, unlike an upwind tack during which the boat virtually stops moving forwards. Therefore a gybe requires a wide turning arc, so before you gybe ensure that there is plenty of space downwind and that there are no other boats in the way. A boat that is gybing has no rights of way over a boat sailing a course.

The boat should be upright and under control before entering a gybe. It must also be travelling at good speed to survive the gybe. If you let the boat slow down, the apparent wind will increase, put more power in the sail and send it crashing across the boat with greater force. If you keep the speed up the apparent wind will be kept to a minimum, putting minimum power into the sail and making the gybe much easier to control. The ultimate target is to exit the gybe with the boat travelling as fast as when you enter it. A strong wind gybe can be intimidating because the boat goes fast into the turn. Practice makes perfect.

The helm prepares the crew for the gybe by saying "Ready to gybe". When the moment comes he or she gives the traditional cry of "Gybe-oh!".

GYBING THE PICO

1 Note the tiller position and slight heel to windward as the helmsperson starts the gybe.

2 The helmsperson moves inboard as the boat bears away on to a dead downwind course.

3 He then ducks across the middle of the boat as the boom swings through an arc to the new side.

4 Then he changes front and back hands to sort out steering and sheeting.

5 He powers up the Pico on a new reaching course, with the boat flat as it powers away.

GYBING THE RS200 ....

1 The helmsperson stands to steer through the gybe. The crew ensures the arc of the gybe is clear.

2 In this position the helmsperson can balance the boat and trim the sail, before ducking for the gybe.

3 The crew pulls the boom across by the kicking strap and the boat points downwind.

4 Both move smartly to the new side so they are sitting out as the boat starts to heel.

5 They flatten the boat and allow it to bear away on the new reaching course.

Gybe technique – light winds

The helmsperson first bears away onto a dead downwind course, then bears away a little further until the crew can goose-wing (wing on wing) the jib. The helmsperson bears away some more to initiate the gybe. He or she flips the tiller extension so that it points to the new side, and moves across the boat at the same time turning through 180 degrees, facing forwards to see ahead. He or she changes tiller and mainsheet hands while in the middle of the boat.

The gybe will be more controlled if the helmsperson pulls in some mainsheet before the boom starts to move across the boat. The further out the mainsheet is, the further you have to turn before the mainsail will gybe. Pulling in the mainsheet will not only start the gybe movement, but also limit the arc the boom can travel through and reduce the shock when it stops at the other side. The mainsheet can then be run out for the new course.

As the boom crosses the boat, the crew changes side. Watch out for the boom and kicking strap, which can be equally dangerous as they swing to the new side.

If the helmsperson is not in full control the boat may start heeling, and the crew must be prepared to jump to the new windward side to level the boat.

Gybe technique – stronger winds

Everything happens much faster in a gybe as the wind increases, and all mistakes are more costly. If the mainsail is well powered up it will need a tweak to encourage the gybe. This can be vital when gybing onto a reach. If the boat turns onto the new reaching course before the sail gybes, the build-up of power will send the boom across the boat like a sling-shot. You need to gybe the boom while the boat is still heading downwind, by either tugging on the top part of the mainsheet or using the kicking strap as a pulling handle.

Steering through the gybe becomes more important as the wind increases, and it's a common mistake to let the boat follow its natural inclination, which is to turn into the wind once the sail has gybed. A fast gybing boat can spin through almost 180 degrees in a second, and comes to a grinding halt as rapidly increased apparent wind hits side-on and knocks the boat flat. Always bear away onto the new course as soon as the gybe is completed and keep the boat flat to maintain maximum steerage.

Keeping the boat flat can be very difficult in a strong wind, but if the boat tips it is vital that the boom end doesn't catch the water, which can trip the boat. The kicking strap should be tight enough to control the mainsail and prevent rolls to windward, but not so tight that the boom end is bound to catch. Sheet-control will also help prevent the boom end catching.

Different boats react in different ways to their centreboard or daggerboard when gybing. Modern skiff-style designs with narrow, high aspect foils can generally gybe with the foil fully down. More conventional dinghies with wide, low aspect foils need more careful treatment. The traditional advice is that you need the foil about halfway down to provide sufficient resistance to rolls to windward when going into the gybe, but not so far down as to act as a deep water pivot during the gybe, spinning the boat round and capsizing it to leeward.

Managing the rig

Hiking out or using the trapeze will help keep the boat level, but will inevitably be insufficient beyond a certain wind strength. When that happens, you have three choices, which can be summarized as basic response, reefing and rig tuning.

Basic response

A gust hits, the boat heels, and no matter how hard you hike out the boat continues to heel. To bring the boat back upright you have three options:

Bear off with the gust An old-fashioned seaman's response of "running before a storm", meaning to head in the direction the wind sends you, which is not very practical when sailing a dinghy.

Let the sheet out The sail will flap, the boat will slow down and it will come back upright. This is an uncomfortable way to continue sailing, frightens the crew, creates a great deal of drag and could damage the sails.

Luff to windward If you're sailing to windward and a gust hits, you can ease your grip on the tiller and let the boat turn further into the wind. This will depower the front of the mainsail, while still leaving enough drive in the back of the sail to

ABOVE **The Pico helmsperson is at full stretch in a comfortable hiking position. He can react to gusts by sheeting out or luffing.**

REEFING A PICO ....

1 The Pico uses a similar system to the Topper, which has rolls round the mast acting as reefs.

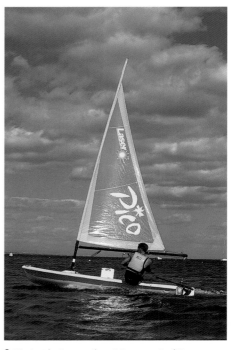

2 Having lost more than 30 per cent of its area, the sail still provides good performance.

push the boat forwards. Used in conjunction with easing the mainsheet, it is likely to be the best solution for survival in comfort if there is too much wind.

Reefing

Some dinghies will sail well with the jib dropped or furled; others may prove impossible to sail to windward. This is a matter for experiment.

Reefing the mainsail is only possible on a limited number of dinghies, mainly cruiser and cruiser-racer designs such as the Wayfarer or Laser 2000. Roller-reefing is a basic mainsail reefing system. The mainsail is rolled around the boom, and when the area is sufficiently reduced the boom can be locked onto its gooseneck and the halyard tensioned. However roller-reefing only works with a transom

mounted mainsheet, it is difficult to fit an effective kicking strap, and the shape and performance of the sail is often severely compromised by the effect of rolling the sail.

Slab reefing, reducing the size of the sail panel by panel, is a more sophisticated reefing system. The mainsail is marked into

ABOVE **The Wayfarer helmsperson and crew look comfortable as the helm eases the mainsheet and sails free and fast through choppy water.**

SLAB REEFING THE MAINSAIL ON A WAYFARER ....

1 Secure the new tack position at the junction of the mast and boom.

2 The new clew position is pulled down and along the boom.

3 Excess sail is tidied away along the side of the boom.

4 The Wayfarer handles well with the first of two reefs in.

one, two or even three parallel slabs. These can be pulled down onto the boom one at a time, using a hook and cringle to secure the new tack position by the junction of the mast and boom, and using a pennant (reefing line) to pull the new clew down and out along the boom. The excess sail can be rolled into a neat sausage, which is secured by shockcord along the boom. This system can produce an effective sail shape, and allows the use of a centre mainsheet and conventional kicking strap.

Prevention is better than cure, and reefing the mainsail is best tackled ashore. With practice it is certainly possible on the water, but it will always be tricky in a strong wind and while completing the reef the boat is likely to be blown a long way downwind.

RIG TUNING

Many modern dinghies have sophisticated rigs that can be tuned both on the beach and while sailing to maximize their performance in different wind strengths. The principal aims of rig tuning are to vary the amount and position of camber (fullness) and twist (leech shape) in the sails by using various controls.

All dinghies need to be tuned and set up in different ways, and are often provided with excellent tuning manuals, but the following are general rules for all classes.

Camber

A full sail is usually preferred for light winds and a flat sail for strong winds. However in very light winds a comparatively flat sail may perform best. The point of maximum camber tends to be blown aft in stronger winds, and needs to be pushed forward to maintain control.

Sail twist

A sail will naturally curve off at the top and act like a twisted wing. In light winds the twist may suit a slightly more open wind angle at the top of the mast. In moderate winds the twist needs to be tightened up and the leech straightened to power-up the sail. In strong winds the twist at the top will help exhaust excess power over the leech, while the bottom of the sail is effectively sheeted in at a closer angle.

ABOVE **The Pico sail twists from top to bottom, with excess power exhausting over the leech.**

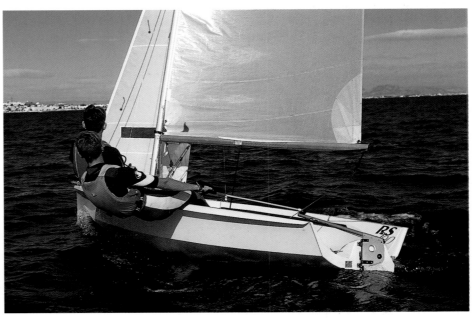

ABOVE **The cunningham is used to control mainsail luff tension while sailing, and is pulled half-down on the RS200 shown here. If the wind increases the crew will increase the tension to flatten the sail.**

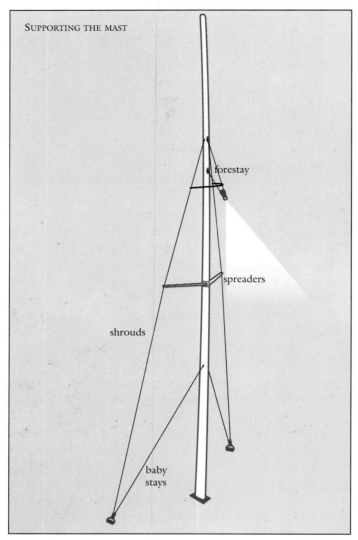

SUPPORTING THE MAST

forestay

spreaders

shrouds

baby stays

ABOVE **A heavy crew sails with a stiffer, more powerful mast than a light crew, who need to depower the rig when sailing upwind. Spreader length dictates how much the mast bends sideways, the longer the spreader the less bend. Not all boat types have baby stays, which help support the mast's lower half.**

ABOVE **The RS200 is heeling much too far, slipping sideways and slowing down due to increased hull resistance. The crew need to depower the rig with cunningham and kicker tension, and could even try hiking a bit harder.**

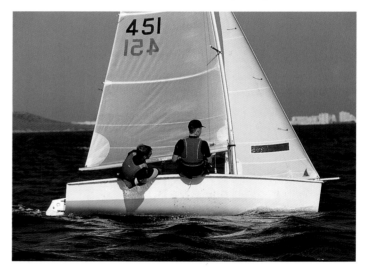

ABOVE **Note the clean mast bend of the RS200 and the lack of any major creases in the sail. In this instance the crew should definitely be hiking harder.**

Mast rake

Raking the mast forward by shortening the forestay and lengthening the shrouds will move the centre of effort forward improving control in stronger winds. Raking the mast back can improve pointing performance in lighter winds.

Mast bend

A heavier crew can sail with a stiffer rig than a lighter crew. The stiffer rig will hold more power and support a heavier crew; the softer rig, which bends sideways and backwards will exhaust more power and be manageable by a lighter crew. Mast bend can be tuned by spreader length (longer

equals stiffer) and mast gate position (a wider gate lets the mast bend more). Lower shroud tension can be increased to stiffen the bottom half of the mast and power up the rig in medium winds; and reduced to allow the bottom half of the mast to flex and lose excess wind in gusts, as well as creating a wider slot and less power between mainsail and jib.

Luff tension

Increased luff tension, using the downhaul or cunningham controls, flattens the camber in the mainsail and keeps it well forward. On modern rigs this is a key control to sail power, and on some high

performance boats the downhaul can be played or adjusted by the crew while sailing upwind. A vertical crease near the mast indicates too much tension.

The wrong tale

Due to turbulence around the mast, the lower mainsail telltales nearest the luff will not function correctly when sailing upwind. The lower leeward telltale should always be horizontal; if the lower windward telltale is horizontal, the sail needs easing until it begins to lift.

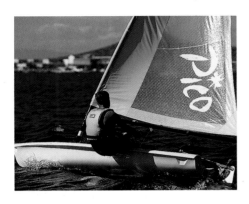

LEFT **Creases appear in the luff panel next to the mast when the unstayed rig of the Pico becomes well powered up, but the sail still provides good control and drives the boat forward.**

Sailing in very light winds

- Getting the best performance out of a boat in very light winds requires intense concentration.
- Don't rock the boat. Keep as still as possible, with your weight trimmed so the stern is lifted and the boat heeled enough to keep the sails filled.
- Do not oversheet the sails, particularly after a tack. The aim is to slowly build up speed without stalling the airflow.

Outhaul tension

Increased outhaul tension flattens the sail, but is very much a secondary control and much less effective than adjusting luff or kicker tension. A horizontal crease near the boom indicates too much tension.

Mainsheet tension

Modern rigs are designed around maximum mainsheet tension to bend the top of the mast, flatten the top of the sail, reduce twist, increase jib luff tension and provide maximum pointing ability and power when sailing upwind. Easing the mainsheet promotes fullness and twist in the sail, unless balanced by kicking strap tension.

Kicking strap/Vang/Gnav tension

The original role of the kicking strap was to hold the boom down. On modern rigs it has become a far more sophisticated depowering sail control, which plays a dual role with the mainsheet. It bends the top of the mast, flattens the top of the sail, reduces twist, increases jib luff tension and provides maximum pointing ability and power on all points of sailing.

Jib sheets

Easing the jib sheet to open the slot can be the most immediate and effective way of temporarily depowering the rig. Moving jib fairleads forward flattens the jib, closes the luff, reduces twist and narrows the slot between jib and mainsail. Moving jib fairleads aft increases jib twist, opens the leech and widens the slot, which will help if the crew is overpowered. The performance of the jib will also depend on whether the jib is new and in good condition or old and blown out of shape.

RIGHT **The slot between the jib and the mainsail plays an important role in driving a two sail boat forwards. Easing the jib, and so opening the slot, has the effect of immediately depowering the rig.**

ABOVE **Modern rig controls coupled with sophisticated sail materials allow relatively simple boats such as the Pico to cope with a wide range of wind conditions.**

Sailing in waves

On the sea, sailing with the waves can make a huge difference to both speed and controlling the boat when sailing downwind.

- Watch the waves coming up from behind the boat.
- Bear away to catch a wave face at about 90 degrees to your transom, so you are travelling directly with it.
- As the boat accelerates down the wave, sheet in to match the new wind angle as the apparent wind moves forward with your increased speed. You may need to move crew weight quickly forward to help initial acceleration on the wave face, and quickly back to avoid a nose dive into the next wave.
- Luff across the face to stay with the wave for as long as possible.
- Look for gaps, and avoid ploughing into the back of the next wave.

Capsize and recovery

Capsizing is all part of the fun of dinghy sailing, and should hold no fears. A capsize used to be a long, cold, messy business during which crews got freezing cold and boats were swamped and had to be painstakingly bailed out. Modern crews have the advantages of highly efficient clothing coupled with dinghies that are designed to float high and drain any water immediately once they are righted. That should make capsizing less of a worry, but it can still pose problems.

LEFT **Modern dinghy designs allow capsizes to be a relatively relaxed affair, and the RS200 floats at just the right height to make things easy. If the helm rights the boat now, the crew can simply roll into the bottom of the boat.**

CAPSIZE TO LEEWARD

This is the conventional capsize, when the boat is simply blown over due to a combination of too much wind and the crew failing to ease the sheets or luff to windward.

Going over

The boat will be blown on to its side. It reaches a point of no return, after which the final stages of the capsize are a relatively slow and graceful process.

Do not throw yourself on to the sail. You may break battens or rip the sail, and your weight may sink the mast (few masts are completely buoyant) and turn the boat upside down. As the boat goes over on its side, try to step over the top of the hull so you can sit astride the gunwale ready to stand on the centreboard or daggerboard.

Different boats behave in different ways as they go over. If the boat starts to invert, get on to the centreboard or daggerboard immediately. If there is only room for one on the centreboard or daggerboard, it should be the helmsperson.

If the mainsheet or jib sheet is still cleated, the crew will need to uncleat them so they run free when the boat is righted. It may also be necessary to push the centreboard or daggerboard in or down.

RIGHTING THE RS200 AFTER A CAPSIZE ....

1 The helmsperson stands on the centreboard, facing the wind with both hands on the gunwale.

2 As he pulls back and the boat comes up, he lifts himself on to the side of the boat.

3 The helmsperson goes in head first while the crew simply rolls in on the downhill side.

4 The wind (blowing from the right) blows the boom across.

5 So the crew gets out smartly to prevent a complete 180 degree roll.

GETTING THE CREW ON BOARD AFTER A CAPSIZE ON THE RS200..

1 A more conventional method is for the crew to get back in over the stern.

2 Once the boat is righted, it sits in a stable position beam-on to the wind.

3 The crew gets on without tipping the boat, and is ready to go sailing.

Blowing downwind

It is important to right the boat as quickly as possible. Give it time, and the capsized boat will turn so the hull (windage) is blowing downwind of the rig (drag). This is true of most modern dinghies that have high buoyancy and float very high in the water. Once the hull is downwind of the rig, righting the boat becomes more difficult. As you pull the boat upright, the wind will help it on its way up. However as can often happen, it may also be too helpful so that the mast tip describes a complete 180 degree arc, which means the boat comes up and capsizes on top of you and you have to start all over again. If the boat is starting to turn downwind, the crew should get in the water, grab the forestay and swim the bows around so that it points upwind.

Righting

The helmsperson should be able to stand on the centreboard or daggerboard and lean back with one or both hands on the gunwale lip. Try stepping back as far as you dare for extra leverage, but don't risk breaking the foil. Try leaning back while holding onto a line so you can get further outboard, but don't use the mainsheet. Some dinghies have special righting lines attached along the hull. If the boat still won't come up, ask your crew to hang on the centreboard or daggerboard tip from underneath (very tiring) or clamber up on the foil behind you if it will take the weight.

You can feel the boat come up. As the mast tip breaks free of the surface of the water the rig will start to accelerate.

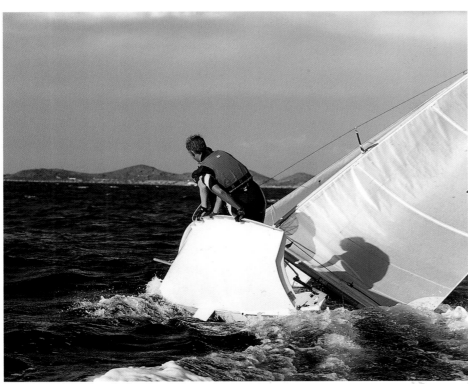

ABOVE **Once a boat goes this far, capsize is often inevitable. The helm is in a perfect position to hop onto the top side, and should be able to get on the centreboard and right the boat without getting wet.**

Getting back into the boat

This can be a difficult manoeuvre with the crew in the water. There are two methods:

- When the helmsperson is on the centreboard or daggerboard and ready to right the boat, the crew lies in the water alongside the cockpit area. Providing all goes well he or she will be scooped up and dumped in the bottom of the cockpit as the boat comes upright.
- An alternative method is for the crew to lie in the water parallel to the forestay, while keeping the boat pointing into the wind. As the helmsperson pulls the boat upright, the crew lifts his or her feet up onto the deck either side of the forestay, stands up and steps back into the cockpit.

You must control the rate of lift so it doesn't build up enough momentum to throw the rig into a 180 degree capsize. Step off the centreboard or daggerboard as soon as you can get on to the windward deck, and prepare to balance the boat. If your crew is still in the water, he or she should be ready to hold down the leeward side. You can then help the crew to get in over the stern.

Recovery

Once righted the boat will sit side-on to the wind with the sails flapping. Capsize can be tiring and disorientating, so take a breather, look around, decide what to do next, indicate to any would-be rescuers that you are OK and, if you need to start bailing, roll up your sleeves. Most modern dinghies will self-drain as soon as you get the boat moving.

CAPSIZE TO WINDWARD

A capsize to windward (backwards) normally results from a windward roll while sailing on a broad reach or dead downwind. It can happen when travelling fast, and is likely to be fast and unexpected, as opposed to the slow and graceful leeward capsize.

Going over

As the boat goes over grab something, such as the mainsheet or footstrap, so you don't get left behind. The boat will capsize with the hull downwind of the mast. In a light or moderate wind it should be possible to right the boat from the leeward (top) side.

Capsize rules

- Try to stay with the boat as it goes over. Modern dinghies float high and can be blown downwind faster than you can swim wearing a buoyancy aid, dinghy boots and hi-tech clothing. Catch a rope as the boat goes over.
- If you find yourself under the sails or tangled in sheets and lines, don't panic. Your buoyancy aid will keep your head well clear of the water, and you have plenty of time to extricate yourself.
- Beware of highly buoyant dinghies that float very high. Some float so high that it is very difficult to get up onto the centreboard or daggerboard once you are in the water.
- Try to prevent the boat turning turtle. You may bury the mast tip in the mud at the bottom, which makes righting difficult and can lead to a broken mast.
- If the boat turns turtle and you are underneath, don't panic. There will be plenty of air in the cockpit, so when you are ready you can take a deep breath, duck down and escape from the transom or side.
- When things go wrong avoid a pattern of repeat capsizes. Each attempt to right the boat becomes more physically draining, and all the time you may be being blown further out to sea. Don't hesitate to accept outside help.
- If you can't right the boat, grab hold of something and stay with the boat until rescue comes. Never leave the boat and attempt to swim to shore – an upturned boat will float and is much easier to spot than a sailor lost in the sea.

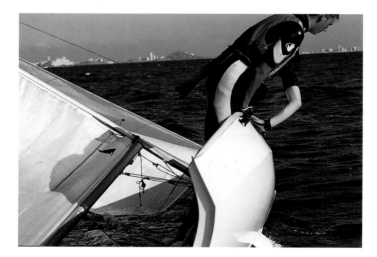

LEFT **No hope. The boom is pressing on the water, keeping the sail powered up and the boat pinned down. Think where you are going to go, and make sure you grab something and do not lose the boat.**

EASY UP WITH A WAYFARER...

1 The Wayfarer is a stable and fairly heavy boat, and not prone to capsizing.

2 But if it does go over, it comes up more sedately than any lightweight flyer.

3 The water will drain out through the stern flaps once the boat gets moving.

UN-TURTLING THE RS200..

1 A turtled boat can be brought upright by the helmsperson standing on the gunwale and pulling on the tip of the centreboard.

2 The crew helps by swimming the bows into the wind, which will blow under the deck rather than on to the hull.

Recovery

You need to scramble aboard very quickly as the boat comes up. Be prepared to throw your weight to windward in order to prevent the boat performing a complete 180 degree flip. In stronger winds it will be necessary to swim the bow round until it points almost into the wind, and then right the boat from the windward side.

Turning turtle

If the boat turns turtle, try standing on the underside of the lip of the gunwale with your back to the wind and lean back with both hands holding the end of the centreboard or daggerboard. Having the crew hold on to the bow will help spin the boat into the wind.

LEFT **Either the result of sailing by the lee unsuccessfully or pulling out of a strong wind gybe, the RS200 is about to roll all the way over to windward. The crew can expect a speedy capsize.**

Capsize tricks

If the capsized boat is lying downwind of the rig, try a San Francisco Roll (a variation on a kayak Eskimo Roll) to prevent the rig doing a 180 degree flip on top of you. One of the crew hangs on to the tip of the daggerboard or centreboard as the boat comes upright, is pulled through an underwater arc beneath the hull, and shoots out and breaks surface on the windward side. He or she can then immediately grab the windward deck and weigh down the boat to prevent it tipping any further.

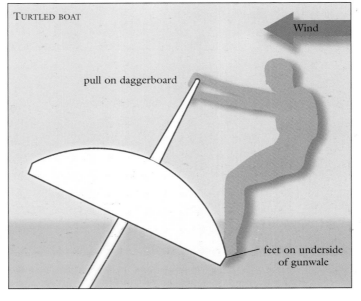

TURTLED BOAT

Wind

pull on daggerboard

feet on underside of gunwale

LEFT **Turning turtle is unusual with a monohull, but may happen if the crew push the rig down and the mast sinks. Getting the boat up again requires a little time and patience, and the crew must take care not to dig the mast into the bottom.**

Trapeze techniques

The trapeze is the most effective lever for keeping a dinghy level. It is generally much less tiring than hiking, and a lot more fun as you fly across the water.

The trapeze handle should be easy to grab, which usually means around eye level when you are sitting on the side of the boat. The handle has to carry all your weight in short bursts, so make regular checks that it is up to the job.

Trapezing in bare feet is seldom a good idea. You need grippy, lightweight boots that allow maximum movement but also give good protection to the ankles.

Modern trapeze hooks only stay hooked under tension. If you dangle from the trapeze wire by hanging on the handle, the hook will probably fall off.

If the boat capsizes while you are on the wire, try to avoid dropping into the mainsail from a great height. It's much better to squat down, unhook and drop in by the centreboard or daggerboard before the boat starts to turn right over.

If you're hooked on under the sail after a capsize to windward, don't panic.

Knock the ring off the hook, moving your hips forwards or up to give a little slack if necessary.

Getting out

Make sure there is enough power in the rig to support your weight before going out on the wire. The helmsperson may need to ease the mainsheet while the crew is getting prepared.

Sit on the side deck, sheet and cleat the jib, and hold it with your back hand. Then hook onto the ring with your front hand and grab the trapeze handle to lift yourself off the deck – all in one smooth movement. Slide out over the side in a semi-hiking position with the trapeze wire taut. Do not ease your weight, or the ring may drop off the hook. To get out into the trapezing position, bend your front leg and lift your front foot onto the side of the boat then push your front leg straight. At the same time push off from the side of the boat with your back hand while lifting your back foot onto the side and straightening the back leg. Let the jib sheet

ABOVE **On the wire, feet close together, looking ahead, staying relaxed, that's the way trapezing should be.**

run through your hand as necessary. Keep both feet as close together as possible and lean back until your shoulder straps start to pull taut. You can then let go of the handle.

TIGHTENING UP A TRAPEZE HARNESS ....

1 Pull the leg straps of your trapeze harness tight first.

2 Then tighten the shoulder straps until your body starts to bend.

ABOVE **The trapeze allows the crew to greatly increase leverage on the 29er, but will require good technique on such a short and frisky boat.**

Newcomers to trapezing often find letting go of the handle a major challenge, but it soon becomes a delight to swing free with the jib sheet in one or both hands.

Staying there

You may feel unsteady on your feet as the boat pitches through waves and the trapeze wire pulls you forwards. Try bracing your front foot against the shroud plate, and keep the back leg flexed so that you are leaning slightly back towards the transom – do not stand straight out at 90 degrees to the boat. Your front leg supports most of your body weight, while your back leg is used for balance. Get used to moving your weight in and out on the trapeze by bending your legs so the helmsperson can respond to lulls and gusts without the boat tipping to windward. If the wind is fluky you may have to come in and go out like a jack-in-the-box and adopt an ungainly crouching attitude on the side deck.

The traditional style of trapezing requires a dead straight body for maximum leverage. However, on modern skiff-style boats this has been superseded by a more comfortable, sit-up posture in which the sailor sits upright in the harness. This provides increased vision and allows better control and faster responses when sailing a fast moving, gennaker-powered boat at the expense of slight loss of leverage.

On a fast and gusty reach – particularly with a gennaker – the crew needs to keep well braced to avoid being thrown round the forestay if the bows go down. This will

GETTING OUT ON THE WIRE

1 Grab the hook and handle.

2 Hook on with the back hand.

3 Take the weight and move out.

4 Use the back hand for support.

5 Step out with the front foot.

6 Follow with the back foot.

almost certainly result in a major wipeout, and the sling-shot effect can cause damage to crew or equipment. If it helps, the crew can grab the helmsperson's shoulder to hold back; or use a special restraining line that clips on to the hook as when sailing a performance catamaran.

Coming in

Take the jib sheet in your back hand. Grab the handle with your front hand, and pull up so you can slide your back leg in over the side deck. Bend your front leg, using the handle to lift your backside onto the deck. Unhook for the next manoeuvre.

STAYING OUT ON THE WIRE

1 Brace the front leg and hold the jib sheet with your back hand.

2 Angle your feet so that you can lean and look forwards.

3 If conditions are marginal, then bend your legs and move in.

Trapeze height

For upwind sailing the trapeze ring should generally be adjusted so it is just clear of the deck. It is theoretically most efficient to trapeze parallel to the deck of the boat. However at that height waves will almost certainly hit your body, so you need to lift the trapeze ring enough to clear them. Do not lift the ring too high, or you will topple into the boat every time it heels.

All good trapezes need a system to lift or lower the ring, which can be used while on the wire. This is normally an adjustable length, two-part purchase led through blocks and locked by a friction cleat. Unless you are strong and experienced, adjusting ring height is a two-handed job. Cleat the jib, take your weight on the handle with your front hand, and use your right hand to pull the line through the adjuster. Be very sure that the line is firmly locked before you let go.

"Moon walking"

In stronger winds and on reaching courses, the crew will need to move back along the side deck to stop the bow burying. The more you move back, the greater the forward pull on the trapeze

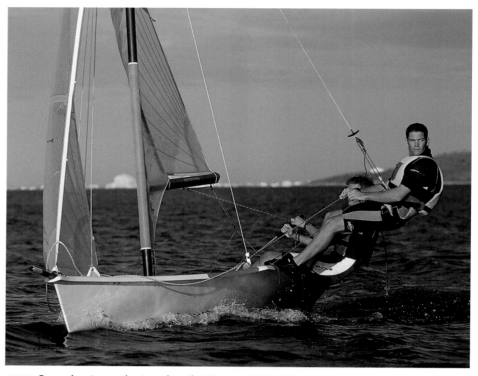

ABOVE **On modern trapeze boats such as the 29er an upright sitting position is common. It allows maximum control of the sails, plus a good view of the surroundings.**

wire becomes, and the more you need to lean back towards the stern with your back leg well bent and the front leg straight. You also need to set your feet

wider apart for greater stability. Moving back effectively shortens the length of the trapeze wire. You will need to lengthen it for a reaching course, or risk being pulled forward into the boat.

Trapeze tacks

When you are ready to tack, pull up on the handle in order to take your weight, and let the rig slide off the hook, with the pull of the shockcord retainer helping it. As the boat goes through the tack, wait until the last moment before coming in over the side and uncleating the jib. Cross to the new side taking the new leeward jib sheet with you – a continuous jib sheet makes this much easier.

Newcomers to trapezing will want to hook on before going out on the wire on the new side. Once you become more experienced, you can grab the handle on the new side with your new front hand, and push yourself straight out in the trapezing position. Sheet in and cleat the jib, while still hanging on the handle. Use your back hand to grab the ring, hook on and let the trapeze harness take your weight.

GETTING THE HEIGHT RIGHT ....

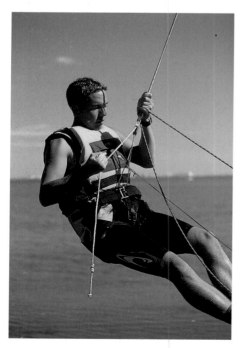

1 Take your weight on the back hand and shorten or lengthen the height of the hook.

2 Make very sure that the adjustment line is firmly locked in position.

HELMING OFF THE WIRE

This is a skilled art, whether on a two-handed or single-handed boat requiring plenty of practice. In most cases the helmsperson will have to manage both rudder and mainsheet and is unable to move in and out as quickly or easily as the crew. The crew will generally go out on the wire first and come in last, and should take responsibility for weight trim and respond to lulls and gusts, while the helmsperson stays out and concentrates on keeping the boat powered up.

When tacking the helmsperson will normally come in off the wire ahead of the crew, using the mainsheet hand to knock off the trapeze ring.

When the wind goes aft of a beam reach, helming from the wire becomes extremely difficult. It's much faster to be in control and hike, than out of control and on the trapeze.

Getting in and out

Before the helm goes out on the wire, he or she needs to hold both mainsheet and tiller in their back hand, in order to grab the trapeze ring and hook on. There is a natural tendency to pull the tiller with you when going out on the wire. This makes the boat bear away and can throw the crew forwards at an inopportune moment. To avoid it happening, try crooking your tiller

TACKING ON THE WIRE ....

1 Cross quickly to the new side, grabbing the handle with your front hand.

2 Go all the way out on the handle, while sheeting in with the back hand.

3 Bring the sheet hand into your body and use it to hook on.

4 Easy on dry land – not as easy on the water with the wind and the waves.

arm so you can hold the tiller by the side of your head. Straighten your arm as you go out on the wire, and the rudder will stay centred. Avoid pushing the tiller away and luffing the boat as you come in off

the wire. Slide your hand as far down the tiller extension as it will go, and then bend your arm as you come in to keep the rudder straight.

Tricks and tactics

The helm needs to trapeze from a slightly higher position than the crew to get an unobstructed view forwards.

Your front hand can manage small sheeting movements while on the wire. If you need to take in or let out a lot of mainsheet, you will need to use the back hand, which is holding the tiller, as a mainsheet clamp.

Do not let the tail end of the mainsheet drop in the water and drag. Lay the amount of slack that's needed for mainsheet adjustments over your thighs, with the remainder of the sheet thrown down in the cockpit.

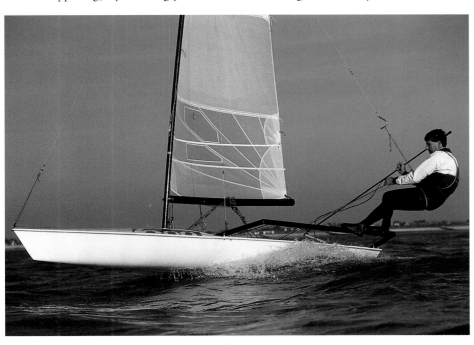

LEFT **Helming off the wire is a refined but very satisfying skill, particularly when out on the racks of a demanding single-hander such as the RS600.**

Gennaker techniques

A gennaker is a general term for an asymmetric spinnaker that is a pure reaching sail. Many people would agree that gennakers are a lot simpler and a whole lot more fun than conventional symmetric spinnakers, which are primarily for downwind sailing. Most gennakers have a clearly defined triangular shape: the leech is shorter than the luff and the mid-girth (halfway measurement) is shorter than the foot. The sail tapers from foot to head, unlike a spinnaker, which gets wider in the middle.

A gennaker can be effectively used on any point of sailing between a broad reach and close reach. However on a close reach in light winds there comes a point where a gennaker will drive a boat more sideways than forwards.

The key technique on a gennaker-driven boat is to luff to build boat speed. This creates a stronger apparent wind and closes the apparent wind angle so the sailor can bear off with the wind. If it's windy a fast boat such as a 49er or International 14 can sail a blistering close reach on a course that's almost dead downwind.

Hoisting, gybing and dropping the gennaker requires excellent co-ordination and communication between the crew. The object is to keep the boat level and sailing fast throughout these manoeuvres. Ratchet blocks and gloves are necessary to handle the loads generated by a gennaker. Travelling at speed helps reduce loads, which could otherwise overpower the crew.

Socks and bags

The main difference in technique for hoisting and dropping the gennaker is likely to revolve around whether the boat is equipped with a bag or a sock (also known as a shute) to stow and launch the sail.

A sock stows the gennaker neatly and automatically. It also allows the gennaker to be hoisted and dropped on either tack, so long as the mouth of the sock is in front of the forestay.

A bag on the other hand is able to hold a larger size gennaker and there is no friction in the hoist. However, the gennaker has to be gathered and packed manually every time it is dropped, and the sail must be hoisted on the same side as the last drop.

ABOVE **The gennaker looks great and is brilliant fun to sail with, adding a lot of downwind power to a boat like the RS200.**

SOCK VARIATIONS ....

The Laser 4000 has a moulded bridge at the mouth of the sock.

On the RS200 the sock is simply laid along the foredeck.

SAILING WITH A BAG ....

1 The 29er uses a gennaker bag, mounted behind the mast, with an elasticated opening.

2 When not in use, the bag shuts like an oyster and is held together by velcro.

HOISTING FROM A SOCK ON AN RS200 ....

1 It's often a good idea to talk through the sequence before you start.

2 On the RS200 the crew launches the gennaker while the helm sails the boat.

3 The pole pulls right out before the gennaker starts to go up and fill.

4 The helmsperson bears away to blanket the gennaker behind the mainsail.

5 The crew cleats the gennaker halyard when he is sure it is all the way up.

6 The helm luffs to help power up the gennaker while the crew sheets in.

Standard hoist

Bear away well downwind before the hoist. If the helmsperson does not bear away enough the gennaker may become wrapped round the forestay. During the hoist the helm can stand with legs astride to balance the boat and keep it level. A slight luff lifts the windward side; a slight bear-off lifts the leeward side.

The crew usually launches the gennaker by pulling in the halyard very fast, hand over hand. On some boats this action will automatically pull out the gennaker pole, which comes out of its hole in the bow rather like a torpedo; on others the pole may need to be pulled out separately before the halyard. The hoist needs to be as fast as possible to avoid the sail dropping and being run over, or the boat slowing to a crawl while sailing downwind.

The point where the gennaker is fully hoisted should be clearly marked on the halyard. Once the gennaker is sheeted and fills, it is very difficult to hoist the halyard further in anything other than a light wind, and performance and control will be compromised. The crew takes in the sheet and moves out to the windward side, or goes straight out on the trapeze if fitted. At the same time the helmsperson locks the pole at a suitable angle to windward, and luffs onto a reaching course to build up speed and apparent wind as the crew sheets in. If the helm wants to get out on the trapeze, the crew may need to depower the gennaker for a couple of seconds to help him or her onto the side.

Bag hoists

A leeward side hoist is easiest from a bag. The crew can manage the hoist from the windward side, and the helmsperson can sail a reaching course.

If a windward side hoist is necessary, most likely after dropping the gennaker on the wrong side for the next hoist, the helm

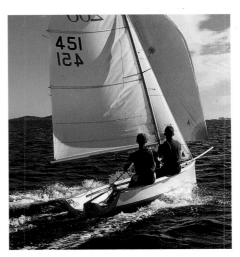

7 The boat accelerates and they bear off on the apparent wind.

must bear off downwind to ensure the gennaker goes up cleanly. Don't stay downwind too long – a fast hoist and a slight luff will help ensure the gennaker floats around the front of the boat without wrapping its luff around the forestay.

DROPPING INTO A SOCK ON THE RS200 ....

1 The helm bears away to blanket the gennaker, while the crew lets go of the sheet.

2 The crew pulls in hand over hand on the retrieval line.

3 The gennaker is drawn into the bag without wrapping or snagging it around the bow.

Standard drop

The helmsperson temporarily takes the gennaker sheet as the crew comes inboard, and bears off dead downwind as the crew moves to the middle of the boat.

The helm keeps the boat trimmed, while the crew prepares to uncleat the halyard. On some boats, particularly catamarans, you can throw the bundle of excess halyard over the bag so it streams out in a straight line. This guarantees it will run free.

Sock system

The crew uncleats the gennaker halyard and pulls hand over hand on the retrieval line, which will drag the gennaker into the sock and the pole into the bows. The helm may need to uncleat the pole angle controls to allow this.

Bag drop

Unless the wind is very light, the drop is best done on the windward side so the crew does not have to move down to leeward and risk heeling the boat. It is also very uncomfortable trying to retrieve the gennaker when you are squashed under the boom. The long, continuous gennaker sheet must be tensioned and cleated when not in use, to prevent any chance of it falling off the bows and under the boat.

For a windward drop the crew grabs the windward sheet, lets the leeward sheet fly, pulls the sail round the forestay or jib luff and gathers in the foot while letting go of the halyard. Within a few feverish seconds he or she drops the sail in the cockpit, rapidly bundles it into the bag, and finally secures the top with velcro straps so that none of the corners pull out while sailing. The helmsperson may need to uncleat the pole launch system to let the pole slide back into the boat while this is going on.

If dropping to leeward, bear away enough to prevent the sail blowing back and catching on the ends of the battens. The helm may need to stand and grab the leeward sheet to get it within the crew's reach. The crew then pulls in the foot with the leeward sheet, taking great care to bring the sail under the leeward jib sheet.

A gybe drop lets you drop the sail to windward, without having to bear away and pull it round the forestay. As the boat gybes, the crew crosses to the new windward side but keeps pulling in on the old sheet. As the boom goes across, he or she grabs the gennaker clew, lets go of the halyard, and catches the sail as it drops on the windward side.

Gennaker gybing

Gybing requires good balance and trim, with the boat travelling at maximum speed to reduce apparent wind and potential overloading of the sails. The faster the gybe, the smoother and more effortless it should be. Both crew come inboard as the helmsperson begins to bear away. The helmsperson keeps the boat level as the boat turns past dead downwind ready to give a tug on the mainsheet to help gybe the mainsail.

DROPPING THE GENNAKER IN STRONG WIND ....

1 The helm bears off and lets the main flog as the crew prepares to let go the gennaker sheet.

2 The crew pulls it down and into the sock at top speed. Any wraps or snags would be a disaster.

3 On a gusty day, the helm needs to sheet in and head up straightaway to keep the boat upright.

The crew waits to let the old gennaker sheet run free. If it is let go too soon it may blow forwards and wrap round the forestay. Sometimes it will unwrap with a tug; at other times it is necessary to gybe back onto the old course. The crew lets the sheet off so both boom and gennaker cross to the new sides together, with the clew of the gennaker just brushing the forestay.

The helmsperson continues to steer through the gybe. If the jib is set, a good trick is for the crew to cleat the gennaker on the new leeward side before moving to the other side of the boat. The crew then sheets in fast, and goes out on the side or wire.

Once the sail is powered up on the new gybe, the helm starts to luff to build up to full speed and the crew sheets in to match the apparent wind angle. If the boat heels over and does not power out of the gybe, the gennaker must be eased off by letting out the sheet slightly. If the boat loses speed at the end of the gybe, the helmsperson must luff before bearing away on the apparent wind and a suitable downwind course.

GYBING WITH THE GENNAKER ON THE RS200

1 The helmsperson stands up to bear away and grab the boom.

2 He flicks it across, while the crew moves across and lets go of the gennaker sheet.

3 The helm balances the boat with his feet while the crew pulls the gennaker round the forestay.

4 The crew then sheets in, powers up and flattens out the boat on the new course.

GYBING WITH THE GENNAKER ON THE RS200 IN STRONGER WIND

1 The boat is moving fast on a broad reach as the helm starts to bear away.

2 The helmsperson stands to give the boom a flick to the new side as the boat turns downwind.

3 The helmsperson ducks while the crew lets the gennaker sheet fly and pulls in on the new side.

4 The helmsperson concentrates on steering and levelling out the boat on the new course.

5 The helmsperson luffs to build speed while the crew sheets in.

6 As apparent wind increases they start to bear away at full speed.

Gennaker trimming

With the apparent wind coming from ahead, a gennaker tends to be more stable and easier to trim than a spinnaker, but there is skill in getting it powered up to maximum advantage. As with the mainsail and jib, the trick is to sail with the gennaker on the edge. Let the sheet out until the luff starts to curl inwards near the top, and from there trim it back in until the curl is just hovering on the edge. If the gennaker keeps collapsing, it could be that the halyard is not fully up or that the helmsperson needs to sail a lower course. If the boat lacks power in light winds, the probable solution is to head up. If the pole can be trimmed to either side, a task performed by the helmsperson, it should be trimmed a few degrees to windward. The further downwind you are heading and the lighter the apparent wind, the further to windward it needs to be so it is kept well clear of the mainsail. Pole trim will also need to be adjusted every time the boat gybes.

When a gust hits, the gennaker sheet is eased to compensate for the apparent wind shifting forward, as the helmsperson bears

GENNAKER

head

luff

gennaker

leech

clew

foot

tack

LEFT The gennaker is essentially a free floating, overlapping jib (genoa), which has a very full shape owing to its loose luff. It retains the same clew, head and tack as any headsail.

away to maximize downwind course and prevent the boat from heeling. As the boat accelerates even faster the sheet must be trimmed in. In strong winds, the helm can steer the boat to keep the gennaker on a finely tuned edge, bearing off when the luff curls in and luffing when the luff lifts outwards. The crew may need to ease the gennaker to help the boat bear away in gusts.

The jib can be sheeted for a close reaching course, easy with a self-tacking jib as on the 49er. Other dinghies may have self-furling jibs, so on a more downwind course it is easier to furl the jib leaving the area between the mast and gennaker totally unobstructed. This gives a better view when trimming the gennaker. The jib can then be unfurled just prior to dropping the gennaker and changing course upwind.

TRIMMING THE GENNAKER ON A 29ER

1 The crew bear off on a gust with everything pulling hard.

2 The apparent wind drops and swings aft, collapsing the gennaker.

3 The helm luffs and the crew sheets in to power up the sail.

TACKING DOWNWIND AND REGAINING CONTROL ....

1 The boys in the RS200 are on a blast, sailing flat out downhill on the apparent wind.

2 Time to put in a downwind tack, so the helmsperson says, "let's go for it!".

3 All's well as the boat slews round onto the new course.

4 But they have a few problems getting the boom across.

5 The momentum of the gybe looks set to flatten the boat, but the helm keeps the tiller up.

6 The helm can now bear away while the crew helps flatten the boat.

Tacking downwind

A gennaker should never be used for sailing dead downwind. The object of a gennaker is to be able to sail a downwind course on a succession of very fast broad reaches, with gybes in between. The skill is to be able to build up apparent wind on a beam reach, and then bear off and head downwind holding the same speed. The exception is in very light winds, when it may pay to sail a more direct downwind course without luffing.

All gennaker boats have an optimum velocity made good (VMG) downwind sailing angle, which is determined by different wind speeds. The difference between optimum VMG and being slightly off the angle, either sailing too high or too low, will be proportionally greater as a boat becomes lighter, faster and starts to plane. The angle between a luffing course to build speed and bearing off with a gust can be as much as 90 degrees. A gennaker boat therefore sails a kind of slalom course, luffing and bearing off to maximize its downwind VMG.

Gybing angles are more difficult to guess than tacking angles on a course sailed in gusts and lulls. As an average rule, the gybing angle needs to be about 45 degrees or more to the course of the boat.

ABOVE **Judging how deep you can sail downwind and when to tack is largely a matter of "seat of the pants" experience and watching other boats. There is a constant trade-off in the search for maximum velocity made good (VMG).**

Spinnaker techniques

The spinnaker is a traditional symmetrical sail for downwind sailing. Most spinnakers are fuller than gennakers and considerably more full than the mainsail or jib. The amount of fullness or flatness helps determine how efficient a spinnaker is on a dead run, and how close to the wind it can be carried on a reach. A spinnaker is only useful when the wind is aft of the beam. If the wind goes forward of the beam, the fullness of a spinnaker will heel the boat over and pull it sideways. It is also likely to become less controllable than a gennaker. Unlike a gennaker, the velocity made good (VMG) of a spinnaker can be maximized by taking the shortest course downwind, when the difference between true wind and apparent wind is less critical than when tacking downwind with a gennaker.

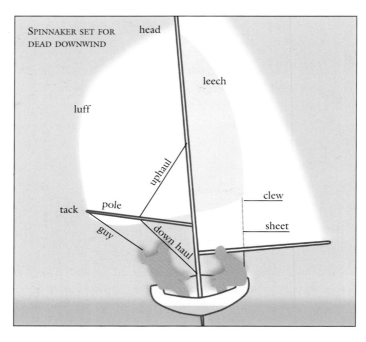

SPINNAKER SET FOR DEAD DOWNWIND

head
leech
luff
uphaul
pole
tack
guy
down haul
clew
sheet

LEFT **The clew and sheet of a spinnaker are to leeward and the tack, pole and guy are to windward. Both sides of the sail are interchangeable unlike a gennaker where tack and clew are in fixed positions.**

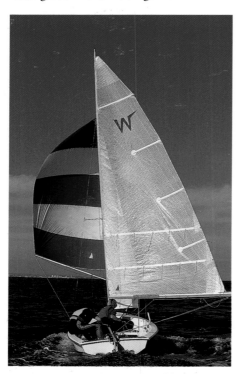

ABOVE **Both tack and clew of the spinnaker are level as the Wayfarer runs downwind, and the spinnaker is pulled well round to the windward side so it is not blanketed by the mainsail.**

Spinnaker controls

A spinnaker has control lines to both sides of the sail, unlike a gennaker, which has sheets led to a single clew and is closer in use to an oversized jib. The control line on the leeward side of the spinnaker is the sheet. This is attached to the clew and controls the leech by means of constant trimming. The control line on the windward side of the spinnaker is the guy. This is attached to the tack and is also clipped into the outer end of the spinnaker pole. The guy controls the luff, and once a course is set is cleated in a fixed position. Since the spinnaker is symmetrical, the luff/leech, tack/clew and guy/sheet swop roles every time the boat changes tacks.

To avoid being blanketed by the boat, crew or mainsail, the spinnaker is held out to windward by a spinnaker pole while sailing downwind. The vertical angle of the spinnaker pole is adjusted by an uphaul and downhaul line. The more downwind the course, the higher the end of the pole should be. The horizontal angle of the spinnaker pole is adjusted by the guy. The pole should be set at approximately 90 degrees to the apparent wind.

Spinnaker hoists

A spinnaker will begin to fill the moment it leaves its bag or sock. If you hoist while bearing away and are still on a beam reach, the top of the spinnaker may fill and capsize the boat; if you wait until the boat is dead downwind, lateral stability becomes poor and the boat may start rolling as the spinnaker goes up.

The centreboard or daggerboard needs to be lifted at least halfway. This is a compromise between providing enough resistance to windward rolls and letting the boat slide leeward rather than trip on its board; the side pressure from a partly filled spinnaker can capsize a boat with the board fully down.

To start the hoist, the crew rigs the spinnaker pole, which has identical clip fittings at both ends. The outer end is clipped over the guy and then the inner

SPINNAKER HOIST ON A WAYFARER

1 The helmsperson bears off downwind. The crew picks up the spinnaker pole.

2 The crew clips the outer end of the pole to what will be the guy.

3 She clips the uphaul/downhaul to the middle of the pole, and clips the inner end to the mast.

4 The spinnaker is hoisted from its bag, and goes up on the leeward side of the sail.

5 The crew pulls in on the sheet after the helm has pulled back the guy.

6 The spinnaker sets perfectly.

end is clipped to the mast with the vertical angle of the pole pre-set for the course. On many boats, the helmsperson stands and faces forward while pulling up the halyard. In this way the person can use their legs to balance the boat, as well as pulling in a lot of halyard with each heave. Meanwhile, the crew pulls in on the guy to get the pole round to windward. The guy should be locked with the pole at 90 degrees to the wind, pointing across the boat for a dead downwind course, and in line with the boat for a beam reach. Never let the pole push against the forestay on a beam reach. The crew sheets in and trims the spinnaker for the course.

Trimming the spinnaker

As with a gennaker, the spinnaker should always be sheeted so that it is on the edge of collapse with the top of the luff starting to curl inwards but not collapsing. If the spinnaker collapses the crew needs to sheet in or the helmsperson needs to bear away, with the pole eased forwards for the new course.

Running with a spinnaker

As the boat bears away, the crew pulls the pole right back. This lets the spinnaker lift and fly as far forward as possible, so it can

pull the boat with minimal effect from wind shadow or turbulence. The helm usually sits to leeward on the same side as the mainsail boom, with the crew to windward on the same side as the spinnaker pole. Both crew need to move aft where the hull is flattest and most stable. The crew must keep trimming the boat, laterally and longitudinally, when sailing

TRIMMING THE SPINNAKER

and surfing with following waves. Beware of a sudden death roll caused by a clumsy crew movement or sudden rogue wave.

To provide roll resistance the centreboard or daggerboard should be part-way down. The mainsail should be sheeted in a short way off the shroud, and the spinnaker slightly over-sheeted to prevent it swinging from side to side.

1 If the luff of the spinnaker collapses, the crew needs to sheet in or the helm has to bear away.

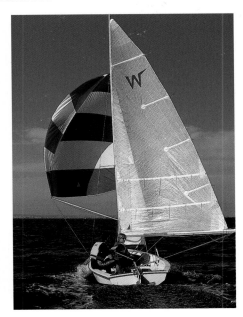

2 The spinnaker is just on the curl. A quick tug on the sheet will bring it back and halt its collapse.

Reaching with a spinnaker

The pole should be at around 90 degrees to the wind with the tack and clew as level as possible to maintain the sail's symmetrical shape. Pulling in the sheet for a reaching course will automatically pull the clew down, and the tack needs to be pulled down to the same height.

In anything more than a light wind, the crew will need to hike or trapeze to keep the boat flat. The guy is pushed out of the way under a clip by the windward shroud, which also holds the boom down.

The difference between true and apparent wind poses more problems with a full bellied symmetric spinnaker than a flat bellied asymmetric gennaker. If the boat accelerates and drives the wind forward, the helmsperson must bear away to continue to carry the spinnaker and keep the boat level. On a reaching course a spinnaker will start to collapse or pull the boat sideways well before a gennaker, and it is an important skill to be able to judge when a spinnaker ceases to be an advantage and should come down.

A boat that is well powered up and flying with a spinnaker will make the rudder seem finger light, exerting only

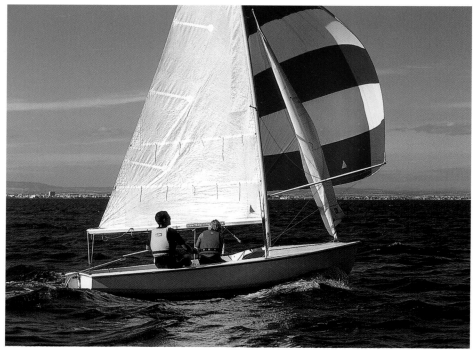

ABOVE **When reaching, the spinnaker pole is let forward, but must always be pulled back off the forestay. The pole should be pulled down a little harder than is shown here. The jib should either be furled or sheeted in and cleated, even though it will produce negligible drive.**

marginal control. If the boat suddenly heels and goes into an involuntary luff, the top of the spinnaker will power up and take control of the boat. It is a top priority for the helmsperson and crew to keep the boat flat, with the crew depowering the spinnaker to let the helmsperson bear away in gusts.

GYBING THE WAYFARER WITH A SPINNAKER

1 The helm bears away, pulling in the guy while the crew eases the sheet.

2 The helm pushes the tiller over to gybe the boat, while the crew gives a sharp pull on the kicker.

3 Both crew move to the new side while the helm centres the rudder to keep downwind.

4 The crew unclips the pole from the mast, and clips this end of the pole onto the new guy.

5 She pushes the pole forward, releases the old guy, and clips the pole's new inner end to the mast.

6 The crew sheets in as helm pulls in on the new guy and heads up onto the new reaching course.

Spinnaker gybes

The spinnaker gybe is more complex than the gennaker gybe, and provides more opportunity for getting things wrong.

The centreboard or daggerboard must be raised at least halfway; down enough so it won't roll going into the gybe, and up enough so it won't trip and heel the boat when luffing out of the gybe. The helmsperson plays a major role, steering the boat through the gybe, balancing the boat and managing the spinnaker controls all at the same time.

The helmsperson bears away until the boat is sailing by the lee, with the spinnaker pulling well out to the windward side and the clew floating close to the forestay. The helm steers the boat through the arc of the gybe, standing in order to balance the boat, holding the spinnaker sheet in one hand and guy in the other, and steering with the tiller between his or her legs. This allows the crew to unclip the inner end of the pole from the mast, and clip this end (the old inner end) to the new guy (old sheet). He or she then quickly unclips the old outer end from the new sheet (old guy) – there is usually a line along the spinnaker pole to facilitate this – and supports the pole with both hands for a second before pushing it out towards the new tack and clipping the new inner end to the mast. Meanwhile the helm steers the boat through the gybe, keeping the boat level and the spinnaker filled so no speed is lost and the apparent wind does not power up at an inopportune moment.

In light to moderate winds the main boom will gybe of its own accord; in stronger winds the momentum may throw the boat on its side, so the crew will need to yank the boom across by pulling the kicking strap just before clipping the pole to the new side. As the boom comes over and the boat powers up, the crew is ready to hike or trapeze the boat, having taken the guy and sheet from the helm who has already set them for the new course.

Spinnaker drops

The traditional spinnaker drop is on the leeward side, with the sail coming down the same way that it went up. With the

LEFT **When gybing there is no need to let the downhaul and spinnaker go up in the sky. Keep them down with the pole level or the boat will go out of control if a gust hits.**

spinnaker blanketed by the mainsail, the crew lets off the guy and halyard, then pulls the spinnaker in from the clew (via the sheet) to bundle it into its bag; or alternatively pulls it back into its sock or shute with a retaining line. Once the spinnaker is stowed with halyard and sheets tensioned and cleated, the crew can unclip and stow the pole.

If the next spinnaker hoist is on the opposite tack, the crew will need to drop the sail on the windward side of the boat. Having let go the sheet and halyard, the crew grabs the tack via the guy and pulls the sail down into its bag. Care is needed to ensure that the spinnaker and all associated lines are pulled in under the jib sheet to avoid a mess at the next hoist.

SPINNAKER DROP ON THE WAYFARER ....

1 The crew passes the sheet to the helm, unclips the pole from the mast and lets go of the guy when the spinnaker is blanketed by the mainsail.

2 She drops the pole into the cockpit, having unclipped the downhaul/uphaul line, and stows it ready to drop the spinnaker halyard.

3 The spinnaker is dropped on the leeward side of the mainsail where it is kept under control.

4 The crew sits inboard to cram the spinnaker into its bag, letting the three corners protrude.

Catamaran Sailing
Techniques

Catamarans go fast because they have a wide, stable platform that can support a big and often oversized rig, combined with pencil-slim hulls that create minimal wetted surface area. The result is a very different boat from a monohull; it is invariably wider, frequently faster and usually requires a very different style of sailing.

Not everyone likes catamarans, which are very much in a minority compared with monohulls in most countries – notable exceptions are Holland and France. Catamarans are ungainly and take up a lot of space on land, can be rather slow and unresponsive in light winds, do not sail well when heading dead downwind and may lack the super-sensitive feel of a finely tuned dinghy. But in return they can be brilliant fun, fast and tremendously powerful, with rudder foils that literally hum with glee as the wind passes Force 3 (10 knots). From there on a catamaran's sensational performance really kicks in, with the promise of the windiest, wildest and wettest rides of them all.

Rigging and tuning

Most aspects of assembling, rigging and tuning a catamaran are similar to those of monohull dinghies though there are important differences.

The platform

The hulls, beams and trampoline of a catamaran form a platform that is equivalent to the hull and deck of a monohull. The main problem for designers and builders is to ensure the platform is as rigid as a monohull, with minimal amount of flex and perfect parallel alignment between the two hulls. The platform also needs to be light, and the correlation between light weight and speed is more marked in catamarans than monohulls.

Each hull is an individual sealed unit accessed by inspection hatches. The platform is created by joining the hulls with two crossbeams, which are usually bolted to the top of the hulls or slide and lock into moulded slots. Crossbeams are invariably made from aluminium extrusions, while carbon fibre is a much

more expensive option. The front crossbeam may have a dolphin striker – a V-shaped brace – to help support the load of the mast without bending. The rear beam carries the mainsheet loads, and will usually incorporate a full length track for the mainsheet traveller.

The self-draining, mesh trampoline forms the deck of the boat, and has to be rigid enough to support the crew as well as helping to stiffen the whole platform. Most trampolines are fed into slots along the beams and sides of the hulls, and tensioned with lashings at the rear beam.

The rig

All catamaran masts are stepped on the front beam, and most can rotate through an arc so they line up with the mainsail. This is achieved by a shaped cup at the mast base, which fits over a raised ball that is similar to a towball on a car. A pin locks the mast cup securely onto the ball, and the mast is held up by a single forestay that splits into a V-shaped bridle

leading to each bow, and conventional shrouds allow enough twist for the mast to rotate from side to side.

Most catamarans have an elliptical wing shape mast with zero or minimal taper. The mast will bend sideways, but not fore and aft, and due to its size is considerably heavier than the mast of a comparable monohull. Catamarans also have mainly aluminium masts, but carbon fibre is increasingly taking over despite being more expensive:

- Carbon is considerably lighter, which makes the mast easier to hoist or lower when rigging and reduces pitching when sailing.
- It is also more likely to float, which prevents a catamaran turning turtle when capsized.

All high performance catamarans are fitted with flat-sided, square-section booms, and they had loose footed mainsails long before the trend became accepted by monohulls. Aluminium is the favoured material; carbon fibre is the lightweight option.

LEFT **Formula 18 catamarans such as the Dart Hawk can carry a big, powerful rig thanks to the righting moment leverage created by wide-spaced hulls and both crews on trapezes.**

ABOVE **The platform of a catamaran features a quick-draining mesh trampoline suspended between the two main beams. On the Dart 6000 the beams slot directly into the hull mouldings.**

THE CATAMARAN
(DART 16)

mast

mainsail

shroud

trapeze wire

jib

mainsheet system

traveller

rudder
stock

front beam

forestay bridle

forestay striker
beam

transom

rudder
blade

bow

skeg

hull

trampoline

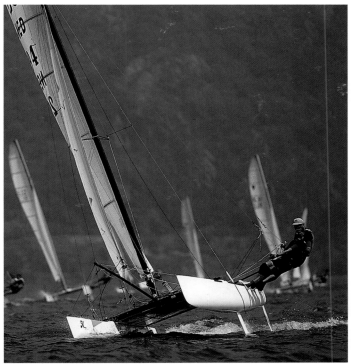

ABOVE **Formula 18s charging upwind. Long, deep daggerboards that give tremendous lift to windward are only practical for sailing in deep water.**

LEFT **Catamarans have several design features not found on other high performance boats. Twin hulls make the trampoline and twin foils necessary while the sails are flatter, and the mainsail has full length battens (not shown) to keep it tensioned to help the sailor cope with the higher speeds.**

The foils

Catamarans can be fitted with centreboards or daggerboards to provide resistance to sideslip and upwind lift. Long, narrow, straight-sided daggerboards are favoured for top performance, and are used on classes such as Formula 18 and A Class single-handers. They are not advised for the faint-hearted or inexperienced sailing in shoal waters – if you hit the bottom at 20 knots, you will certainly smash a foil and possibly rip open the entire hull.

Another disadvantage is that they are clumsy to put in and take out, and protrude way above the deck when retracted. Centreboards, which are used in the Tornado, are more user-friendly since they flip up inside the hulls and barely protrude above the deck line when lifted. However, they do not give the same upwind lift as a high aspect daggerboard, and, unfortunately, they increase the difficulty and cost of manufacturing a catamaran hull.

Beware of sand, grit or pebbles getting into the cases and jamming the tightly fitting boards when you pull the boat on to the beach.

Another option is to have no boards at all and rely on the speed of the catamaran to ensure that it still makes reasonably good upwind progress. Cats in this category include the Hobie 16, which relies on the flat outer sides of its asymmetric hulls to prevent leeway, and the Dart 18, which has small, built-in keels known as skegs running under its hulls.

All catamarans have twin rudders, twin tillers, and a single tiller bar and tiller extension. Aluminium is the favoured tiller material. Rudder alignment is critical on a catamaran when the effects of weather helm (tiller pulls away from you) or lee helm (tiller pushes towards you) are pronounced since the leeward rudder is effectively doing all the work. The rudders should feel balanced and light at all speeds.

If there is an uncomfortable pull:

- Check that both blades are locked fully down. Most catamarans have a tiller-lock, which lets the rudder flip up if it hits the bottom.
- Check the blades are aligned. Measure between the leading edges and trailing edges, and adjust the tiller bar to equalize any difference.

ABOVE **The transoms of a catamaran need protecting when left on its trolley on rough ground. This French built Diam Formula 18 has a beautiful set of Sailworks wood and laminate rudders from Sweden.**

Mainsail

All catamarans have fully battened mainsails that act like semi-rigid aerofoils. Since the battens push against the luff there is a great deal of friction inside the mast track, and it can be difficult to hoist or lower the mainsail unless guidelines are followed:

- The leading edge of the mast must point directly into the wind with the trailing edge correctly aligned for the sail.
- Hoisting is often a two-person job. One feeds the sail into the track from the front beam, while the other pulls the halyard from wherever gives as straight a lead as possible.

Catamaran controls

The size of the catamaran mainsail, combined with the power generated from sailing at speed on the apparent wind, requires sophisticated controls to handle the boat when you are out in winds of up to Force 4 (11–16 knots).

Mainsheet

A catamaran mainsheet needs to be sheeted in whenever the apparent wind is forward of the beam.

The mainsheet controls sail twist in the top of the leech. For normal sailing and maximum pointing ability, it should be pulled in hard enough so the leech points backwards without curling to windward. If the sail is overpowered and the boat starts

Righting lines

Most catamarans need a righting line to pull the boat back up after a capsize. At its simplest, a righting line is a rope that is about 3m (10ft) long, thick enough to be comfortable on the hands, but thin enough to take a hitch round a trapeze hook. Secure one end to the base of the mast or dolphin striker, and stow the rest in a trampoline pocket where it comes easily to hand.

ABOVE **A righting line is a critical requirement when attempting to right the majority of cats. The Dart 16 shown here will come up easily.**

ABOVE **The very wide trampoline of an Olympic Tornado is left relatively uncluttered, allowing the crew more room to move, because the boat has no gennaker.**

ABOVE **The Tornado control lines are led down from the boom, under the trampoline and out to the sides of the boat so they can be adjusted while the crew is on the trapeze.**

to heel, easing the mainsheet will open the leech and promote sail twist with excess wind spilling out of the sail. The mainsail will need to be sheeted in and out continuously to keep the boat flat and moving fast on a gusty day. This is hard

work. To make it easier, the 17sq m (183sq ft) mainsail of a Formula 18 has an 8:1 multi-purchase mainsheet complete with ratchet-block control, and most catamarans are fitted with similarly powerful sheeting systems.

HOISTING A CATAMARAN MAINSAIL

1 The headboard of the mainsail is reinforced for high loadings.

2 The bolt rope must be carefully fed into the mast slot.

3 Keep the mast pointing directly into the wind. This is vital to ensure the fully battened mainsail, which is under tension, will slide freely up the mast slot.

Halyard locks

Most catamarans feature a halyard lock that locks the sail to the top of the mast, of which the two following examples are typical. The Hobie 16 has a V-shaped cleat on the leading edge of the mast and a ferrule (basically a lump on the halyard) that fits over it. The Dart 16 has a hook on the trailing edge of the mast and a ring on the end of the halyard that fits over it. Both systems require a similar technique for hoisting:

- With the downhaul let right off, the halyard is pulled to the top using maximum tension.
- On the Dart the ring rises onto the hook, while on the Hobie the ferrule has to be dropped into its cleat.
- Easing the halyard will drop the top of the sail enough to lock the ring onto the hook and the ferrule into the cleat, so long as they are correctly aligned.
- Tensioning the downhaul ensures the halyard is totally locked.

A similar technique is required for dropping the mainsail:

- With the downhaul let right off, the halyard is pulled to the top of the mast using absolute maximum tension.
- On the Dart the ring rises above the hook, while on the Hobie the ferrule rises above its cleat.
- Rotating the Dart mast through 90 degrees should pull the ring away from the hook. Hold the mast in that position and pull the sail down hard until the ring is definitely below the hook. You can then let the mast rotate back to its in-line position, and drop the sail.
- On the Hobie the halyard needs to be pulled forwards and to the side, to lift the ferrule away from the cleat. Keep the halyard in that position while pulling the sail down to get the ferrule above the cleat, and then drop the sail.

ABOVE **The black mast rotation spanner can be seen just above the boom on this Tornado. The red control line is used to lock the angle between mast and sail.**

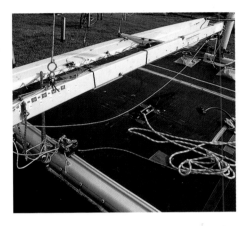

ABOVE **The 1–10 calibration gives precise outhaul control on this Tornado. The mainsheet is led forward along the boom and back under the trampoline to a small cut-out, saving mess and clutter for the crew.**

Jib and jib sheets

The primary role of the jib is to accelerate airflow through the slot between mainsail and jib. The size of the jib is generally small in relation to the mainsail, but speed and the effect of apparent wind means that sheets will often need a 2:1 purchase system. Due to the width of a catamaran, the jib sheet fairleads may be mounted on barber-haulers, which are used to pull the clew of the jib outwards, opening the slot for offwind sailing or strong winds. Jib fairleads may also be adjustable fore and aft to tighten or open the leech.

Traveller

This controls the angle of attack of the mainsail, with the traveller control line usually attached to the end of the mainsheet so that it comes easily to hand. The traveller is generally set in the centreline for beating, and moved out for sailing offwind. It can be let right out to the inner edge of the leeward hull for downwind reaching. The traveller can also be eased away from the centreline to feather the main and make the boat more comfortable, but point lower, while beating in stronger winds.

Mast rotation

The mast rotation spanner usually has a control line led to the boom, which limits the amount of natural rotation. The rotation can be locked at a specific angle, either in-line to flatten the sail and direct wind over the leeward side, or side-on to increase fullness in light winds and downwind.

Downhaul

The downhaul is widely recognized as one of the most important sail controls on a catamaran. Pulling hard on a multi-purchase downhaul will compress and bend the mast, flattening the sail and opening the leech for conditions when the crew are overpowered and cannot keep the windward hull down.

Outhaul

Tensioning the outhaul helps to pull the bottom of the sail flat for when sailing upwind. Easing the outhaul in contrast increases camber for offwind sailing in light wind conditions.

Diamonds

Some catamarans have diamonds (diamond-shaped spreaders) that support side-bend in the mast. Lighter crews need a bendier mast to help depower the mainsail, and can adjust the amount of tension while rigging up. This is used to produce predictable pre-bend for the expected wind speed, after which downhaul and mainsheet are used to control gusts out on the water.

Launching and coming ashore

Most aspects of launch and retrieval are similar with catamarans and monohulls, although catamarans have the advantage of much better stability. There are some important variations.

Trolleys

A simple catamaran trolley comprises an axle, two wheels and two moulded cups to support the hulls. Big wheels with oversize tires make a catamaran considerably easier to push across shingle or soft sand. To get the trolley under the catamaran, one person lifts one bow. This will raise the front enough for a second person to slide the trolley cups beneath each hull. To move the catamaran, the trolley cups need to be pushed just behind the main beam. When it is perfectly balanced fore and aft, one person should be able to walk it across smooth ground.

Do not leave the catamaran with the trolley in the pushing position. Lift the bow and pull the trolley forwards about a metre (yard), so it is approximately halfway between the main beam and bow. In this position the catamaran will sit tail-down. Some catamarans have box-shaped tail protectors to save the gelcoat from scratches. If you leave the catamaran for an extended period, it is best to remove the

ABOVE **With the trolley pulled forward the Formula 18 Diam will rest on its sterns. It is vulnerable to wind, so it is unwise to leave a catamaran unattended for long periods like this.**

trolley so the hulls lie flat on the ground. If there are strong winds forecast, it is a wise precaution to lash the boat down to some suitable anchor since there is considerable windage on the wing mast and trampoline.

Big-wheel catamaran trolleys tend to hold fast on to catamaran hulls due to their own buoyancy, but will float out when given a tug by the crew. They are easily carried up and down the shore.

Launching in onshore winds

When launching in side-onshore or onshore winds, it is important to drive the catamaran free and fast, luffing into the waves as necessary and bearing away to regain speed between crests.

LAUNCHING A DART 16 WITH A CATAMARAN TROLLEY ....

1 The helm lifts one bow, which is sufficient for the crew to push the trolley aft of the mast.

2 In this position the catamaran is perfectly balanced and can be wheeled backwards or forwards.

3 When the catamaran is in deep enough to float, the trolley can be pulled out from underneath.

LEFT **Getting away on a catamaran is easy when you have such a stable platform. The crew gives the Dart a shove away from the wind and pulls himself on board holding the shroud, while the helm sheets in to power away.**

Coming ashore in onshore surf

When coming ashore in breaking surf, the wide turning circle and twin hulls of a catamaran can make it difficult to turn the boat into the wind without being rolled before the 180 degree turn is complete.

One option is to run the catamaran straight up the beach with the rudders kicking up on impact, a trick that boats such as the Hobie 14 and 16 were originally designed for. In extreme conditions the crew will let off the sail controls and lift the boards, drive the catamaran in on the top of a wave, then leap off, pull the boat clear of the water and spin it round into the wind before the next wave hits. This is not for the faint hearted, or for catamarans with relatively fragile hulls and rudders.

A second option is to drop the mainsail and come in under jib alone. With a ring and hook system you can drop the mainsail by heaving-to so that the head of the mainsail turns at 90 degrees to the mast and automatically lifts off the ring. You can then drop the mainsail and roll it up on the trampoline, before heading into shore. This is a technique that requires practice.

Launching in offshore winds

Push the boat into the water with rudders and boards raised. As soon as it's deep enough, approximately shin height, both crew choose a bow and hop on with feet dragging either side. Let the boat blow offshore, pushing down on the starboard bow will turn the catamaran to starboard and vice versa. When it's deep enough, walk back, drop the foils, and bear off downwind.

Coming ashore in onshore winds

Turn the catamaran head to wind. Lift the boards and rudders, and depower the sails. Sit on the bows and steer them towards the beach with the sterns lifted. Hop off at the last moment and grab the bows before the sterns touch the beach.

COMING ASHORE ON A DART 16 ....

1 Make sure the mainsheet is unclipped and the downhaul loosened right off to depower the mainsail.

2 In this situation one crew may need to pull from the sides (using a shroud) to stop the boat slipping.

Catamaran tricks

The stability of two hulls means you can steer the boat downwind without rudders. This feature is useful when launching with offshore winds or coming ashore with onshore winds.

Tacking, gybing and capsize

Catamarans share the same principles as dinghies and use sailing techniques closest to gennaker-driven skiffs. However, there are a number of specific skills for two hulls.

TACKING

Owing to its width and twin hulls, a catamaran is likely to be considerably slower to tack than a monohull, and the tacking circle is wider as the outer hull has further to turn. Stalling is a particular problem with some older catamarans such as the Hobie 16, which are prone to come to a stop halfway through the tack due to their slab sides.

In general catamarans with daggerboards or centreboards will tack more easily since they have something to

pivot around. All catamarans need to be kept moving through the turn, with particular attention to weight distribution, which on some classes may involve lifting the bows.

Tacking technique

The helmsperson steers into the tack, but does not slam the rudders over, which would make them act like two brakes. He or she must keep steering through the tack and not let the rudders centralize halfway, which will stall the boat.

On some catamaran classes both crew need to keep on the windward hull until the boat has passed through the eye of the wind. This lifts and lightens the leeward hull, so that the boat can spin round on

the inside. Other catamarans tack faster if the bows are lifted – don't do this on a Hobie 14 or 16, which can quite easily capsize backwards.

The crew may need to keep the jib sheeted in until the boat starts to bear away on the new tack. This helps pull the bows round. The helm lets the mainsheet out enough for the battens to pop round, while continuing to steer through the tack, bear away, power up the catamaran and luff onto the new beating course.

If the catamaran stalls just as you've got onto the new tack it will soon start to move backwards. Try reversing the rudders and pushing against the boom, which will reverse the boat into the right position to start sailing forwards.

TACKING A CATAMARAN

1 The Dart 16 sails free at good speed as the crew comes in off the trapeze wire.

2 The crew crosses the trampoline as the catamaran turns, keeping forward and away from the helm.

3 Backing the jib helps pull the bows round. Care is needed to prevent stalling at head to wind.

4 The helmsperson crosses to the middle and concentrates on steering the boat round onto the new tack.

5 The helmsperson moves out while the crew sheets in, still keeping his weight forward on the trampoline.

6 The crew goes out on the wire while the helm gets the boat back up to speed before luffing.

GYBING

Catamarans are generally less intimidating to gybe than dinghies since the platform is so stable. However, you may be moving at considerable speed in a strong wind, and this speed must be maintained through-out the turn to keep the apparent wind, and the amount of power in the sails, to a minimum. The danger area during a gybe is when the boat swings dead downwind and starts to slow right down. If the catamaran is fitted with daggerboards or centreboards, the leeward board may need to be lifted halfway to prevent the boat tripping.

Beware of nose-diving during a gybe in strong winds. The leeward bow will go down if you accelerate into the gybe, and down again if the mainsail and boom crash across onto the new gybe. Keep your weight well back and help the mainsail across.

Gybing technique

The helmsperson turns to face aft during the gybe, kneeling by the rear beam in order to grab the falls of the mainsheet

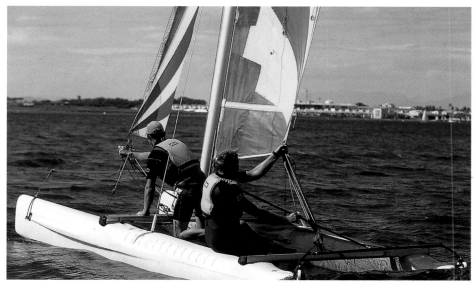

ABOVE **If a catamaran stalls mid-way through a tack, you can back the jib and mainsail and reverse the rudders to pull the bows round.**

and help pull the mainsail over as the catamaran passes downwind. Avoid letting the mainsheet crash across of its own accord as the length of the traveller may generate enough momentum to throw the boat into a violent luff on the new gybe.

The helm must keep steering through the gybe and not let the rudders follow their natural tendency to straighten up. Once the mainsail has gone across the rudders must be straightened for the new gybe to prevent luffing.

GYBING A CATAMARAN ....

1 As the helmsperson bears away the bows tend to go down, so keep weight aft.

2 Both crew move inboard as the helmsperson starts bearing away.

3 The helmsperson turns to face aft and lifts the tiller extension.

4 The helmsperson then flicks the tiller extension onto the new side.

5 At the same time he moves across and pulls the mainsheet falls over.

6 Then he sheets in and powers away on the new gybe.

CAPSIZE

Righting a capsized catamaran presents considerably more of a challenge than righting a monohull, since you have to lift the combined weight of the rig, which with an elliptical mast and fully battened mainsail is heavy anyway, and the upper hull that will have tipped past the vertical.

Capsize technique

A catamaran can be sailed with the windward hull high in the sky, but will reach a point where capsize is inevitable.

Try not to throw yourself into the mainsail, which may break battens or push the boat into a complete inversion. Just slide down the trampoline into the water, and grab a line so you do not get separated from the boat – a capsized catamaran presents a lot of windage, and can blow away quickly. Once in the water, both crew should pull themselves round to the bottom, and clamber up on the side of the lower hull. This is a surprisingly comfortable place to take a breather, with time to assess the situation.

A pitchpole – when the bows drive down and the catamaran goes tail-over-nose – is likely to be considerably more violent than a conventional capsize when the boat blows over sideways. It will happen at speed, both helm and crew will be thrown forwards, and the crew may shoot round the forestay if he or she is out on the wire with the potential for cracked ribs on the gennaker pole. Both crew may also be thrown well clear of the capsized boat, so grab something as you go.

Capsize retrieval

To get a catamaran up, you often need to line up the capsized boat so the platform is lying downwind from the mast top. The wind will then blow directly against the topside of the trampoline, which helps push the platform vertical, and start to blow under the mainsail as soon as the rig lifts from the water. A capsized catamaran

CAPSIZING AND RIGHTING A DART 16 ....

1 A catamaran will usually go over slowly. Do not throw yourself into the mainsail.

2 The helm swims round to the back of the boat while the crew swims to the front beam.

3 The crew gets up on the lower hull and grabs the righting line, which is stowed by the mast foot.

4 He flips it over the top hull and passes the end to the helmsperson.

5 The crew leans out on the righting line while the helmsperson pulls from the main beam.

6 The boat starts coming up slowly, and then as the mast lifts accelerates.

7 Watch out when the top hull comes down. The crew must grab the dolphin striker in the middle.

8 From this position it's easy for the crew to get back on the trampoline.

9 The crew and helmsperson make sure everything is OK, then sail away.

LEFT **Righting a catamaran single-handed can be extremely difficult. Inventions such as this righting pole on a Hurricane 500 give the crew increased leverage, and when not in use stows under the trampoline.**

Capsize problems

In some cases it is virtually impossible to right a catamaran without outside assistance. A rescue boat can aid retrieval by lifting the mast tip until the wind gets under the mainsail and your leverage is enough to pull the boat upright.

- If you are sailing single-handed there may not be enough wind blowing onto the trampoline to help lift the rig from the water.
- If you opt to sail a two-person boat single-handed, you may not have enough weight to lift the mast.
- The mast of a Tornado has internal halyards and will sink rapidly. Combined with its extreme width, this makes the Tornado prone to turn turtle and difficult to right.

will generally blow round into this position given time, but you can accelerate the process by standing on the lower bow. This lifts the stern and helps the boat pivot downwind.

Make sure all sheets are free and, if it's windy, let off the downhaul to fully depower the mainsail. With both crew standing on the lower hull, grab the righting line and throw the free end over the top of the upper hull. One crew leans back on the righting line until there is enough leverage to start lifting the mast off the water. Leverage can be increased by taking a turn round the harness hook, with both crew leaning out together – the crew can even sit on the helm's shoulders.

The rig will start to lift slowly, and then accelerate as it comes clear of the water. Stay under the trampoline as it comes upright, and watch out for the upper or leeward hull, which will come down with an almighty crash – don't let it fall on your head. The crew must be ready to grab the dolphin striker on the lower or windward side to prevent the boat blowing right over. The helm still holds the righting line so as not to be separated from the boat – a catamaran with a fully battened mainsail may try to sail off. The helmsperson can then climb in over the rear beam, and help the crew up over the front beam, ready to sort out the boat and sail away.

Turning turtle

If a catamaran turns turtle (upside down) it is still possible to get it upright.

Get up on the underside of the trampoline and take a breather. Make sure all control lines are free. Lead the righting line over the windward hull, then stand on the back of the leeward hull and pull.

This should raise the bows of the windward hull clear of the water, encouraging the mast to float upwards. Walk your weight forward to level out the leeward hull as the windward hull lifts above you. Continue to right the catamaran as normal.

PITCHPOLING AN OFFSHORE CATAMARAN..

1 An 8 metre (26ft) long racing catamaran will pitchpole if pushed too hard offwind.

2 Firebird *Orion* drives her bows down so hard that the sterns come right over.

3 Past the point of no return she turns turtle with the crew thrown into the sea.

Sailing upwind

Most catamarans with centreboards or daggerboards perform well with both boards fully down, but on some it pays to lift the windward board, which means the crew has to do a down-up sequence with the board during each tack.

The narrow, twin hulls of a catamaran will tend to stick to the water in light winds, when it is vital to move weight forward, so the crew sits on or even in front of the forward beam. This will lift the sterns and help prevent them dragging, while the crew sit close together and as still as possible in order not to disturb water flow over the hulls or wind flow over the sails. It may pay to heel the catamaran slightly to windward, increasing waterline length while lifting the windward hull if possible. The most important thing is to keep the boat sailing free and moving, with light mainsheet tension.

As the wind picks up the catamaran should be sailed with the windward hull just skimming the surface of the water, if it is lifted any higher the leeward hull will start to dig in and slow you down. Weight still needs to be well forward to lift the sterns. The crew typically trapezes with one leg in front of the shroud, and the helm is directly next to him or her. The mainsheet should be well tensioned without going so far as to hook the leech to windward.

In stronger winds, the crew will need to move far enough back to prevent the leeward bow making a nose dive. Both crew have to work to hold the windward

UPWIND VARIATIONS ON A DART 16

In light winds it's vital to prevent the sterns dragging by moving forwards.

In light winds it also helps to take weight off the windward hull by moving inboard.

Never pinch a catamaran by pointing too high. It's best to go for speed as shown.

The catamaran should be sailed with the windward hull just skimming the water.

Let the hull get this high and you dig in the leeward hull and slow right down.

As the wind increases the crew can move back, but not so far that you sink the stern.

hull just clear of the water, with the crew setting the downhaul to depower the mainsail until it's at maximum tension.

From then on the helm will need to ease the mainsheet from its hard-in setting while sailing into gusts, which can be both tiring and difficult when the helm also has to contend with directing the boat through waves. On some smaller catamarans it pays for the crew to play the jib, which opens the slot and depowers the boat enough to bring the windward hull back down. On larger catamarans the crew may need to cleat the jib and take the mainsheet, trimming to the helmsperson's call. If the boat is still overpowered, easing the mainsheet traveller away from the centreline will make it easier to handle.

Strong arm tactics

If you can't point as high as the next catamaran, it's probably because you are not pulling in enough mainsheet. Try pulling in the mainsheet as hard as you can, and set up a test to discover if you pull in less on port tack (the left arm is the weak arm for most of us) than starboard tack. You can do this on shore:

- Point the catamaran into the wind.
- Hike or trapeze as if sailing to windward and sheet in as hard as you can on one side. Get your crew to mark where the sheet exits from the blocks.
- Repeat the process on the other side, but this time close your eyes so you don't attempt to compensate. Get the crew to mark the sheet once again and you are likely to be amazed at the difference.

The next stage is to get the mainsheet right in on the water. Pull it in as hard as you can when hiking or on the trapeze, then tuck the tiller under your back arm so you have both hands free to haul the mainsheet in some more.

ABOVE **On the Tornado it's normal for the crew to play the mainsheet, which requires a lot of strength while the helm plays the traveller.**

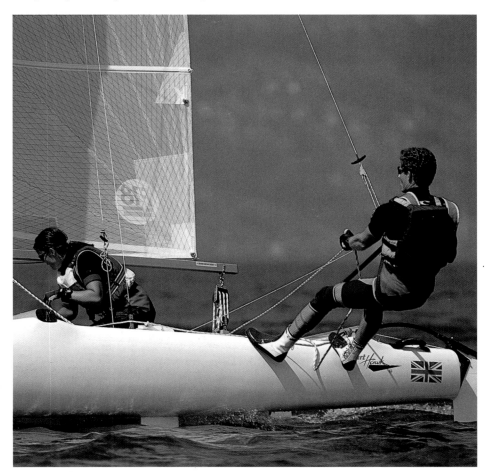

ABOVE **The helm has his hands full getting the mainsail hard in on this Formula 18 while his crew sorts out packing the gennaker.**

Weather helm

This will be most pronounced when sailing upwind, and is usually caused by poorly adjusted rudder blades. There should be no backward movement when the blades are locked fully down – the slightest tilt is enough to cause weather helm.

If you have weather helm on one tack and lee helm on the other, it is probably caused by a twisted rudder blade, which will affect the boat upwind and offwind. You can diagnose the problem by sailing the boat in a moderate wind on a broad reach, lifting first one and then the other rudder, and repeating the process on both tacks. If one rudder is clearly at fault, it may need to be replaced.

Sailing offwind

On a reaching course you should aim to fly the windward hull, with the leeward board down and the windward board retracted. The traveller should be eased away from the centreline to remove twist from the leech, keeping the sail powered up to the maximum when sheeted hard in.

The helmsperson needs to bear away in gusts and luff in lulls to maximize apparent wind and keep the boat moving at full speed, as well as using waves to help acceleration. In survival conditions bear away and sail low to reduce the apparent wind. Keep bearing away in big gusts until you are effectively dead downwind or even by the lee, but luff when the gust has passed.

Tacking downwind

Most catamarans will sail downwind fastest when they gybe from reach to reach with both boards fully retracted, using the apparent wind to build speed, which is substantially faster and more fun than sailing on a dead downwind course. The only time when a dead downwind course might be faster is in very light winds.

An effective method of judging downwind angles is to use a wind indicator mounted on the bridle, and steer a course at 90 degrees to the apparent wind. If the wind indicator points back, bear away to sail lower; if it points forward, head up to build speed.

Preventing a nose dive

All catamarans are prone to nose dives when sailing on a fast reach in moderate to strong winds. A leeward nose dive can lead to a cartwheel on any reaching course; a double nose dive can lead to a pitchpole, and only occurs on a very broad reach typically when the apparent wind has suddenly swung aft due to the boat stopping. Nose-dives in general can be caused by:

* Crew weight too far forward.
* Not easing the sheets when you bear away.
* Too much power in the rig, which is the result of failing to bear away in a gust.
* Driving the boat into the back of a wave where it comes to a dead stop.
* An uncontrolled gybe when the bow goes down due to gybing too tightly in strong winds, letting the boom crash across, or letting go of the tiller.
* Insufficient buoyancy in the bows, which is a design problem.

ABOVE **The Hobie 16 enjoys a wild ride on a downwind course, while the wind indicator shows that the apparent wind is on the beam.**

Keeping the crew weight back is the best way of preventing the catamaran from nose diving. If it's a twin wire boat, the helmsperson will have better control sitting in by the rear beam. The crew can

DOWNWIND VARIATIONS ON A DART 16...

Sailing in a light wind of Force 1-2 the crew need to concentrate on lifting the windward hull so that it does not stick to the surface.

When the wind picks up to Force 3–4 (7–16 knots) the crew moves aft and stands by the helmsperson to prevent the bows burying.

Deep downwind in a strong wind, with the traveller right out, the crew sits inboard to help lift the windward hull.

ABOVE **A wildthing variation is possible on the Dart 16 although, with no centreboard or daggerboard to push against and help hold the hull up, it's less effective.**

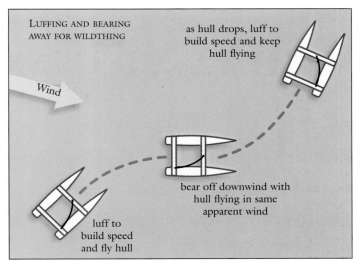

LUFFING AND BEARING AWAY FOR WILDTHING

Wind

as hull drops, luff to build speed and keep hull flying

bear off downwind with hull flying in same apparent wind

luff to build speed and fly hull

ABOVE **Wildthing means following a course like a snake, with constant repetitions of luffing to fly the hull and bearing away to go deep downwind.**

move right back and straddle the helm, using a rear foot loop for security, or clipping onto a retaining line attached to the rear beam, which will prevent him or her being pulled forwards. If the leeward bow goes down:

- Let off the jib.
- Move your weight back.
- Let the jib fly.
- Let off the mainsheet.
- Do not luff or bear away, which can make it worse by holding the leeward bow down or accelerating the boat.

Wildthing

Australian catamaran champion Mitch Booth – Tornado winner of Bronze and Silver Medals at the 1992 and 1996 Olympics – is credited as the inventor of wildthing.

The object of wildthing is to sail as deep as possible while flying downwind on a single hull. If you get it right it is the fastest way to go downwind, depending on the catamaran you are sailing it can be effective in winds from about Force 3 (10 knots) upwards. The trick is to build

apparent wind by luffing, hold it when you bear away, and with the reduced wetted area of one hull streak away from catamarans that are sailing downwind with both hulls stuck to the water. To keep the boat flying the crew must sit down to leeward, which requires plenty of nerve and firm control in strong winds, with the leeward centreboard or daggerboard down to give the windward hull something to push against.

The helmsperson sets the main traveller close to the leeward footstrap, sheets in hard, luffs, flies the hull and accelerates. As this happens the helmsperson bears away quickly and smoothly so that the boat keeps flying and accelerating, easing the mainsheet if the boat fails to bear away. When the hull begins to drop, the process is repeated, resulting in a kind of tightly spaced slalom on a dead downwind course.

ABOVE **Wildthing was first used on the Tornado. Despite the sails being sheeted hard in, this boat is sailing downwind.**

Whistle-stop

The sound of rudder blades whistling at speed pleases some people and convinces others that turbulence is slowing them down. If it displeases you, try lightly filing and flattening the trailing edge of the blades at 90 degrees; if that doesn't work, try the same treatment at 45 degrees both sides.

Gennaker basics

The principal difference between sailing with a gennaker on a catamaran and most monohulls is that the gennaker can only be launched from behind the jib – normally from a bag on the trampoline.

Chutes and gennaker poles

Some catamarans have a chute, but this has to lie down one side of the trampoline where it gets in the way and doesn't have the advantages of a monohull chute that launches with the gennaker in front of the forestay. Another important difference is that the gennaker pole is permanently rigged between the front hulls and bridle, and not launched from the boat as on most monohulls. To avoid having to use an oversize section, the pole is usually pre-bent to stiffen its middle section and inhibit flex when pulled by the gennaker.

Slow upwind

With a fixed pole and bag there is a lot of extra clutter on a catamaran fitted with a gennaker, and it will be slower upwind than an identical catamaran sailing with mainsail, jib and no gennaker. This has been proven by trials with Tornados, with and without gennakers. The gennaker slows the boat for various reasons:

- Extra weight and windage.
- The halyard breaking up air flow round the elliptical mast.
- Clutter on the trampoline slowing down tacks.
- Pole length making manoeuvres, such as pushing in on the start line or crossing tacks, more difficult.

Fast downwind

A gennaker is certainly more effective downwind, allowing the catamaran to sail deeper even if it doesn't go faster. However time lost hoisting and lowering the gennaker, as well as dealing with the

LEFT **The gennaker is a mixed blessing when sailing a catamaran as the additional clutter and weight of a fixed pole and bag slows the boat down going upwind.**

problems that an out-of-control gennaker can cause, means that it needs a very long downwind leg for a gennaker-driven catamaran to win back lost ground. The conclusion is that, unless courses are predominantly downwind, a gennaker adds both hassle and expense to a catamaran in return for a marginal improvement in performance. However,

broad reaching with a gennaker is considerably more fun than with jib and main alone, and for that reason the gennaker seems destined to become a common accessory on most catamarans.

Gennaker techniques on catamarans are virtually the same as on gennaker-driven skiffs fitted with a bag, but some points need to be highlighted.

ABOVE **Offwind the gennaker is a total blessing: it looks great, feels great, is a lot of fun to sail with and helps the catamaran go deeper downwind.**

ABOVE **The skipper lifts both windward foils to maximize offwind performance on the Hobie Tiger.**

Hoists and drops

The gennaker can only go up on the same side as it comes down, which makes it important to drop the gennaker on the right side for the next hoist during a race.

Hoisting to leeward is favourite. The gennaker goes up on the correct leeward side of the mainsail, and the helm bears away from a beam reach in anything more than light winds. Hoisting to windward requires turning well downwind to let the gennaker blow out to the end of the pole, before the helmsperson luffs to blow it

RIGHT **This Hawk looks neatly controlled as it sails a gybe-to-gybe downwind leg.**

across the forestay onto the leeward side. All this must be done quickly to avoid the gennaker taking a wrap.

Dropping to windward is favourite, but the helm has to turn well downwind to float the gennaker round the forestay to the windward side. Allowing the gennaker to drop between the hulls and then running over it is a disaster. The sail must be pulled in fast and the halyard must run free; if in any doubt, throw the coiled halyard over the rear beam and let it stream astern.

Dropping to leeward has the disadvantage of putting the crew down on the leeward side of the catamaran. In anything more than very light winds the helmsperson would need to bear right away to manage this without the windward hull lifting. Beware of catching the gennaker round one of the mainsail batten ends.

A drop-gybe lets you drop the gennaker on the windward side of the catamaran, without having to bear away and pull it round the forestay:

- Reach in on port tack.
- Helm bears away and gybes mainsail.
- As the boom comes across, the crew moves to the new windward side of the boat (starboard side), drops the gennaker, which is immediately to hand and on the right tack for a port tack hoist.
- Always remember to pull the gennaker and all its ropes in under the jib sheet during the drop.

ABOVE **You can only sail so high with a gennaker. Any more wind, and the helm will need to bear away to maintain control.**

Reaching control

Keeping control of a catamaran and its gennaker follows the same main principle as on a monohull, if the sail collapses or a gust hits you need to bear away and go with the apparent wind.

You will need both centreboards or daggerboards right down to minimize leeway on a reach. To maximize leeway when sailing downwind, pull them right up. If you are bearing away to absorb a gust on a reach and the boat trips on the leeward board, you need to half-raise both boards, although the windboard could be further down to allow for lift out of the water.

In extreme conditions the elliptical mast of a catamaran will pant – flex rapidly from side to side – when you let the gennaker flog in a hard gust. This is a clear indication that the time has come to get it down.

Capsizing with a gennaker

If you capsize with a gennaker, do not attempt to right the boat with it up unless the wind conditions are very light. Lower the gennaker while the catamaran is on its side, and bundle it on top of its bag where it will sit while the catamaran is being righted.

Dinghy and Catamaran
Classes

The following selection does not aim to be fully comprehensive, but includes many well-loved favourites, which give some idea of the breadth of contemporary dinghy sailing. There is of course a good deal of crossover between the categories of the various classes (specific dinghy designs) and we can only apologize to those whose personal favourites have been left out.

There are three types of classes: one design, restricted and development. In a one design class every boat must be as identical as possible in every detail down to ropes and cleats. Careful policing by class authorities ensure consistency among the small numbers of licensed builders. Restricted classes allow a certain amount of freedom in choice of fittings, sails or construction, but are still restricted by rules that ensure the boats remain similar. Development classes allow a wide degree of latitude in important areas such as hull shape and sail plan. The most open-ended development classes have rules that govern little more than maximum length and sail area.

Other details on each class featured includes the overall length (LOA) and the maximum upwind sail area, which generally relates to the mainsail and jib, or mainsail alone.

Cruising dinghies

A cruising dinghy needs to be roomy, stable and above all seaworthy. It should be able to undertake extensive coastal cruises in comfort and safety, and be the perfect boat for family sailing with the option of propulsion by oars or a small outboard. Any cruising dinghy worth the name should also provide enough speed and performance to be satisfying to sail, and the potential for good racing is a bonus.

Laser 16/13

Bruce Kirby of Laser 1 fame designed the Laser 16 as a comfortable and very stable cruising dinghy. With modern, handsome lines and a big, reefable rig it delivers good performance and can carry four adults in reasonable comfort. Due to its ballasted centreboard, the Laser 16 can be safely left on a mooring during the sailing season and bridges the gap between a dinghy and keelboat.

The Laser 13 was introduced as a smaller sister to the Laser 16, following the same concept for a smaller number of crew. It had the bonus of being considerably lighter with a conventional dinghy centreboard, and therefore much more appropriate for dry sailing with a trolley.

ABOVE **The Laser 13 provides comfortable cruising in a modern package.**

Designer Bruce Kirby (Canada)
First launched 1980/1982
Type One-design
LOA 5.19m (17ft)/4.05m (13ft)
Beam 2.06m (6¾ft)/1.72m (5½ft)

Minimum hull weight 250kg (551lb)/ 132kg (291lb)
Upwind sail area 14.02 sq m (151 sq ft)/ 10.4 sq m (112 sq ft)
Spinnaker 11.54 sq m (124 sq ft)/ 10.5 sq m (113 sq ft)

LEFT **The Laser 16 is a considerably bigger boat than the Laser 13, and is stable and heavy enough to be safely left on a mooring during the summer season.**

Laser Stratos

Both the Laser 16 and 13 enjoyed a comparatively brief period in production before being replaced by the Laser Stratos, a novel approach to the concept of a cruiser-racer dinghy designed by Phil Morrison. In its cruising mode the Stratos can be fitted with a ballasted centreboard to provide stability on a mooring; in its performance mode a conventional centreboard coupled with optional gennaker and trapeze gives racing-dinghy-style sailing. In between

ABOVE **The Drascombe Lugger and associated range of different length Drascombes are modern cruising classics that sail far and wide. Cruises in company are very popular, and crews adapt their boats to live on board.**

ABOVE **The Laser Stratos is a multi-package approach to modern dinghy design, which can be optimized for racing or cruising according to requirements. The race version shown here is fitted with trapeze and gennaker; the cruiser version has a ballasted centreboard and can be left on a mooring.**

those two extremes the Stratos retains room to go sailing with the family, and features a unique capsize safety system. This floods the down-side of the hull during a capsize to ensure the boat floats low enough for the crew to get on the centreboard and right with ease, after which the water drains out again.

Designer Phil Morrison (UK)
First launched 1999
Type One-design
LOA 4.94m (16ft)
Beam 2m (6½ft)
Minimum hull weight 170kg (375lb)
Upwind sail area 14.53 sq m (156 sq ft)
Gennaker 12.54 sq m (135 sq ft)

RIGHT **The Wayfarer has proved exceptionally successful as a dinghy that is equally suitable for cruising, racing or teaching novices to sail. With a history spanning more than 40 years, it is also widely available second-hand.**

Drascombe Lugger

The Drascombe Lugger started a popular trend for traditional dayboats built in modern materials, and was followed by a range of different size Drascombes and similar craft from other designers, which can be either trailer-sailed or left on a mooring.

The double-ended traditional design is both seaworthy and handsome, with loose footed tan sails, sliding gunter rig and small mizzen, all designed for ease of handling. It has a short wooden mast and no boom. A sprayhood and boat tent can be used to convert the Lugger into a fair weather cruiser with room for two to camp on board. If the wind fails, alternative propulsion is provided by an outboard in the transom, or rowing.

Luggers and similar craft have enjoyed a long period of success for all kinds of small boat cruising: adventure sailing along open coastlines, fishing and exploring backwaters, as well as running up on deserted beaches.

Designer John Watkinson (UK)
First launched 1965
Type One-Design/Restricted
LOA 5.72m (18½ft)
Beam 1.9m (6ft)
All-up weight 340kg (750lb)
Upwind sail area 12.26 sq m (132 sq ft) including mizzen

Wayfarer

Having over 10,000 boats registered, Ian Proctor's Wayfarer has enjoyed a long life as a well established cruiser-racer dinghy. It is stable and roomy enough to have been a firm favourite with both sailing schools and families, but also possesses a good enough turn of speed for enjoyable and competitive racing. A Wayfarer World Championship is held once every three years and the 1998 event was held in Denmark.

The Wayfarer has also enjoyed a great deal of fame as a long-distance cruising dinghy, and many Wayfarer sailors dream of emulating the feats of Frank and Margaret Dye who cruised their wooden Wayfarer (number 48) over thousands of miles around Norway and Iceland in the years soon after the design first appeared. The class association holds an extensive library of cruises undertaken by members all round the world, as well as organizing regular cruises in company.

Continuous updates in construction have ensured that the tough, seaworthy and versatile Wayfarer keeps pace with the times. The design was brought right up to date by the all-fibreglass Wayfarer World in 1996, which featured a self-draining floor through to the transom. A 17 sq m (183 sq ft) gennaker is optional and, while not class legal for racing, has proved extremely popular for cruising and learning.

ABOVE **The Wanderer gives a good turn of performance, while maintaining good sea-keeping qualities when cruising.**

Designer Ian Proctor (UK)
First launched 1957
Type Restricted One-Design
LOA 4.82m (16ft)
Beam 1.85m (6ft)
Minimum hull weight 168kg (370lb)
Upwind sail area 8.8 sq m (95 sq ft) mainsail plus 4.3 sq m (46 sq ft) genoa or 2.8 sq m (30 sq ft) jib
Spinnaker 13.5 sq m (145 sq ft)

Wanderer

Ian Proctor designed the Wanderer as a little sister to the Wayfarer. It has less capacity, lower weight and a much smaller rig, which is easier to handle when sailing, as well as when it is on a slipway or on a trailer. In that role it has proved popular for family sailing, cruising and gentle racing.

Designer Ian Proctor (UK)
First launched 1978
Type Restricted
LOA 4.27m (14ft)
Beam 1.78m (6ft)
Minimum hull weight 129kg (284lb)
Upwind sail area 10.68 sq m (115 sq ft)
Spinnaker 9.94 sq m (107 sq ft)

Dinghy cruising

With skill and a certain amount of daring, it is possible to undertake extended inshore cruises in a stable and roomy dinghy. The advantages over a yacht cruise are that you can trail the dinghy to an ideal starting point and from there explore anchorages and landing places that are too shallow or confined for bigger sailboats. Careful planning combined with good weather are essential for enjoyment, and for those who get it right the experience of pulling up on a remote, isolated beach is likely to be unforgettable.

As with any land-based camping trip, trim the amount of gear being carried to a practical minimum, store it with extreme care and ensure that everything that needs it has waterproof protection.

Routes must be planned with great care, taking note of weather forecasts and tidal streams and ensuring every landfall is made at least two hours before sun-set.

Dinghies for young sailors and learners

Children can start learning to sail properly from about the age of eight, and this selection primarily spans the 8–18 period during which a nervous first-timer out in an Optimist can be transformed into a full-on skiff sailor blasting in a 29er. However, while the Optimist and Cadet are specifically for young sailors, classes such as the Topper, Pico, Laser Radial and Topaz are equally suited to adult use.

International Cadet

This is a classic junior two-up racing class for under-18 sailors of optimum crew weight of around 86 kg (189 lb). Originally designed by Jack Holt in 1947 for low-cost, marine-ply construction. The design, concept and performance are now very dated, but with World and European championships, competition up to international level remains extremely tough.

Designer Jack Holt (UK)
First launched 1947
Type Restricted
LOA 3.22m (10½ft)
Beam 1.27m (4ft)
Minimum hull weight 54kg (119lb)
Upwind sail area 5.16 sq m (55 sq ft)
Spinnaker 4.25 sq m (46 sq ft)

LEFT **The International Optimist has worn its years well, and has even bounced back to become undisputed as the world's top racing class for young single-handed sailors involving racing that is extremely tactical.**

International Optimist

The Optimist is an old timer that has bounced back to become the number one worldwide racing and learning class for young single-handed sailors, and the calibre of international championships ensures that top sailors frequently move on to contest the Olympics. Racing is restricted to under-16s with an optimum crew weight of around 50kg (110lb), but it is common to find sailors of half that age learning to sail in these boats. The Optimist was originally designed for plywood construction, but is now widely available with both marine ply and fibreglass foam sandwich hulls, while the quaint looking sprit rig remains the same.

Designer Clark Mills (USA)
First launched 1947
Type Restricted
LOA 2.3m (7½ft)
Beam 1.13m (3¾ft)
Minimum hull weight 35kg (77lb)
Upwind sail area 3.5 sq m (37.7 sq ft)

International Topper

The Topper is a hugely popular one-design with more than 40,000 boats on the water. Originally designed to be carried on a roof rack, the Topper was re-designed for rotomoulded polypropylene construction, and is the epitome of a low-cost, super-durable, zero upkeep funboat. The Topper can be sailed by one or two children from about the age of ten upwards. It is also an excellent solo boat

LEFT **The International Cadet was once renowned for producing future world champions in all of the leading adult classes. Although it can no longer claim that role, the level of competition remains extremely keen.**

LEFT **The International Topper combines maximum durability with an extremely user-friendly design. It is at its best when sailed single-handed by lighter weight sailors, but can also be enjoyed by two children or a heavier adult.**

ABOVE **The Topaz is an ultra durable, multi-purpose boat which can be sailed both as a single-hander, or two-up complete with trapeze and gennaker.**

for moderately agile adults and is very popular for learning as well as providing excellent competition.

Designer Ian Proctor
First launched 1976
Type One-design
LOA 3.4m (11ft)
Beam 1.2m (4ft)
Minimum hull weight 43kg (95lb)
Upwind sail area 5.2 sq m (56 sq ft)

Pico

Laser introduced the Pico as an all-round funboat for learners and families, with special appeal for sailing schools and holiday centres that need a boat that is very easy to sail and even easier to right after a capsize. The Pico's tecrothene construction combines rotomoulded plastic with foam sandwich for the best combination of durability and rigidity and, with all that foam, the Pico has enough buoyancy to carry two (not too large) adults or four children – at a squeeze. Design features include an excellent

ergonomic cockpit, with a small jib available in Pico Plus mode.

Designer Jo Richards (UK)
First launched 1996
Type One-design
LOA 3.5m (11½ft)
Beam 1.37m (4½ft)
Minimum hull weight 60kg (132lb)
Mainsail 5.9 sq m (63½ sq ft)
Optional jib 1.09 sq m (12 sq ft)

Topaz

The Topaz is a clever triple concept design that was introduced as a direct competitor to the Laser Pico. The hull is produced using similar rotomoulded, foam-sandwich polyethylene construction to maximize low cost and durability, with three rig options to suit different requirements. Topaz Uno has a simple, unstayed una-rig for learning and general fun sailing in the style of the Topper. Topaz Duo has a much more sophisticated two-sail rig with tapered mast, fully battened mainsail, shrouds and trapeze wires. Topaz Tres includes a full gennaker.

Designer Ian Howlett (UK)
First launched 1998
Type One-design (three versions)
LOA 3.86m (12½ft)
Beam 1.42m (4½ft)
Minimum hull weight 60kg (132lb)
Upwind sail area 5.2 sq m (56 sq ft)/ 8.35 sq m (90 sq ft)
Gennaker 9 sq m (97 sq ft)

International 420

The 420 was first introduced as a junior partner to the 470, and adopted by the French as their principal youth trainer for teenage crews. It maintained that role for more than 30 years and over 50,000 boats were sold worldwide and, despite its age and dated design, it became the automatic twin-crew choice when the ISAF Youth World Championships were

LEFT **The Laser Pico has become established as a great favourite with sailing schools since it is durable, simple, has good performance and is an excellent weight carrier for all ages.**

ABOVE **The International 420 has enjoyed over 30 years as a junior racing class, but is being challenged by more modern designs.**

first held in the late 1990s. The class also holds annual World and European championships where the competition is intense.

Designer Christian Maury (France)
First launched 1964
Type Restricted
LOA 4.2m (13¾ft)
Beam 1.62m (5½ft)
Minimum hull weight 80kg (176lb)
Upwind sail area 10.25 sq m (110 sq ft)
Spinnaker 9 sq m (97 sq ft)

International Hobie 405

The single trapeze Hobie 405 was conceived as a high performance youth trainer that would bring dinghy sailing up to date, appealing to young sailors with an optimum crew weight of around 100–120kg (220–265lb), and replace elderly designs like the 420. It was adopted as the official twin-crew youth trainer by the Royal Yachting Association (RYA) in Britain and enjoyed a period of moderate popularity, but by the end of its first decade the design seemed ready to be outphased by even more modern concepts such as the 29er.

Designer Chris Benedict (Canada)
First launched 1991
Type One-design
LOA 4.05m (13ft)
Beam 1.38m (4½ft)
Minimum hull weight 68kg (150lb)
Upwind sail area 7.98 sq m (86 sq ft)
Gennaker 8.8 sq m (95 sq ft)

29er

The 29er is no less than a junior 49er, aimed at giving the same state-of-the-art skiff thrills in a twin crew, single-trapeze package that's ideally suited to experienced teenagers with an optimum crew weight of 110–135kg (242–298lb). The 29er was due to receive international status for the year 2000, with its first World Championship in the same year and, with performance matched by appearance, looks set to become established as a major high performance youth class.

Designer Julian Bethwaite (Australia)
First launched 1998
Type One-design
LOA 4.45m (14½ft)
Beam 1.77m (6ft)
Minimum hull weight 65kg (143lb)
Upwind sail area 12.5 sq m (134 sq ft)
Gennaker 15 sq m (161 sq ft)

International Laser Radial

The optional Laser Radial rig has a different lower mast section and smaller, radial-cut sail compared to the International Laser, but in all other respects is exactly the same. The rig delivers approximately 15 per cent less power, and was introduced as an alternative for lightweight and young sailors who find the Laser's 7.06 sq m (76 sq ft) sail physically too demanding in stronger winds. The Radial has its own keenly fought international race series, culminating in events such as the ISAF World Youth Championships.

Designer Bruce Kirby (Canada)
First launched 1971
Type One-design
LOA 4.23m (14ft)
Beam 1.37m (4½ft)
Minimum hull weight 60kg (132lb)
Radial sail area 5.76 sq m (62 sq ft)

LEFT **The Hobie 405 was introduced at the start of a decade that saw rapid change in dinghy designs and by the end its appeal was eroded by even more modern dinghies.**

ABOVE **The radial rig makes the International Laser much easier to handle for lighter weight and less able sailors. An alternative 4.7 sq m (50 sq ft) sail is available with a shorter mast, and is ideal for learning or for younger teenagers.**

The gennaker generation

The Australian experience combined with rapid developments in the International 14 class spawned a whole host of gennaker-driven dinghies with Phil Morrison the most popular designer. These boats are great fun to sail and seem destined to make the old spinnaker classes obsolete, but come in much more user-friendly packages than the mega-light, monster rig ideal of the true skiff.

Laser 4000

The Laser 4000 has been a huge success, combining modern single trapeze, gennaker-driven, skiff-style sailing in a user-friendly accessible package. It features the Laser crew power equalisation system, with sliding racks and weight correctors, that is designed to provide level racing for a range of crew weights between 118–188kg (260–414lb). Well over 4,000 boats were

sold in the first four years of production, with a high profile in Europe for the annual Audi Laser Eurocup – a major series of events in France, Italy and the UK.
Designer Phil Morrison (UK)
First launched 1995

RIGHT **The Laser 4000 looks great and is a huge amount of fun to sail. Part of its attraction lies in the weight equalization system which allows different weight crews to race on a level basis. The sliding racks are pushed in for heavier sailors.**

LEFT **The Laser 5000 was originally conceived as a new Olympic class, but was beaten by the 49er. It is known as a powerful boat that is a real challenge when the wind gets up.**

Type One-design
LOA 4.64m (15ft)
Beam 1.5–2.3m (4½–7½ft) maximum
Minimum hull weight 80kg (176lb)
Upwind sail area 14.7 sq m (158 sq ft)
Spinnaker 17.1 sq m (184 sq ft)

Laser 5000

The Laser 5000 was introduced as an early Olympic contender to replace the aging Flying Dutchman. It is a super-powerful and almost brutal boat with its gennaker pole extending the overall length to a mighty 11.2m (37ft) but, with a comparatively heavy hull, the 5000 lost out when lined up against the lean and lightweight 49er. Failing to get Olympic selection is no bad thing for a class, and the 5000 has continued as a powerful boat for heavyweights, using the same weight equalisation system as the Laser 4000 and the same EuroCup series.
Designer Phil Morrison (UK)
First launched 1992
Type One-design
LOA 5.0m (16½ft)
Beam 1.9–3.05m (6–10ft) maximum
Minimum hull weight 109kg (240lb)
Upwind sail area 21.16 sq m (228 sq ft)
Gennaker 33 sq m (355 sq ft)

LEFT **The RS400 was originally designed with a spinnaker, but the gennaker was chosen as a more popular option and gives the boat exceptional broad reaching performance. The RS200 is a smaller sister.**

ABOVE **The Laser 2000 was introduced as a stable and well behaved club racer with the appeal of a modern replacement for the Enterprise or GP14.**

RS400/200

The RS400 has rapidly become a modern British classic, with a design pedigree honed on the National 12, Merlin Rocket and International 14 classes and a huge turnout at major championship events in the UK and on the Italian lakes. It is a powerful, gennaker-driven, non-trapeze class that requires a fairly heavy crew weight in the 135–165kg (298–364lb) range for stronger winds. It has impeccably designed ergonomics and sail controls that make it a real delight as a race boat.

The RS200 was introduced in 1995, using the same Phil Morrison design concept but with a much smaller rig for lightweight crews in the 112–137kg (247–302lb) range.

Designer Phil Morrison (UK)
First launched 1993/1995
Type One-design
LOA 4.52m (15ft)/4m (13ft)
Beam 2m (6½ft)/1.83m (6ft)
Minimum hull weight 85kg (187lb)/ 78kg (172lb)
Upwind sail area 14.76 sq m (159 sq ft)/ 11.52 sq m (124 sq ft)
Gennaker 13.94 sq m (150 sq ft)/ 8.29 sq m (89 sq ft)

Laser 2000

Laser introduced the 2000 as their new club racer, aiming to convert the owners of more elderly classic boats with a design that bears comparison with the RS200 as a rival. The difference is that the Laser 2000 is heavier and likely to be more stable, with more appeal to the cruiser-racer type of user who wants a combination of club racing, family cruising and enjoyable but predictable performance.

Designer Phil Morrison (UK)
First launched 1998
Type One-design
LOA 4.44m (14½ft)
Beam 1.85m (6ft)
Minimum hull weight 100kg (220lb)
Upwind sail area 10.78 sq m (116 sq ft)
Gennaker 9.86 sq m/106 sq ft

Iso

The Iso was conceived by John Caig, a multi-championship winner in Fireballs and Toppers. Iso means equal, and his idea was to produce a new high performance dinghy in which a range of crew weights would be equal by using detachable wings. The design was based on an International 14 by Ian Howlett, and as the first of the new style gennaker-driven dinghies the Iso was an immediate

Weight equalization

As boats have become lighter and rigs more powerful, crew weight has become a major influence on the relative speed of boats in a one-design class. In light winds lighter crews have less dead weight to carry, while in stronger winds heavier crews can exert more leverage and keep on more power. But in general light crews have the overall advantage – regatta winds are more often light than strong and, when the wind picks up, lighter crews can use advanced rig control techniques to stay in touch, while heavy crews can never compensate for too much weight.

Laser was first to tackle the problem of light crews making a potential mockery of one-design racing. Their crew power equalization (CPE) system was initially introduced on the Laser 4000 and Laser 5000 using adjustable racks and weight correctors to equalize the weight of crews. At each major

ABOVE **Adjustable racks and weight correctors allow different weight crews to race on a level playing.**

regatta the crew must be weighed in sailing gear, and this produces a total weight and leverage figure that determines which rack setting and correction weights must be used. Random checks are carried out to catch anyone cheating.

ABOVE **The ISO was among the first of the new generation of gennaker dinghies, and proved an immediate hit.**

and rapid success before popularity started to decline in the face of challengers such as the Laser 4000.
Designer John Caig/Ian Howlett (UK)
First launched 1993
Type One-design
LOA 4.74m (15½ft)
Beam 1.75m–2.25m (5¾–7ft)
Minimum hull weight 100kg (220lb)
Upwind sail area 14.3 sq m (154 sq ft)
Gennaker 18.8 sq m (202 sq ft)

Topper Buzz/Spice

The Topper Buzz was introduced as a bouncing baby skiff, which would provide an introduction to high performance sailing in a simple, single trapeze, gennaker-driven package, which could be enjoyed by sailors from teenagers and upwards. The Spice is a big-rig, twin trapeze variation on the same International 14 style hull that takes the boat into pocket rocket territory.

ABOVE **The launch of the Topper Spice coincided with the Spice Girls' early successes and its popularity has lasted just as long as its namesake.**

Designer John Caig/Ian Howlett (UK)
First launched 1994/1997
Type One-design
LOA 4.2m/4.25m (13¾ft)
Beam 1.92m/1.9m (6½ft)
Minimum hull weight 90kg (198lb)/ 85kg (187lb)
Upwind sail area 12.85 sq m (138 sq ft)/ 15.93 sq m (171 sq ft)
Gennaker 17.4 sq m (187 sq ft)/ 21.68 sq m (233 sq ft)

RS800

The RS800 was introduced in late 1999 as an exceptional high performance racer featuring a twin mode form of weight equalization that is usable by a wide range

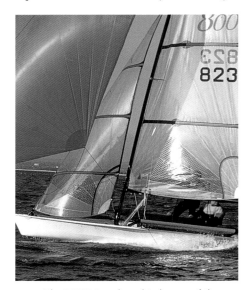

ABOVE **The RS800 is reckoned to be one of the fastest of the new generation dinghies on the water, with a unique single trapeze or twin trapeze weight equalization concept.**

of crews. The boat can be raced with single trapeze or twin trapeze, with weight equalized by weights and the racks. The RS800 is built from epoxy foam sandwich and uses carbon spars.
Designer Phil Morrison
First launched 1999
Type One-design
LOA 4.8m (15ft 9in)
Beam with racks 1.88m–2.89m (6ft 2in–9ft)
Minimum hull weight 78kg (172lb)
Upwind sail area 16.5 sq m (178 sq ft)
Gennaker 21 sq m (226 sq ft)

Boss

A carbon reinforced sandwich hull and carbon spars make the Boss a super-light flying machine and a 2.7m (9ft) pole extension and massive gennaker give a blistering performance offwind. The hull is based on Ian Howlett's world championship International 14 designs, and the rig is designed by Jon Turner to ensure that maximum power is combined with a boat that remains manageable. The Boss was originally conceived to outpace the Laser 5000, though both boats had to give second best to the 49er when it came to Olympic selection.
Designers Ian Howlett and Jon Turner
First launched 1997
Type One-design
LOA 4.9m (16ft)
Beam with racks 2.37m (7¾ft)
Minimum hull weight 85kg (187lb)
Upwind sail area 17.85 sq m (192 sq ft)
Gennaker 33 sq m (355 sq ft)

ABOVE **The Boss is the biggest sister in the Iso/Buzz/Spice family, aiming at the ultimate end of twin wire sailing with performance on par with the Laser 5000.**

Single-handers

The most obvious advantage of sailing single-handed is that you don't need a crew. Beyond that, all decisions and the control of the boat are down to you alone, which can make single-handed sailing the purest and most satisfying form.

International Laser

With over 165,000 boats sold worldwide, the Laser is the most successful sailboat ever. The key to its success is absolute simplicity combined with very low cost, plus challenging performance and the strictest possible one-design rules to ensure that race success is purely down to the sailor. Robert Scheidt of Brazil took the first gold medal at Savannah in the USA in 1976, and the Laser has continued to prosper at all levels of competition with active fleets in over 100 countries.
Designer Bruce Kirby (Canada)
First launched 1971
Type One-design
LOA 4.23m (14ft)
Beam 1.37m (4½ft)
Minimum hull weight 60kg (132lb)
Standard sail area 7.06 sq m (76 sq ft)

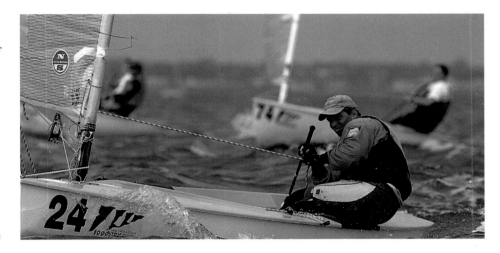

ABOVE **The International Finn is one of the most graceful boats on the water, a heavyweight classic that hails from another era but has been kept alive by the Olympics.**

ABOVE **The International Laser has been a massive success, based on the winning formula of the best possible racing combined with absolute simplicity.**

International Finn

The Finn replaced the Firefly as the men's Olympic single-handed class in 1952, and remained the only single-hander until 1996 when it was joined by the Laser and Europe. With a massive 120kg (265lb) hull weight the Finn remains a heavy classic that demands the services of heavyweight sailors, and 90kg (198lb) is the optimum weight for best performance. As such its appeal is very limited and it is slow by modern standards. Having won a gold medal sailing a Firefly in the Olympics in 1948, the great Danish sailor, Paul Elnström, went on to win three more golds sailing the Finn in 1952, 1956 and 1960, an unsurpassed record.
Designer Rickard Sarby (Sweden)
First launched 1949
Type Restricted
LOA 4.5m (14¾ft)
Beam 1.52m (5ft)
Minimum hull weight 120kg (265lb)
Upwind sail area 10 sq m (108 sq ft)

International Europe

The Europe became the first ever women's single-handed Olympic class at Savannah, USA in 1996 when Kristine Roug of Denmark took the gold medal. Since the boat first appeared as a Moth design in 1960 it has evolved into a small, high performance single-hander, which offers excellent racing for sailors in the 50–70kg (110–154lb) weight range. The class is particularly strong in northern Europe.
Designer Alain Roland (France)
First launched 1960
Type Restricted
LOA 3.35m (11ft)
Beam 1.38m (4½ft)
Minimum hull weight 45kg (99lb)
Upwind sail area 7 sq m (75 sq ft)

ABOVE **The International Europe provides the best possible racing for women, using a design that has been greatly refined since its first appearance.**

OK dinghy

The OK was originally introduced as a smaller, lighter alternative to the Finn, which would appeal to a wide range of sailors in the 70 kg (154 lb) range and be cheaply available in basic, box-shaped marine ply construction. Despite there being little more than 2,000 OKs registered, the class enjoys popularity in many countries with World and European champions drawn from nations as diverse as Australia (which hosted the 1998 World Championships), Poland, Denmark and Sweden.

Designer Knud Olsen (Norway)
First launched 1957
Type Restricted
LOA 4m (13ft)
Beam 1.42m (4½ft)
Minimum hull weight 72kg (159lb)
Upwind sail area 8.5 sq m (91 sq ft)

ABOVE **As a restricted class the OK has been steadily brought up to date, with carbon fibre masts being allowed from the year 2000.**

International Contender

The Contender was designed by Bob Miller, who confusingly changed his name to Ben Lexcen. Great things were expected of the Contender which, with a single-handed trapeze, was extremely radical for its time, and was widely tipped to supplant the aging Finn in the Olympics. Despite winning IYRU trials to find a new single-hander the Contender never made it to the Olympic slot, and its appeal has remained limited with less than 700 boats registered in almost 40 years.

Designer Bob Miller/Ben Lexcen (Australia)
First launched 1962
Type Restricted
LOA 4.87m (16ft)

LEFT **The International Contender is the original single-handed trapeze boat. Despite being a difficult boat to sail, a committed band of enthusiasts continue to race it, and the best fleets are found in the UK and Germany.**

Beam 1.5m (5ft)
Minimum hull weight 83kg (183lb)
Upwind sail area 10.8 sq m (116 sq ft)

International 10 Sq M Canoe

The International 10 Square Metre Canoe is one of the most radical craft of them all with the narrowest beam of any one-design/restricted dinghy the world has ever known. This helps to give it a tremendous turn of speed upwind, making it undisputed as the world's fastest single-handed monohull for more than 50 years. It has a small but dedicated international following and has strong fleets in the UK, USA and Sweden, and regular World and European championships.

Learning to control an International Canoe is a skill that is reckoned to take an experienced sailor three or more years to perfect. Much of the difficulty is due to the enormous sliding seat, which projects more than 3m (10ft) from the centreline of the boat, where the crew hikes off the outside edge. Every tack is an exceptionally tricky manoeuvre.

Designer Nethercot (UK)
First launched 1946

RIGHT **Despite being among the oldest dinghies of them all, the International Canoe remains in a class apart when it comes to upwind speed.**

Type Restricted/Development
LOA 5.18m (17ft)
Beam 1.02m (3½ft)
Minimum hull weight 63kg (139lb)
Upwind sail area 10 sq m (108 sq ft)

International Moth

The International Moth is the boat for radical lightweights. There is no minimum hull weight, which encourages featherweight construction, and the basic rules cover little more than maximum length, beam and sail area. This has helped to take the International Moth design in very extreme directions, with the norm being a super-narrow hull coupled with maxi-wings. The result is a boat that is incredibly unstable and specialised to sail, but a lot of fun for the small band of enthusiasts who frequently build and design their own boats.

Designer Various
First launched 1939
Type Development
LOA 3.35m (11ft)
Beam 2.35m (7½ft)
Minimum hull weight No minimum.
Upwind sail area 8 sq m (86 sq ft)

ABOVE **With super-wide wings mounted on an extra narrow hull you can see why the International Moth is such a tricky boat to handle, but although it is very wobbly, it is also a lot of fun.**

RS600

The RS600 revived the single-handed trapeze concept of the Contender 30 years later in a much lighter, wider and more powerful package. The option of racing with wide or narrow racks provides a weight equalization system that allows technically able sailors across the 65–90kg (143–198lb) weight spectrum to enjoy racing in a single-hander, which is acknowledged as one of the fastest and most demanding dinghies on the water.

Designers Chris Everest and Nick Peters (UK)
First launched 1993
Type One-design
LOA 4.47m (14½ft)
Beam 1.93m (6½ft)
Minimum hull weight 52kg (115lb)
Upwind sail area 12.14 sq m (131 sq ft)

RS300

The RS300 is a very modern, club racing single-hander with a super-wide design concept borrowed from the International Moth, but used in a much more sailor-friendly way. The result is an exciting boat, which has wings spread wide over a narrow waterline, an unstayed carbon mast fitted with a GNAV, and the choice of two sail sizes for weight equalization.

Designer Clive Everest (UK)
First launched 1997
Type One-design
LOA 4.25m (14ft)
Beam 2m (6½ft)
Minimum hull weight 53kg (117lb)
Upwind sail area 9.25 sq m (99 sq ft)/ 10 sq m (108 sq ft)

Laser.eps

The Laser.eps was introduced as a direct challenger to the RS300 in a bid to establish a new, state-of-the-art small single-hander. Designed by Yves Loday, the Laser.eps introduced the mini-stay system with a short forestay and stub shrouds supporting the carbon mast at the gooseneck in order to control the rig while letting the boom right off downwind. The .eps also continues the Laser weight equalization philosophy, with a choice of two rigs for different weight helms and sliding aerowings which are adjusted to equalize leverage.

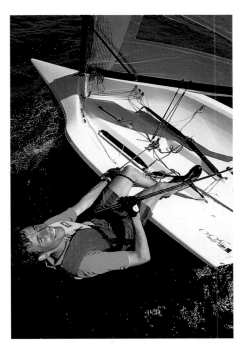

ABOVE **The RS300 is an innovative single-hander, which features wide wings with a surprisingly user-friendly hull design and carbon spars for fast tactical racing.**

Designer Yves Loday (France)
First launched 1998
Type One-design/Weight equalization
LOA 4.3m (14ft)
Beam 1.85–2.4m (6–8ft)
Minimum hull weight 53.5kg (118lb) plus 9kg (20lb) aerowings
Upwind sail area 9.3 sq m (100 sq ft)/ 8.4 sq m (90 sq ft)

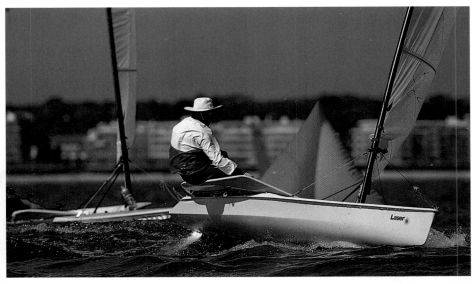

ABOVE **The RS600 is a single-handed trapeze skiff, faster than most two person dinghies and featuring a unique reefing rig system.**

ABOVE **The Laser.eps features weight equalization adjustable aerowings and a mini shroud system, which supports the lightweight carbon mast. It also has two rig options.**

Skiffs

Skiff racing was first held in Sydney Harbour in 1827, and over the next 150 years developed a strong public following due to the spectacular size of the enormous rigs being used. However, it was not until 1975 that skiff development really began to race ahead and change the face of performance dinghy sailing. Dave Porter won the 18 Foot World Championships with KB, the first skiff to be helmed from the trapeze with a three-man crew replacing the conventional four-man crew, and the first boat in the world that would plane continuously on all points of sailing in nine knots of wind.

From then on there were two decades of intense development in lightweight hulls, wings, asymmetric spinnakers and flex-top masts, increasing the speed of the Australian skiffs to the point where they were unchallenged as the fastest boats in the world for round-the-buoys racing. This led directly to the development of the 49er, a miniaturized 18 Foot Skiff with a blistering performance which at a single stroke took Olympic sailing into the 21st century.

Cherub

Despite first appearing almost half a century before the 49er, the Cherub is a clear forerunner of the modern gennaker-driven skiff concept. Just 3.5m (11½ft) long, weighing around 73kg (160lb) fully rigged and with plenty of canvas, it still combines spectacular downhill performance with on-the-edge handling that is only found in true lightweight skiffs and makes them so much fun to sail. The design was originally a one-off commission by John Spencer in New Zealand, which got its name when the owner referred to her as a perfect little cherub to sail. The new class rapidly spread to Australia and from there to Britain, and had rapid development until

ABOVE **A long bowsprit, a big gennaker, a fast ride and the front of the boat flying clear of the water mark out the Cherub as a forerunner of the modern skiff.**

The spinnaker/gennaker connection

In the 1960s the Cherub sported a primitive kind of asymmetric spinnaker mounted on a long boom with tremendous reaching performance, but the concept was soon shelved in favour of a more conventional spinnaker and did not resurface until the 1980s when Julian Bethwaite claims to have invented the asymmetric spinnaker or gennaker.

At the time Julian was looking for ways to simplify his Sydney Harbour 18 designs, which had become so over-complex that the skills required to sail them were overloading the crews. One of his answers to the problem was to replace the conventional gybing spinnaker pole with a fixed bowsprit, and flatten the leech of the spinnaker to give it an asymmetric shape, which would allow the boat to go downwind like an ice yacht. As downwind speed increased, it was found that speed depended on the luff length of the spinnaker rather than its area, with a single continuous sheet controlling the balance of the sail from tack to head with comparatively light sheet loads.

LEFT **Julian Bethwaite's development work on asymmetric spinnakers for the Sydney Harbour 18 class led directly to his design for the 49er more than a decade later.**

ABOVE **Flying high with the front half of the boat lifted clear of the water is the hallmark of an International 14 fully powered up by its gennaker. The class has experienced massive evolution since the trapeze was first introduced and then banned as being an unfair advantage.**

1984 when rules for UK Cherubs and Australian and New Zealand Cherubs went their own separate ways (the UK allowing a bigger rig and a considerably bigger gennaker).
Designers Various (New Zealand, Australia and UK)
First launched 1951
Type Development
LOA 3.7m (12ft)
Beam 1.8m (6ft) maximum
Minimum hull weight 50kg (110lb)
Upwind sail area 12.5 sq m (134 sq ft) (UK)
Gennaker 15 sq m (161 sq ft) (UK)

B14

The B14 is a wonderful little flying machine, which has become popular in the UK. Super-wide racks replace the trapeze for crew power, giving this lightweight boat performance that is both demanding and rewarding, and a phenomenal speed round a race course rated on par with the International 14.
Designer Julian Bethwaite (Australia)
First launched 1985
Type One-design
LOA 4.5m (14¾ft)
Beam 3.05m (10ft) (including wings)
Minimum hull weight 62kg (137lb)
Upwind sail area 17.2 sq m (185 sq ft)
Gennaker 29.2 sq m (314 sq ft)

International 14

The International 14 is a development racing dinghy with a very long and illustrious history, which has kept it at the forefront of small boat technology. Two British designers, Uffa Fox and Morgan Giles, proved that light is fast, and the first weighed less than 100kg (220lb) in the 1920s. In 1938 the class pioneered the use of the trapeze, then banned it for the next 30 years due to protests from the light wind, inland fleets.

In 1984 the class took a big step forward with the introduction of twin trapezes to increase sail carrying power and performance, and in 1988 unlimited asymmetric spinnakers were allowed,

ABOVE **Old meets new. Europe and Australia met head-on to resurrect the International 14, and turned it into a modern classic that rates as one of the most challenging boats on the water.**

following the lead of skiff sailors in Australia and New Zealand. Carbon hulls and masts soon followed.

The parallel development of the Australian 14 Foot Skiff class over a similar period of time led to the two classes merging in 1996, with the first combined World Championship held at San Francisco the following year. Despite being an expensive boat to race the International 14 continues to be one of the most desirable high performance boats the world has to offer and has international fleets in Australia, Canada, Denmark, Germany, Japan, New Zealand, Switzerland, the UK and USA. It had no less than 130 boats on the start line at the 1999 World Championships in Melbourne.
Designer Various
First launched 1908
Type Development
LOA 4.27m (14ft)
Beam 1.83m (6ft) maximum
Minimum hull weight 74.25kg (164lb)
Upwind sail area 18.56 sq m (200 sq ft)
Gennaker Unlimited

LEFT **The B14 has extra-wide wings instead of trapezes. Despite being a comparatively old design, it is a brilliant boat and is a real buzz to sail.**

16 Foot Skiff

The 16 Foot Skiff is a uniquely Australian dinghy, which has seen many developments over more than 100 years. The latest designs feature three crew, with two on trapeze wires, and massive masthead gennakers. Despite being highly demanding, they are one of the most popular high performance dinghies in Australia with more than 150 boats scattered through 12 clubs and 70-strong fleets at major regattas. To prevent costs escalating and provide closer racing, strict design rules were introduced in 1997/98, which fixed hull design and construction for eight years. The rules also limited competitors to having two masts, three jibs, two mainsails and two gennakers, which can be used in different combinations for optimal performance.

Designer Various (Australia)
First launched *c.* 1900
Type Restricted/Development
LOA 4.9m (16ft)
Beam 1.52–1.78m (5–6ft)
Minimum hull weight no limit
Upwind sail area 22 sq m (237 sq ft) maximum
Spinnaker 45 sq m (484 sq ft) maximum

LEFT **Popular modern classes such as the Iso and Laser 4000 have all the hallmarks of skiff development, but lack the super light weight combined with a powerful rig and knife edge handling, which is the hallmark of a true skiff.**

18 Foot Skiff

The Sydney Harbour 18 Foot Skiff is the ultimate triple trapeze development class, and probably the most spectacular dinghy on the water with a racing history that extends back to the 1890s. The first World Championship was held in Sydney in 1938, and Australia remains the home of the class although there are smaller circuits in the UK, USA, New Zealand and Japan as well as individual boats from France, Sweden, Holland, Italy and Canada.

Despite the exotic and extreme nature of the boat, class rules are framed to uphold the original philosophy of a boat within the means of the average man, which provides good competitive racing and attracts public interest. To this end the class currently uses a one-design hull, and an Iain Murray design replacing one by Julian Bethwaite and a list of approved materials that includes epoxy resin and carbon fibre. The maximum sail inventory allowed is two mainsails, two jibs and two gennakers, with mains and jibs constructed from Mylar, Dacron, Aramaid or Spectra at a minimum weight of 38g (1½oz). Each boat is allowed two masts of 10.2m (33½ft) and 9.2m (30ft) built in 6000 Series aluminium with optional fibreglass tops, and a maximum of one boom. In this class, there is also a maximum of one gennaker pole with a maximum length of 3.8m (12½ft) built in 6000 Series aluminium, while the most unlikely rule is a minimum age of 14 for crew members.

Designer Julian Bethwaite, Iain Murray (Australia).
First launched *c.*1890
Type Development
LOA 5.41–5.48m (17¾–18ft)
Beam 1.82–2.44m (6–7½ft)
Wings Not to exceed 2.13m (7ft) from the centreline.
Minimum hull weight 82.5kg (182lb)
Upwind sail area Unlimited
Gennaker Unlimited

ABOVE **Australia's 16 Foot and 18 Foot Skiffs push the limits where other classes dare not go, and provide a unique spectacle of humanity battling against extreme forces.**

ABOVE **It's difficult to believe that the 18 Foot Skiff first appeared in 1899, though there have been a few changes since then. This must be the ultimate fun machine for a three man crew.**

International approval

International recognition is conferred on leading racing classes by the International Sailing Federation (ISAF, formerly known as the IYRU). The ISAF licenses class builders and administers and polices class rules, ensuring that all boats in a class race to a consistent formula wherever events are held in the world.

LEFT **The Europe is one of many internationally recognized classes, policed by the ISAF, which ensures consistency in construction and class rules.**

49er

The 49er set the dinghy world alight when it was selected as the new Olympic high performance dinghy within little more than a year of first taking to the water, making its Olympic Games debut in Sydney in 2000. It is a miniaturized development of the Sydney Harbour 18 Foot Skiff but, with a lower drag factor, is reckoned to need 85 per cent of the 18's relative power to achieve the same speed. In real terms it is rated almost as fast as the 18, despite giving away a tremendous amount in sail area.

With licensed builders around the world, the 49er is built in an epoxy woven cloth laminate with a PVC core using a glass epoxy space frame to handle loads from the rig. It has proved popular and extremely demanding, but while fun on flat water, sailing in wind and waves has a tendency to make it nose dive.

Designer Julian Bethwaite (Australia)
First launched 1995
Type Restricted
LOA 5m (16ft)
Beam 3m (10ft)
Minimum hull weight 62kg (137lb)
Upwind sail area 46.4 sq m (499 sq ft)
Spinnaker 29.2 sq m (314 sq ft)

RIGHT **The 49er brought the skiff story up to date and gave it worldwide respectability, even though it is rated as an exceptionally difficult, and sometimes downright unpleasant, boat to sail.**

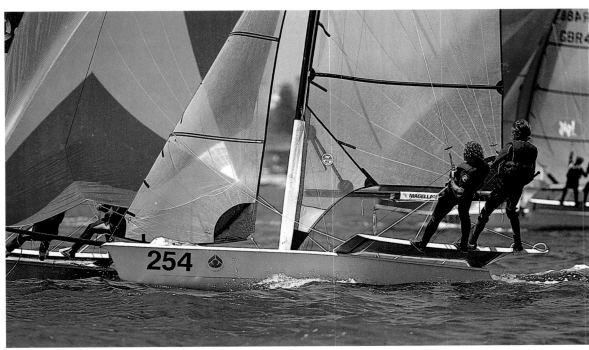

Catamarans

While the best gennaker-driven dinghies may push catamarans hard, two hulls are very fast and top catamarans such as the Tornado remain in a class of their own. Catamarans also provide a different style of sailing and competition, and are recommended to sailors who adore the thrill of speed.

International A Class

The A Class catamaran is the fastest small single-handed sailboat in the world, with a blistering performance that puts it close to the 49er despite its diminutive size. It is a largely unrestricted development class built to a super-light rule, and is at its fastest and most potent when racing inland in light to moderate winds. There is a small but dedicated following for the class led by Germany, Switzerland, Italy, Australia and the USA, while in Britain the Unicorn – a 1967 vintage A Class design by John Mazzotti (UK) – is established as a more popular and less extreme restricted class racer.

Designers Various
First launched 1962
Type Development
LOA 5.5m (18ft)
Beam 2.3m (7½ft) maximum
Minimum platform weight 30kg (66lb)
Upwind sail area 13.94 sq m (150 sq ft)

LEFT **The International Tornado has proved a difficult act to follow. It is exceptionally fast, a delight to sail, and Olympic competitors always rate it as their number one choice.**

International Tornado

The Tornado swept the board at the first ever trials for an Olympic catamaran, and has been an Olympic class at every Games since 1976 in Canada, when Reg White and John Osborn won the first gold medal. More than 30 years of intense competition among the best sailors in the world continuously refined the Tornado and ensured it seldom had a problem proving that it was the fastest racing catamaran in the world. However by 1996 it had become refined to the point where it was turning into a virtual one-design, with almost all boats built by Göran Marström of Sweden. Early attempts to introduce a Tornado Sport with twin trapezes, bigger mainsail and gennaker were defeated, until the ISAF voted to replace the standard Tornado with this option for use in the 2004 Olympic Games.

Designers Rodney March (UK)
First launched 1967
Type Restricted
LOA 6.1m (20ft)
Beam 3.05m (10ft)
Minimum platform weight 127kg (280lb)
Upwind sail area 21.8 sq m (235 sq ft)

ABOVE **The International A Class catamaran has an exceptional power to weight ratio, and is likely to be the fastest boat on the water upwind in a light or moderate breeze.**

ABOVE **Formula 18 is a tightly drafted measurement rule that prohibits the use of carbon. The class has flourished in Europe where it is the top choice for gennaker catamaran racing.**

Formula 18

This was originally a French concept for a restricted measurement class of twin trapeze, gennaker-driven catamarans. Support for the rule spread through Europe, with France, Britain, Italy and Germany leading the way in national and European racing circuits.

The Formula 18 rule was very carefully drafted in an effort to limit an arms war attitude to sailing and premature obsolescence. In this it has been highly successful, and leading designs, primarily the Dart Hawk, Hobie Tiger and Nacra 18 – have stayed competitive over a long period of time and rely on the crew's skills to decide who wins the races.

Designers Various
First launched 1993
Type Restricted
LOA 5.5m (18ft)
Beam 2.6m (8½ft)
Minimum overall weight no limit
Upwind sail area 20.45 sq m (220 sq ft)/ 21.15 sq m (228 sq ft)
Gennaker 19 sq m (205 sq ft)/ 21.8 sq m (235 sq ft)

Dart 18

Following straight on from his design for the ultra elite Tornado, Rodney March demonstrated the breadth of his design skills by introducing the Dart 18 – a single trapeze, performance catamaran that is as simple as possible to own and is suitable for everyone. The Dart 18 has skegs rather than daggerboards, no boom and the most fundamental sail controls, but the result is that it has enjoyed non-stop popularity as an exceptionally user-friendly one-design. It also provides some of the very best class racing on a scale that ranges from club to international championship events in many countries. To help bring it in line with modern skills it can be sailed for fun with an optional gennaker package.

Designer Rodney March (UK)
First launched 1976
Type One-design
LOA 5.5m (18ft)
Beam 2.3m (7½ft)
Minimum platform weight 130kg (286lb)
Upwind sail area 16.072 sq m (173 sq ft)

Hobie 16

Hobie Alter designed his first Hobie 14 as a boat to get out and sail in waves, using distinctive asymmetric banana-shaped hulls with no daggerboards or skegs so it could sail straight up the beach, and a raised trampoline to keep the crew clear of the waves. The 14 became a worldwide success as a fun-racing, single-handed cat, and was soon followed by the two crew, twin trapeze Hobie 16. This was a scaled-up, and even more successful version and is the best selling catamaran of all time selling thousands of boats worldwide and sales still going strong.

The appeal of these early Hobie designs is that they define the phrase beach cat, have an image that has remained attractive, are tough and very durable if somewhat heavy, and still have formidable reaching performance, plus a tendency to indulge in sensational pitch-pole capsizes. While the Hobie 14 has become rather dated, the Hobie 16 has built up and maintained a huge international racing circuit, and even made an unsuccessful bid to replace the Tornado

ABOVE **The Hobie 16 has proved equally successful as a beach catamaran for recreational use and as a racer, which has been selected for major ISAF championships.**

in the 2000 Olympic Games. Both Hobie 14 and 16 have been built in the USA, South America, Australia, South Africa and France, reflecting a worldwide enthusiasm for sailing and racing the original Hobies.

Designer Hobie Alter (USA)
First launched 1970
Type One-design
LOA 5.11m (16¾ft)
Beam 2.4m (8ft)
Minimum platform weight 145kg (320lb)
Upwind sail area 20.26 sq m (218 sq ft)

ABOVE **The Dart 18 is a one-design racing catamaran that is almost as simple to own and race as a Laser. Events for the class are held worldwide and the 2000 World Championship was staged in South Africa.**

OTHER CATAMARAN CLASSES

With the noble exceptions of Holland and France, catamaran sailing and racing tends to be a minority interest when compared to monohulls. Most countries support their own favourite classes, and the following brands are among some of the best known names.

Dart (UK)

Apart from the Dart 18 one-design and Dart Hawk Formula 18 racer, Dart's best known catamaran is the Dart 15, a little sister to the 18, which was designed by Rodney March in 1979. The 15 can be sailed either with two lightweight crew or single-handed.

A more recent arrival to the range is the Dart 16, which was launched in 1997, and designed and developed by Yves Loday and Reg White (both Tornado Gold medalists) who also produced the Hawk.

RIGHT **The Hurricane 5.9, shown here in optional sport mode with a gennaker, has slim, sharp hulls like the Tornado, but is slightly shorter. It is also a lot narrower to make it more practical, with twin trapezes to make up for the loss of leverage.**

White Formula (UK)

Having won the first Tornado gold medal, Reg White was for many years a famous builder of Tornados, before concentrating on the Hurricane 5.9, which he developed as a more user-friendly catamaran offering nearly as good performance. It is narrower than the Tornado, for easy trailing and storage, but has twin trapezes to compensate for loss of crew power. The Hurricane 5.9 built up a popular and very competitive circuit in the UK, with occasional incursions into France, Holland and Italy.

White Formula has also made attempts to produce and market an ultimate catamaran. The 6.5m (21ft) Hurricane 6.5 sported massive racks and a huge rig, but proved too ponderous to sail consistently fast and was very expensive. The Tornado Sport left the standard Tornado in its wake thanks to twin trapezes, bigger mainsail and gennaker, but was rejected by the International Tornado Association. The 6m (20ft) Storm was introduced in prototype form in 1999, and was due for series production in 2000.

Prindle/Mystere (USA/Canada)

The Prindle 16 followed the design style of the Hobie 14 and 16, but with more volume in the hulls for all-round fun use. It proved a big success, and was followed by totally different models such as the Prindle 18.2 and 19. Both of these slim, swift catamarans owed their style to the Tornado, as did the similar Mystere 6.0 from Canada.

Nacra (USA)

The Nacra catamaran range is manufactured alongside Prindle in California, and has replaced it for high performance competition use. Much of the design input and demand for Nacra comes from Holland, a small country that boasts more catamarans and more Nacras

LEFT **These young sailors are having a good time on a Dart 15, but this catamaran has proved equally successful as an adult single-handed racer. It was originally introduced as the small sister to the Dart 8.**

ABOVE **The Dart 16 combines beach friendly moulded plastic hulls with design development led by Yves Loday and Reg White. The result is a catamaran that belies its appearance and is easily controlled and fun to sail. The crew displaying a rather unconventional trapeze stance here.**

LEFT **A fleet of Prindles line up for an offshore marathon. The Prindle 18.2 and 19 were well regarded as high performance racing cats, but the range then switched to the recreational market in favour of Nacra.**

RIGHT **The Nacra (named after the North American Cat Racing Association) enjoyed a period of popularity with the 5.0, 5.5 and 6.0 models before the introduction of the Inter 18 (Formula 18), Inter 20 (Formula 20) and single-handed Inter 17.**

ABOVE **Fast and stately. The Hobie 21 Formula is the biggest Hobie of them all, and a magnificent boat for long distance sailing.**

Marström Sailworks (Sweden)

Göran Marström was the Tornado bronze medal winner at the 1980 Olympics, and became established as the world's most popular Tornado builder over the next 20 years. With the ISAF keen to replace the Tornado for the 2004 Olympics, Marström launched an all carbon 6m (20ft) prototype in 1999 designed to take over from the Tornado as the undisputed fastest catamaran in the world.

ABOVE **The Inter 18 soon established itself as one of the fastest boats in the Formula 18 class, racing with the Hobie Tiger, Dart Hawk and Diam at venues such as the Italian lakes.**

than anywhere else in the world. The Nacra line-up is committed to high performance and includes:

- The Inter 18 is a Formula 18 designed by Gino Morelli of PlayStation mega-cat fame.
- The Inter 17 is a scaled-down, single-handed variation on the 18.
- The Inter 20 is a scaled-up, self-styled Formula 20 suitable for heavier sailors.

Hobie (Europe and USA)

Following the initial success of Hobie Alter, the Hobie business was sold and split between Hobie USA and Hobie Europe, both of which have manufactured the original 14 and 16. Other top Hobie models include the Hobie 17 single-hander (single trapeze with wings), the Hobie 18 and 18 Formula (twin trapeze with optional wings), the Hobie Tiger Formula 18 and the mighty Hobie 21 (twin or triple trapeze).

ABOVE **Will Sunnucks sets a new Round Texel Race record in an early Tornado Sport, originally developed by Reg White, Yves Loday and Mitch Booth to replace the classic Tornado.**

Index

Useful addresses and acknowledgements

SAILING AUTHORITIES

Australian Yachting Federation
Locked Bag 806, Milsons Point,
NSW 2061, AUSTRALIA
tel: 02 99224333
ausyacht@ausport.gov.au
www.aussailing.org

Osterreichischer Segel-Verband
Zetschegasse 21,
A-1230 Vienna, AUSTRIA
tel: 01 662 44 62-0
oesv@sailing.or.at
www.sailing.or.at

Federation Royale Belge du
Yachting
Halve Maanstraat 2C, 8620
Nieuwpoort, BELGIUM
tel: 058 23028

Canadian Yachting Association
1600 James Naismith Drive,
Gloucester
Ontario KIB 5N4, CANADA
tel: 613 7485687
sailcanada@sailing.ca
www.sailing.ca

Danish Sailing Association
Idraettens Hus, DK 2605
Broendby, DENMARK
tel: 043 262189
dan.ibsen@sejlsport.dk
www.sailing.dk

Finnish Yachting Association
Radiokatu 20, Helsinki,
FIN-00093 SLU, FINLAND
tel: 058 9 348121
aarne.kusi@splfsf.slu.fi

Federation Francaise de Voile
55 Avenue Kleber, 75784 Paris
Cedex 16, FRANCE
tel: 0144058112
barbierm@compuserve.com
www.ffv.fr

Deutscher Segler-Verband
Grundgenstrasse 18, 22309
Hamburg, GERMANY
tel: 040 6320090
100763.105@compuserve.com

Hellenic Yachting Federation
51 Poseidonos Avenue, 18344
Moshato, GREECE
tel: 01 9404825
webmaster-eio@eio.gr
www.eio.gr

Irish Sailing Association
3 park Road, Dun Laoghaire,
Co.Dublin, IRELAND
tel: 01 2800239
isa@iol.ie
www.sailing.org/isa

Federazione Italiana Vela
Corte Lambruschini, Paizza Borgo

Pila 40, Torre A - 16 piano,
16129 Genova, ITALY
tel: 010 5445 41
federvela@federvela.it
www.federvela.it

Malta Sailing Federation
PO Box 65,
Valletta, MALTA
tel: 056 337777

Yacht Club de Monaco
16 Quai Antoine 1er
MC 98000, MONACO
tel: 077 93 106300
ycm@yacht-club-monaco-mc
www.yacht-club-monaco-mc

Koninklijk Nederlands Watersport
Verbond
Postbus 87, 3980 CB Bunnik
THE NETHERLANDS
tel: 030 6566550
info@knwv.nl
www.knwv.nl

Yachting New Zealand
PO Box 33 789, Takapuna,
North Shore City
Auckland, NEW ZEALAND
tel: 09 488 9325
mail@yachtingnz.org.nz
www.yachtingnz.org.nz

Norwegian Sailing Federation
Serviceboks 1, Ullevaal Stadion,
0840 Oslo, NORWAY
tel: 021 029711
seiling@nif.idrett.no
www.nif.idrett.no/seiling

Polski Zwiazek Zeglarski
Chocimska 14,
00791 Warsaw, POLAND
tel: 022 495731
pya@polbox.com.pl
www.sailing.org.pl

Federacao Portuguesa de Vela
Doca de Belem,
1300 Lisboa, PORTUGAL
tel: 021 3647324
fpvela@fpvela.pt
www.fpvela.pt

All Russia Yachting Federation
Luchnetskaya nad.8, 119270
Moscow, RUSSIA
tel: 095 725 4703
ilyin@yachting.ru

South African Sailing
5 Vesperdene Road, Green Point,
8051 Cape Town
SOUTH AFRICA
tel: 021 4391147
e-mail: sailsa@iafrica.com
web: www.sailing.org/rsa

Real Federacion Espanola de Vela
Luis de Salazar, 12,
28002 Madrid, SPAIN

tel: 091 5195008
info@rfev.es
www.rfev.es

Swedish Sailing Federation
Af Pontins väg 6
S-115 21 Stockholm, SWEDEN
tel: 08 4590990
ssf@ssf.se
www.ssf.se

Swiss Sailing Federation
Haus des Sportes, Laubeggstrass
70 3000 Bern 32,
SWITZERLAND
tel: 031 359 7266
swiss_sailing@compuserve.com
www.swiss_sailing.ch

Royal Yachting Association
RYA House, Romsey Road,
Eastleigh, Hampshire SO50 9YA
UNITED KINGDOM
tel: 023 8062 7400
racing@rya.org.uk
www.racing.rya.org.uk

US Sailing
PO Box 1260, 15 Maritime Drive,
Portsmouth, RI 02871-6015
USA
tel: 401 6830800
ussailing@compuserve.com
www.ussailing.org

ACKNOWLEDGEMENTS
The author would like to thank the
following for their help, which has
often been extensive:
Firstly Frazer Clark, Gael Pawson
and Peter Spence of Yachts &
Yachting, followed in no particular
order by the RYA, ISAF, Rockley
Watersports and Sail France,
Minorca Sailing Holidays, Sunsail
at Port Solent and in Turkey,
Crewsaver, Musto, Brian Phipps of
Windsport, Robin Smith, Roger
Tushingham, Rob and Reg White,
Rodney Pattisson, Lewmar, the
Laser Centre, RS Racing, UK Sails,

Sobstad, Topper International,
Clamcleat, Hobie Cat and John
Pierce plus a host of dinghy
classes that have provided
invaluable information.

The publishers would like to thank
everyone at Team Unlimited in
Spain. This book would not have
been possible without their help.
Thanks also to the models Rob
Andrews, Sonia Kirk, Ioan R.
Leavey, Andrew Moore, Mark
Reynolds, Ewan McNeill, Felix
Thornton-Jones and Ben Donald.
Lastly, special thanks to Richard
Langdon and Marie Rondoz of
Ocean Images for the specially
commissioned photography, and
extensive use of their picture
library.

PHOTOGRAPHY
All photography by Richard
Langdon unless otherwise stated.
© **Agence D.P.P.I.**: page 7br.
© **Brigid Tiernan**: page 139tr.
© **Cherub Association**: page
150t.
© **Jacques Vapillon**: page 21tr.
© **Laser**: page 68.
© **Minorca Sailing Holidays**:
page 52b.
© **Ocean Images/Richard
Langdon**: pages 4, 6, 7bl, 18t,
19tl, 19b, 21bl, 21br, 22br, 23bl,
23br, 24b, 25, 27, 28, 30b, 31b,
35t, 39tr, 41tr, 41br, 42, 43, 44,
45, 46, 47, 48r, 49t, 51b, 52tl,
52tr, 53tr, 53b, 54, 55, 56t, 56b,
57, 58tr, 60, 61, 62, 63b, 64, 65,
66, 67, 74, 105tl, 105c, 70t, 118,
120l, 121t, 131, 132t, 133b, 134,
135, 136, 138, 139tl, 139b, 140,
141, 142br, 143bl, 143br, 144,
145, 146tl, 147, 148, 149, 150b,
151tr, 152b, 153, 154t, 154br,
155t, 157bl, 157br.
© **Pat Collinge/Sunsail**: pages
10t, 10bl, 12b, 16b, 19tr, 48l,
69b.
© **Peter Bentley/Hobie Cat**:
page 157tr.
© **Prindle**: page 157tl.
© **Richard Neal**: pages 11bl, 40bl,
56c, 69t.
© **Ross Laney Photographic Ltd**:
page 129bl, 129bc, 129br.
© **RS Racing Sailboats**: pages
107b, 146c.
© **Sue Pelling**: page 142tr.
© **Written Products/Jeremy
Evans**: pages 7bl, 10br, 11br, 12t,
13, 14, 15, 16t, 17, 18bl, 18bc,
18br, 21tl, 26tl, 26tr, 29t, 29c,
30t, 31tr, 33, 49b, 50, 51t, 53tl,
58tl, 58b, 63t, 80t, 80c, 81t,
82bc, 85, 120r, 121b, 122cl,
122cr, 123, 124t, 129t, 142tl,
146tl, 146bl, 151b, 154bl, 155b,
156t, 156c, 157c.